PCs
FOR
DUMMIES
A Wiley Brand

13th Edition

PCs

FOR DUMMIES®

A Wiley Brand

13th Edition

by Dan Gookin

FOR DUMMIES®
A Wiley Brand

PCs For Dummies®, 13th Edition

Published by: **John Wiley & Sons, Inc.,** 111 River Street, Hoboken, NJ 07030-5774, www.wiley.com

Contents at a Glance

Table of Contents

Introduction

. . . .

*I*t may have been more than 30 years since that first IBM PC rolled off the assembly line, but that timespan doesn't make the entire realm of computers easier to understand. For all the advances, the graphics, the fun, and the availability of computers for sale in the same place you buy your booze, a PC remains a daunting, intimidating piece of technology. That can make you feel like a dummy.

This book's job is to convince you that you're not a dummy. Computers are intimidating only when you believe them to be. Peel back that sleek case and you find a timid, frightened beast that wants only to help you. This book takes you on a journey that makes that task easy, fun, and enjoyable.

Oh, and don't peel back the skin on your computer. It doesn't hurt the computer if you do so, but you can better get in touch with your PC's emotional core in ways that don't require tin snips and a blow torch.

What's New in This Edition?

Hey! Thanks for continuing to read this Introduction. Most people don't bother, so you're special! I mean, why read all this nonsense when you could open the book to some random page, stroke your chin, and say, "Wow! This is really appealing." Anyone watching would be impressed. But no, you're reading the very front of the book. The best you can hope for is that any onlooker believes you can't find the price or are trying to look up a relative on the details page. Sorry about that.

This is the 14th edition of *PCs For Dummies,* which begs the question, "What the hell happened to the 13th edition?" That's right, the publisher just skipped over 13 as if it would belie the fact that only 16 percent of Americans bothered to visit a bookstore last year and most people steal this book online. Still, if you want to be specific, this book's 12th edition was titled *Windows 7 Edition.* Then when the 13th edition came out, the publisher called it the 12th edition. So now you're all caught up.

Beyond updating many of this book's less important parts to reflect the Windows 10 operating system, I've invigorated the text with all the new whiz-bang technology introduced since the last edition. Here I address some new topics that have arisen, including

- Updates on new PC features that have become standards, such as USB 3.0, media cards, and solid-state drives (SSDs)
- Details on cloud storage and how it's used to synchronize your files across multiple devices
- Sharing media on the cloud
- Connecting your PC to another gizmo, such as a smartphone, camera, or tablet
- Updates on security and the ever-looming threats on the Internet
- A new, sassy attitude that didn't involve heavy drinking

As in years past, I present all the information in this book in a sane, soothing, and gentle tone that calms even the most panicked computerphobe.

Where to Start

This book is a reference. You can start reading at any point. Use the index or table of contents to see what interests you. After you read the information, feel free to close the book and perform whatever task you need; there's no need to read any further. Well, unless you just enjoy my pithy writing style.

Each of this book's 27 chapters covers a specific aspect of the computer: turning it on, using a printer, using software, or heaving the computer out a window without incurring back injury. Each chapter is divided into self-contained sections, which are nuggets of knowledge all relating to the major theme of the chapter. Sample sections you may find include

- Restarting the PC
- Using the Internet to set the clock
- Ejecting media
- Stopping a printer run amok
- Obtaining software from the Internet
- Connecting to a wireless network
- Accessing cloud storage pictures

You don't have to memorize anything in this book. Nothing about a computer is memorable. Each section is designed so that you can read the information quickly, digest what you have read, and then put down the book and get on with using the computer. If anything technical crops up, you're alerted to its presence so that you can cleanly avoid it.

Conventions Used in This Book

Menu items, links, and other controls on the screen are written using initial-cap text. So if the option is named "Turn off the computer," you see the text Turn Off the Computer (without quotes or commas) shown in this book, whether it appears that way onscreen or not.

If you have to type something, it looks like this:

Type me

You type the text *Type me* as shown. You're told when and whether to press the Enter key. You're also told whether to type a period; periods end sentences written in English, but not always when you type text on a computer.

Windows menu commands are shown like this:

Choose File⇨Exit.

This line directs you to choose the File menu and then choose the Exit command.

Key combinations you may have to press are shown like this:

Ctrl+S

This line says to press and hold down the Ctrl (Control) key, type an *S*, and then release the Ctrl key. It works the same as pressing Shift+S on the keyboard to produce an uppercase *S*. Same deal, different shift key.

Foolish Assumptions

You have a PC, which is an acronym for Personal Computer and describes all computers that run the Windows operating system. You do not have a Macintosh. And you are not a superintelligent gerbil desiring to program an Arduino in FORTRAN.

This book was updated to coincide with the release of Windows 10, a deadline I missed by two months. The book primarily covers Windows 10, although I pay homage to Windows 7, which is the most popular version of Windows as this book goes to press. I do not cover the horrid atrocity that was Windows 8, nor will you find material here on Windows XP or other primitive operating systems.

When this book refers to Windows without a specific edition or version, the information applies generically to both Windows 10 and Windows 7.

Icons Used in This Book

This icon alerts you to needless technical information — drivel I added because I can't help but unleash my inner nerd. Feel free to skip over anything tagged with this little picture.

This icon indicates helpful advice or an insight that makes using the computer interesting. For example, when you're dunking the computer into liquid nitrogen, be sure to wear protective goggles.

This icon indicates something to remember, like wearing pants.

This icon is a reminder for you not to do something, like trying to use a leaf blower to dry your hair.

Where to Go from Here

This book features an online support page, which you can find here:

www.dummies.com/extras/pcs

This book's online cheat sheet, which was once included with the book before the publisher got all cheap, can be located at this web page:

www.dummies.com/cheatsheet/pcs

And bonus material is located on this page:

www.dummies.com/extras/pcs

My email address is listed here, in case you want to send me a note: dgookin@wambooli.com.

Yes, that's my email address, and I respond to every email message. Expect a fast answer when you write a short, to-the-point message directly related to this book. Longer messages take me longer to read — sometimes weeks — but I will get back to you. Also, please understand that I cannot troubleshoot or fix your PC.

You can also visit my website, which is chock-full of helpful support pages, bonus information, games, and fun. Go to www.wambooli.com.

With this book in hand, you're now ready to go out and conquer your PC. Start by looking through the table of contents or the index. Find a topic and turn to the page indicated, and you're ready to go. Also, feel free to write in this book, fill in the blanks, dog-ear the pages, and do anything else that would make a librarian blanch. Enjoy.

Part I
Hello, PC!

In this part . . .

- ✔ Discover what a PC is and what it can do
- ✔ Explore the various parts of a computer
- ✔ Set up and configure a PC
- ✔ Cope with turning a computer on or off

Chapter 1

What Is This Thing, This PC?

In This Chapter

▶ Answering some common PC questions

▶ Understanding basic computer concepts

▶ Knowing about hardware and software

▶ Buying a computer

▶ Realizing that your PC is quite dumb

I wish that computers were evil. It would be easier to understand the computer if it were upfront about being evil and expressed its malevolent desire to get you. Minus that negative assurance, you end up operating the PC under a constant suspicion. That's not healthy. So instead of fearing, try understanding. Maybe Mr. PC isn't so bad after all?

Some Quick Questions to Get Out of the Way

Doubtless, your mind is abuzz with various questions about computers. I ask myself computer questions often, so don't think that your curiosity is unusual. Trust me: Few people over the age of 26 are comfortable when first encountering anything high-tech.

"What is a PC?"

A *PC* is a computer — specifically, an acronym for *personal computer*.

Historically, the beast was known as a *microcomputer*. That's because back in the 1970s, computers were huge, room-sized things that required legions of bespectacled scientists to operate. Individuals didn't own such computers — well, unless you were eccentric or enjoyed printing your own phone bill. So mere mortals were sold a smaller version, which the Computer Professionals Union insisted be called a *micro*computer.

Micro means teensy. The term is preferred by computer scientists because you can't wear a white lab coat and be taken seriously when you use the word "teensy."

Actually, the term *micro* comes from *microprocessor,* the main computer chip inside the early personal computers.

When IBM unveiled its first business microcomputer back in 1982, they called it the IBM Personal Computer — or PC, for short. All of today's personal computers are descended from that original model, so they've inherited the term *PC.* Figure 1-1 displays a timeline of the PC's history, in case you're curious.

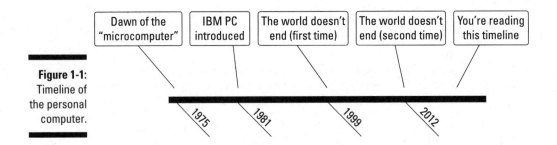

Figure 1-1:
Timeline of the personal computer.

The only PC that's not called "PC" is Apple's Macintosh computer. Mac users refer to their computers as *Macs.* That's based on an old IBM–Apple rivalry that no one cares about any more. Still, many Mac users get all huffy when you call their computers PCs. So it's fine by me to tease those crybabies by referring to their expensive toys as PCs.

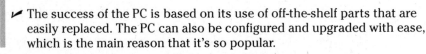

✔ The term *PC* generically refers to any computer that can run the Windows operating system.

✔ Although your car or sewing machine or the machine that goes "boop" at the hospital may contain computer electronics, those devices are not PCs.

✔ Curiously, IBM got out of the PC manufacturing business in the early 2000s.

✔ The success of the PC is based on its use of off-the-shelf parts that are easily replaced. The PC can also be configured and upgraded with ease, which is the main reason that it's so popular.

"Why not just use a tablet or smartphone instead of a PC?"

Sure, you can get by in today's well-connected, digital world by getting yourself a tablet or smartphone. To hell with computers!

Smartphones and tablets can send and receive email, browse the web, play games, and do all sorts of interesting things. They have several downfalls when compared with PCs:

- ✔ Mobile devices are designed for data consumption, not data production. If you're merely passing through this digital life, you can get by with a phone or tablet and never own a PC. If you need to create something, you need a computer.

- ✔ PCs offer several input devices — specifically, the keyboard and the mouse. You can even add a touchscreen to a PC, if you're into that touchy-tappy-swipey stuff.

- ✔ Mobile devices lack the expandability of a PC. You can upgrade a PC, adding more storage, memory, a better monitor, a mouse with 20,000 buttons, and so on.

- ✔ The typical computer lasts for years. A mobile device is usually replaced every other year.

Now, if you've changed your mind about getting a PC, remember that you cannot return this book once you've started reading this material.

"Should I buy a Dell?"

I get this question all the time, though "Dell" might be replaced by some other brand name. See the later section "Buy Yourself a PC!"

"Will my computer explode?"

This question is important, so please skip all the other questions I've placed before this question and read this question first!

If you're a fan of science fiction television or film, you're probably familiar with the concept of the exploding computer. Sparks, smoke, flying debris — it all appears to be a common function of computers in the future. Sure, they could just beep and display error messages when they die, but that's not visually exciting.

The answer is no, your computer will not explode. At least, not spontaneously. If you pour fruit punch into the computer or lightning strikes or the power supply unexplainably fails, the most you may see is a puff of blue smoke, but no explosions.

Basic Computer Concepts in Easily Digestible Chunks

You either use or are about to purchase one of the most advanced pieces of technology ever made available to humans. Why not be a sport about it and take a few moments to not avoid some of the more technical mumbo jumbo surrounding that technology? Don't fret: I'll be gentle.

What a computer does

Computers can do anything and try to do just about everything. At their core, however, computers are simple gizmos. Their advantage is that computers have oodles of potential.

A computer takes input, processes it, and then generates output. That's kind of how a baby works, though to keep you from being utterly befuddled, you can refer to Figure 1-2, which completely illustrates that basic computer concept.

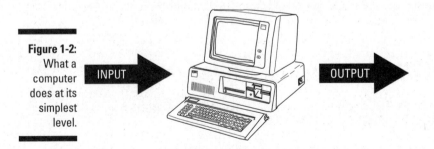

Figure 1-2: What a computer does at its simplest level.

INPUT

OUTPUT

The "input goes into the computer, gets processed, and then produces output" equation is the foundation of these three primary computer concepts:

- ✔ I/O
- ✔ Processing
- ✔ Storage

I/O: I/O stands for input and output. It's pronounced "I owe," like *Io,* the
third-largest moon of Jupiter. I/O is pretty much the *only* thing a computer
does: It receives input from devices — the keyboard, mouse, Internet. It generates output, displayed on the screen, printed, or sent back to the Internet.
That's I/O.

Processing: What the computer does between input and output is *processing.*
It's what happens to the input to make the output significant. Otherwise, the
computer would simply be a tube, and computer science would be the same
as plumbing.

Processing is handled inside the computer by a gizmo known as (logically
enough) a processor. See Chapter 5 for more information on the processor.

Storage: The final part of the basic computer equation is storage, which is
where the processing takes place. Two types of storage are used: temporary
and long-term. Temporary storage is the computer *memory,* or *RAM.* Long-
term storage is provided by the computer's storage media.

Computer memory is covered in Chapter 6. Long-term storage is covered in
Chapter 7.

Hardware and software

The computer universe is divided into two parts. One part is hardware. The
other part is software.

Hardware is the physical part of a computer: anything you can touch and
anything you can see — or anything that smells like burning plastic. The computer console, the monitor, the keyboard, the mouse. All that physical stuff
is hardware.

Software is the computer's brain. Software tells the hardware what to do.

In a way, it helps to think of hardware and software as a symphony orchestra. For hardware, you have the musicians and their instruments. Their software is the music. As with a computer, the music (software) tells the musicians and their instruments (hardware) what to do.

Without software, hardware just sits around and looks pretty. It can't do anything because it has no instructions and nothing telling it what to do next. And, like a symphony orchestra without music, that can be an expensive waste of time, especially at union scale.

To make the computer system work, software must be in charge. In fact, software determines your computer's personality and potential.

- ✔ If you can throw it out a window, it's hardware.
- ✔ If you can throw it out a window and it comes back, it's a cat.
- ✔ Computer software includes all the programs you use on the PC.
- ✔ The most important piece of software is the computer's *operating system.* That's the main program in charge of everything.
- ✔ Chapter 13 covers Windows, which is the PC's least popular yet most common operating system.
- ✔ Chapter 14 covers computer programs, also considered software.

Buy Yourself a PC!

If you don't yet have a PC, you can rush out and buy one. My advice is not to rush, despite having just directed you to do so.

A computer is a complex piece of electronics. Buying one isn't like purchasing a riding lawnmower or nose-hair trimmer. To make your purchase a successful one, consider my friendly, 5-step method for buying a PC.

1. **Know what it is that you want the computer to do.**
2. **Find software to accomplish that task.**
3. **Find hardware to match the software.**
4. **Locate service and support.**
5. **Buy the computer!**

Yes, it's really that easy. If you obey these steps and pay attention, you'll be a lot more satisfied with your computer purchase.

Step 1. What do you want the PC to do?

Believe it or not, most people don't know why they want a computer. If that's you, consider what you're getting into. Computers aren't for everyone, especially with smartphones and tablets available at far less cost.

If you really do need a computer, figure out what you want it to do for you. Do you just want to do some word processing, emailing, and social networking? Perhaps you want a machine that plays the latest games? Or maybe you need some graphics horsepower to create illustrations or animation? Limitless possibilities exist with a computer, but the more you know about what you want to do, the better you can get the perfect PC for your needs.

Step 2. Find software

Software makes the computer go, so before you discuss PC brand names or big box stores, you need to look at the programs you plan on using. That's because some software — games, video production, graphics — requires specific computer hardware. Knowing about that hardware ahead of time means you'll be happier with your purchase.

By recognizing which software you need first, you can easily move on to the next step.

Step 3. Match hardware to the software

How can you match hardware to the software you need? Simple: Read the software requirements. These are listed on the side of the software box or on the software developer's website. The requirements explain exactly what kind of hardware is required. Specifically, the requirements suggest what kind of processor is best, how much memory is preferred, and how much storage the software demands. You might also learn of other requirements, such as a high-end graphics card or a specialized interface.

✔ For general computer uses, any PC that can run the Windows operating system will probably work just fine for you. When you have specific software you plan on running, however, you should make sure that the computer you get has the hardware you need.

✔ All that hardware nonsense is covered later in this book. Don't worry about trying to understand software requirements when you're just starting out. Use this book's index to help you learn about different PC hardware thingies.

Step 4. Locate service and support

Most people assume that Step 4 would have to do with brand names or famously-not-bankrupt brick-and-mortar stores. Nope! What's more important is ensuring that you get proper service and support for your new computer purchase — especially when you're just starting out and you blanch at the thought of opening the computer's case.

Service means one thing: Who fixes the computer? That's the main reason I recommend buying a PC at a local, mom-and-pop type of store. You develop a personal relationship with the people who service your computer. If you choose not to buy at a local store, you must ask to discover who really fixes your computer and where it gets fixed.

Support is about getting help for your computer. Some people need lots of help. If that's you, buy from a place that offers free classes or has a toll-free support number. That support may add to the purchase price, but it's worth every penny if it saves you aggravation in the future.

Step 5. Buy it!

The final step to getting a new computer — or your first computer — is to buy it. Do it!

The hesitation many people have about buying a new computer is that a newer, better, faster model is coming down the pike. That's always true! So rather than wait forever, just get up and buy the computer! 'Nuff said.

What To Do With An Old Computer

For heaven's sake, don't throw out your old computer! That's because a computer can be recycled.

The first stage for recycling is to use the old keyboard, mouse, and monitor with your new PC. If you know this recycling tidbit before you buy the new computer, you can save money by buying just the *console,* or the main part of the PC.

The second stage for recycling is to turn in your old PC to a recycling center. Though the computer guts may be useless to you, they do have value.

Of course, you can always hang on to your old PCs for a while. In fact, I keep my old PC on the network for a few weeks to ensure that the new one has everything I need. If not, I can fire up the old one and copy over files or jot down information.

Eventually my old computers end up in my garage on some shelves. I call it the Bone Yard. After a few years, I recycle the old computer.

- ✔ If the new PC comes with its own keyboard and mouse, keep the old ones as spares.

- ✔ You can always retire the old PC to the rumpus room for the kids to use. They'll hate you for it and whine about buying a new one. Don't worry: You'll give in soon enough.

- ✔ Old PCs can be donated to charities, but call first to see if they want one. Sometimes old computers aren't worth the trouble. (Ask your kids.)

- ✔ One item you might not want to recycle is the old PC's hard drive. If possible, remove it from the old computer's console. If the hard drive contains sensitive information, have it destroyed. Outfits that shred documents offer hard drive destruction services, should security be a concern to you or your presidential campaign.

A Final Thing to Remember

Computers aren't evil. They harbor no sinister intelligence. In fact, when you get to know them, you see that they're rather dumb.

Now robots, on the other hand! Well, that's a topic for another book.

Chapter 2

The PC Knobs, Buttons, and Doodads Tour

*I*f I were to use one word to describe the typical PC design, that word would be *uninspired*. Face it: The PC is a box. It's not aerodynamic or sleek or award-winning. No one will confuse a PC sitting on your desk with modern art. People in the year 2045 won't hang posters of early 21st century PCs on their walls. Sad, but true.

Forgiving its utilitarian look, it's important to identify some of the basic parts of a computer system, as well as know the purpose behind the many buttons, holes, nooks, and crannies that festoon the plain, dull tin can known as a PC.

The Big Picture

Figure 2-1 shows a typical personal computer system. It may not match what you have, because I'm trying to label the pieces and not stalk you.

Here are the important items to note in a typical computer system:

Console: The main computer box, and centerpiece of the computer system, is the console. It is *not* the CPU, though plenty of dorks out there refer to it as such. The console contains the computer's electronic guts. It's also home to various buttons, lights, and holes into which you plug the rest of the computer system.

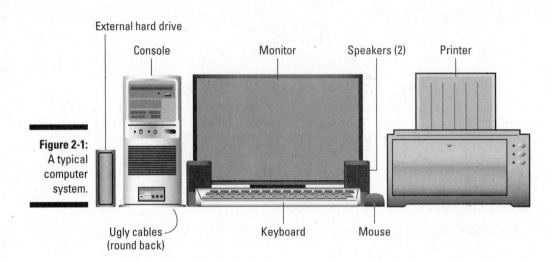

External hard drive

Console   Monitor   Speakers (2)   Printer

Figure 2-1:
A typical
computer
system.

Ugly cables
(round back)   Keyboard   Mouse

Monitor: The monitor is the device where the computer displays information — its output. On an all-in-one PC, the monitor and console are the same thing. Otherwise, don't assume that the "computer" is inside the monitor. The monitor merely displays stuff.

Keyboard: The keyboard is the thing you type on and is the primary way you communicate with the computer.

Mouse: No rodent or pest, the computer mouse is a helpful device that lets you work with graphical objects displayed on the monitor.

Speakers: PCs bleep and squawk through a set of stereo speakers, which can be external jobbies you set up (refer to Figure 2-1), speakers built into the console or monitor, or headphones. Pay more money and you can even get a subwoofer to sit under your desk. Now, *that* will rattle the neighbor's windows.

External hard drive: You may or may not have one (yet), but an external hard drive is used to *back up,* or create a safety copy of, the important stuff you store on your computer.

Printer: The printer is where you get the computer's printed output, also called *hard copy.*

You may find, in addition to these basic items, other gizmos clustered around your computer, such as a scanner, a second monitor, a high-speed modem, or one of many, many other toys — er, vital computer peripherals.

One thing definitely not shown in Figure 2-1 is the ganglion of cable that dwells behind each and every computer. What a mess! These cables are required when you want to plug things into the wall and into each other. No shampoo or conditioner on Earth can clean up those tangles.

- Take a moment to identify the basic PC pieces in your own computer system.

- The printer can be attached directly to the console, or it might be available through the computer network.

- Chapters in Part II go into more detail on the computer components introduced and illustrated earlier, in Figure 2-1.

- CPU stands for *central processing unit.* It's another term for the computer's processor. See Chapter 5.

All Around the Console

The pride and joy of any computer system is the console, the main box into which all the other pieces plug. Because of the console's importance, and its surplus of interesting buttons and such, consider reviewing this section to better familiarize yourself with the typical computer console.

There is no typical console

Thanks to major conspiracies and a wicked sense of humor in the computer industry, not all PC consoles look the same. To keep you confused, manufacturers like to shake it up a bit when it comes to PC design. So while all the consoles do feature the same basic components and connections, no single prototype or base model exists for me to show you. Instead, I offer Figure 2-2, which illustrates six common PC configurations.

Mini-tower: The mini-tower is the most popular console type. It can sit on top of a desk, right next to the monitor (refer to Figure 2-1). It can also be tucked away out of sight, below the desk.

Desktop: The desktop console type sits flat on the desk. The monitor usually squats on top of the console in the traditional PC configuration.

Mini-desktop: The mini-desktop console is just too cute and tiny, about the size of a college dictionary. That makes it ideal for places where space — and money — is tight. The downside is that these consoles lack internal expansion options.

Mini-Tower

Desktop

Mini-Desktop

Figure 2-2:
The gamut
of PC con-
sole
configura-
tions.

All-in-One Desktop

Two-in-One Tablet

Laptop

All-in-one desktop: A popular and trendy computer design combines the console and monitor into a single unit. From the front, the console looks like a monitor, though it's thicker. On the sides, you find the myriad of connectors and other computer doodads.

Two-in-one tablet: This ultrathin, portable PC comes in two pieces: screen and keyboard. The keyboard detaches, allowing you to use the tablet PC's touchscreen for input.

Laptop: The traditional portable computer, the laptop is a handy, lightweight package, ideal for slowing down the security checkpoints in airports. Laptop PCs work just like their desktop brethren; any exceptions are noted throughout this book.

Choosing the proper PC configuration depends on your needs. Power users love the expandability of the tower. Those on a budget may go for a mini-desktop. Folks on the go love laptops.

✔ No matter how big your computer, the amount of clutter you have always expands to fill the available desk space.

✔ The two-in-one model is also called a tablet PC. It features an optional digital stylus for input, which is another handy and expensive thing to lose.

✔ More laptop, two-in-one, and tablet PC information is in my book *Laptops For Dummies,* 6th Edition (Wiley), available at fine bookstores wherever fine bookstores still exist.

✔ Not shown in Figure 2-2 is the tower console configuration. A taller version of the mini-tower, it boasts more internal expansion options. I've not seen this model for sale to the general public in a few years, but it's still a confirmation option from some computer manufacturers.

✔ The amount of space a PC console occupies is often referred to as its *footprint.* Smaller consoles are *small footprint* PCs.

Major points of interest on the console, front

After many years, PC manufacturers discovered that it works best to put those items designed for you, the human, on the *front* part of the console. I'm not joking: Nearly everything you needed to connect to an early PC required that you pull the console away from the wall, crane your neck, and hope for the best. So consider yourself blessed and use Figure 2-3 as your reference as you go hunting for the following items:

Optical drive: Don't worry if your PC lacks one of these storage devices; they're being phased out. You can use the optical drive to read optical discs, CDs, and DVDs. The problem is capacity: These discs don't store as much information as is needed for a modern computer.

Future expansion: Most consoles feature blank spots. They may look interesting or useful, but they're not! They simply cover holes used for adding new hardware to your PC.

Media card slots: Use these slots to read media cards, such as those used by digital cameras and other portable electronics. Your PC may have only one media card reading slot. In Figure 2-3, you see the common 19-in-1 card reader, which accepts all media card formats.

Power button: No longer a plain on–off button, the *power button* can do more than just turn the computer on or off. See Chapter 4 for the details.

Lights: A staple of computers in the movies, the PC console may not have any lights. Some PCs have a power lamp, which illuminates when the system is on. A hard drive lamp may flicker as the mass storage device is accessed. That's pretty much it.

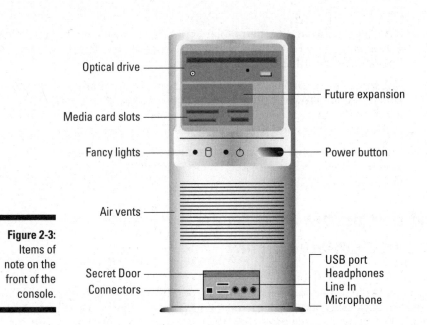

Optical drive

Future expansion

Media card slots

Fancy lights

Power button

Air vents

Figure 2-3:
Items of
note on the
front of the
console.

Secret Door

Connectors

USB port
Headphones
Line In
Microphone

Air vents: Air vents aren't impressive, but they're necessary. They keep the console cool by helping air circulate inside. The thing's gotta breathe.

I/O panel: Your PC most likely features a clutch of various connectors somewhere on its front, covered by a door or not. Nestled in that area are places to connect joysticks, microphones, headphones, thumb drives, or other handy gizmos you may need to plug and unplug from time to time.

You might be lucky and find other fun and unusual items living on the front of your PC's console. They're probably particular to a certain computer brand or model. Consider them a bonus.

✔ Some newer computers have stickers that show the secret Windows code number or proclaim such nonsense as "I was built to run Windows Optimus Prime" or "An Intel hoohah lurks inside this box."

✔ For more specific information on the connectors lurking behind a secret panel, see the section "The I/O panel," later in this chapter.

✔ Don't block the air vents on the front of the console. If you do, the computer may suffocate. (It gets too hot.)

✔ The all-in-one type of PC features all its holes, switches, and slots on its sides or back.

✔ A hard drive lamp can be red or green or yellow, and it flickers when the mass storage device is in use. The flickering is not an alarm, so don't let it freak you out! The PC is just doing its job.

Stuff found on the console's rump

Just like an exotic dancer, the console's backside is its busy side. That's where you find various connectors for the many devices in your computer system: a place to plug in the monitor, keyboard, mouse, speakers, and just about any other gizmo you desire to have in your computer system.

Use Figure 2-4 as a guide for finding important items on the back of the PC's console. Note that some things may look different and some may be missing; not every console is the same.

Power: The console needs power, and the power connector is where you plug in the power cord. The other end of the power cord plugs into the wall.

Fan: Air gets sucked in here. Or it might be blown out. I forget which.

On-off switch: This isn't a power button, it's an on/off switch. Don't use it to turn off the PC! Its purpose is to disable the power supply for troubleshooting or repair. Keep the switch in the On position. Not every PC features this switch.

Voltage selector: Use this switch to change power frequencies to match the specifications for your country, region, or planet. This switch is part of the power supply.

Expansion slots: These slots are available for adding new components on expansion cards to the console and expanding your PC's hardware. Any connectors on the expansion cards appear in this area, such as the video connectors on a graphics adapter (refer to Figure 2-4).

Vents: The breathing thing again.

I/O panel: Aside from the power cord, and anything attached to an expansion card, the rest of your PC's expansion options and plug-in-type things are located in a central area that I call the I/O panel. Details of what you can find there are covered in the next section.

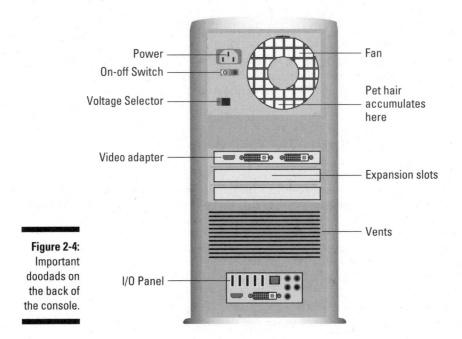

Power

On-off Switch

Voltage Selector

Fan

Pet hair accumulates here

Video adapter

Expansion slots

Vents

Figure 2-4:
Important doodads on the back of the console.

I/O Panel

The I/O panel

To either help keep all connectors in one spot or just create an intensely cable-crammed location, your PC's console features an I/O panel on its rear. That location is where you add various expansion options to the PC as well as plug in the standard devices shown way back in Figure 2-1.

Use Figure 2-5 as your guide for what's what. The items you find on your PC's I/O panel may be labeled with text or may include the symbols listed later, in Table 2-1. Also keep in mind that Figure 2-5 is only a guide; your PC console may have a different layout and sport more or fewer items on the I/O panel.

Here are some of the things you may find on the I/O panel:

USB: Plug snazzy devices into these Certs-size Universal Serial Bus (USB) slots. See Chapter 10 for more information about USB.

Video: Your PC's monitor can plug into one of the video adapters on the I/O panel. You may find a traditional VGA adapter, a digital video adapter, an HDMI adapter, or a combination of all three. See Chapter 8 for more information on computer video.

Table 2-1	Shapes, Connections, Symbols, and Colors		
Name	*Connector*	*Symbol*	*Color*
Digital video			White
HDMI		HDMI	Black
Microphone			Pink
Network			None
Power			Yellow
Speakers/headphones			Lime
USB			Black/blue
VGA video			Blue

Network: Plug in a local area network (LAN) connector or attach a broad-band modem to the PC.

The good news? You connect all this stuff only once. Then your PC's butt faces the wall for the rest of its life and you never have to look at it again — well, unless you add something in the future or you just enjoy looking at PC butts.

✔ Connectors for a microphone and headphones are also found on the PC's front I/O panel, illustrated earlier, in Figure 2-3.

✔ Older PCs may sport ports not shown in Figure 2-5. These ports include separate mouse and keyboard ports, the IEEE port, and even the ancient COM, printer, and joystick ports. The functions of these ports have been replaced with USB ports, which are plentiful on modern PCs.

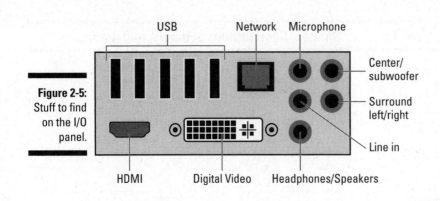

USB   Network   Microphone

Center/
subwoofer

Surround
left/right

Line in

Figure 2-5:
Stuff to find
on the I/O
panel.

HDMI   Digital Video   Headphones/Speakers

Helpful hints, hieroglyphics, and hues

Even though most PC connectors are different, manufacturers have relented and agreed upon a set of common colors and symbols used to label the various holes, connectors, and ports on the console's hindquarters. They're listed in Table 2-1 to help you find things, in case the need arises.

Chapter 3

PC Setup

I could lie to you and say that setting up a PC is so simple that a child could do it. A Vulcan child, perhaps. Even so, setting up a computer isn't as difficult as assembling backyard play equipment or programming 1980s VCRs. The process does, however, involve a lot of cable plugging, which must be done properly if you want the computer system to work.

Computer Assembly

Consider yourself lucky if your new PC pops right out of the box, ready to run. Many all-in-one PCs work that way — or close to it. Laptops come out of the box ready to go (well, perhaps needing a battery charge). For the rest of the lot, peruse this section on how to get your PC out of the box and assembled.

Unpacking the boxes

Your computer runs faster when you take it out of the box.

If you purchased a computer system, open the console's box first. It may contain a roadmap or diagram of how to attach the other pieces.

As you open boxes, check to ensure that you have all the parts necessary for your computer system. Look through all the packing materials inside the box. Sometimes, manufacturers stick important items inside boxes inside boxes, or nestled in the Styrofoam. Refer to the packing slip or invoice for the list of parts. If you're missing anything, call someone!

✔ Keep the packing slip, warranty, sales receipt, and other important pieces of paper together.

✔ Don't fill out the warranty card until after the computer is set up and running fine. If you have to return the computer, the store prefers that the warranty card *not* be filled in.

✔ Keep all boxes and packing materials. You need them if you have to return the computer. Also, the boxes are the best way to ship the computer if you ever have to move. Some movers don't insure a computer unless it's packed in its original box.

Setting up the console

The *console* is the main computer box, the locus of all PC activities, so you should set it up first. Put the console in the location where you've always dreamed it would be. If you plan to put the console beneath your desk, put it there now.

Don't back the console up against the wall just yet, because you need to plug things into the console's rump. Not until everything is connected to the console do you want to push it up against the wall. (Even then, leave some room so that you don't crimp the cables.)

✔ The console needs to breathe. Don't place it in a confined space or inside a cabinet where there's no air circulation.

✔ Avoid setting the console by a window where the sun will heat it up. Computers don't like to operate in extreme heat — or extreme cold, for that matter. A PC is happiest when it operates at temperatures between 40 and 80 degrees Fahrenheit or, for the world outside the United States, between 4 and 27 degrees Celsius.

✔ Also avoid humidity, which can gum up a computer. Readers in tropical climes have reported mold growing inside their PCs — the humidity was that bad! If you compute where it's humid, do so in an air-conditioned room.

✔ Don't put the console in a cabinet unless the cabinet is well-ventilated. Shoot some bullet holes in the cabinet if it requires more ventilation.

✔ A computer by a window makes a tempting target for a smash-and-grab thief.

Plugging in and connecting

After setting up the console, your next job is to obtain the various other devices — the *peripherals* — and attach them to the console. You'll also need to plug things in to a power supply.

I recommend setting up a peripheral, connecting it to the console, and moving on to the next peripheral. For example, set up the monitor, and then plug it into the console. Set up the keyboard, and then plug it into the console. For specific directions on connecting individual items, refer to the next section.

Some computer peripherals get their power directly from the wall socket. I recommend that you plug in their power cords last. Helpful tips on connecting your PC and its components to a power source are covered in the later section "It Must Have Power."

The Plugging-Things-In Guide

It's tempting, but avoid the urge to use glue and adhesive tape when you first set up the computer. Attaching high-tech electronics to each other requires some finesse, and on that topic I'm willing to share my decades of experience.

✔ All major parts of a computer system plug directly into the console, which is why I recommend unpacking and setting up the console first.

✔ If this is the first time you're setting up the computer, don't plug in the console yet. You can turn on the console after connecting all the pieces.

✔ Plug things into the console before you plug them into the wall.

✔ It's generally okay to plug something into the console while the computer is on. Exceptions exist to this rule, so read this section carefully!

✔ Also see Chapter 10 for information on using USB devices, which includes just about every peripheral known in the PC kingdom. That chapter also covers using Bluetooth to wirelessly connect peripherals to your PC.

Know your computer cables

A computer cable is known by which hole, or *port,* it plugs into. For example, USB cables plug into USB ports.

The ends of a computer cable are configured so that you cannot plug in the cable backward: The connector for the console is one shape, and the connector for the gizmo is another shape. When the connectors are the same shape, it doesn't matter which end plugs in where.

All cables fasten snugly. Network cables have little tabs on them that snap when the cable is properly inserted. You must squeeze the tab to remove the cable. Some video connectors have tiny thumbscrews on the side, which help cinch the cable to the connector.

Some cables are permanently attached to their devices: The mouse and keyboard have this

type of cable, for example. Other cables are separate; remember to plug in both ends.

Extra cables, if you need them, can be purchased at any computer or office supply store. As a suggestion, measure the distance for which you need a cable and then double it to get a cable of the proper length. For example, if it's 2 feet between your console and where you want a printer, get a 4-foot printer (USB) cable.

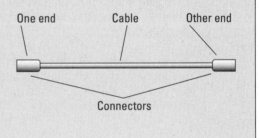

Attaching the keyboard and mouse

Set up the keyboard right in front of where you sit when you use the computer, between you and the monitor. The mouse lives to the right or left of the keyboard, depending on whether you're right- or left-handed.

- ✔ The PC keyboard plugs into a USB port. The mouse plugs into a USB port. It doesn't matter which one.

- ✔ If the keyboard features its own USB port, connect the mouse to that USB port.

- ✔ Some PCs sports a mixture of USB 3.0 and older USB ports. The USB 3.0 ports are color-coded blue. Save those ports for high-speed devices, like external hard drives. Plug the keyboard and mouse into the older (non-blue) USB ports.

Setting up the monitor

Set the monitor atop your desk, generally away from where you sit, to accommodate room for the keyboard. For the best results, the monitor should face you.

The monitor's cable may be attached or separate. If separate, attach the cable to the monitor. Plug the monitor's cable into the console's graphics adapter jack. Several jack types are available, though I recommend using either the digital (white) or HDMI (black) jack. Choose the cable that matches the jack.

The monitor also requires power. See the later section "It Must Have Power."

- ✔ If the console has two sets of connectors, use the one on an expansion card rather than the one found on the console's I/O panel. That expansion card jack indicates a high-end graphics adapter, which offers better features.

- ✔ Many high-end graphics adapters feature two digital video jacks. If the PC has only one monitor, you can use either jack. The second digital video jack is for a second monitor.

- ✔ HDMI stands for High-Definition Multimedia Interface.

- ✔ See Chapter 8 for more information about PC monitors and graphics.

Connecting to the network

Plug the network cable into the network jack on the back of the console. This is how you connect your PC to a network, a gateway, a broadband modem, or any of a number of oddly named networking things. Well, unless you have a Wi-Fi (wireless) connection.

For more info, refer to Chapter 17, which covers computer networking.

Adding a printer

You can add a printer to the computer system at any time. Try to position the printer where it's within arm's reach of the console so that you can reach over and pluck out whatever it is you're printing.

The printer connects directly to the PC with a USB cable. However, you might need to install the printer's software before you make the connection.

You can also access printers on the network, in which case connecting the network also connects the printers. Job finished!

- ✔ The printer requires power, so you need to plug it into a wall socket. See the section "It Must Have Power," later in this chapter.
- ✔ See Chapter 11 for all things printer.

Hooking up the speakers

Computer audio involves both output and input — the famous I/O you probably sang songs about when you went to computer camp as a teen.

Both headphones and speakers use the Line Out, headphone, or speakers jack. Furthermore, speakers may need to be plugged into the wall for more power; see the section "It Must Have Power," later in this chapter.

Connect the microphone to the Mic or Line In jack. When both jacks are available, use Mic for a microphone because Line In is for unamplified sound sources.

Table 3-1 lists the common color codes for any additional audio connections your PC might require. These colors are found on the ring of the jack where you connect the PC audio device.

Table 3-1	PC Audio Color Codes
Jack Type	*Color*
Center/subwoofer	Brown
Line In	Gray
Microphone	Pink
Speakers/headphones	Lime
Surround left/right	Black

- ✔ All computer audio uses the standard *mini-DIN* connector, which looks like a tiny pointy thing. Just plug it into the appropriate, color-coded hole.
- ✔ Be sure to check the front of the console for another spot to plug in the headphones or microphone. This location is much handier than using the connector on the back.

✔ Some PCs have special audio hardware, which you can determine by
      looking at the console's rear for audio connectors on an expansion slot
      cover. If your PC is configured this way, be sure to plug the speakers into
      the audio card's output jacks, not into the standard audio output jacks
      on the I/O panel.

    ✔ Refer to Chapter 12 for more information on PC audio, including some
      speaker layout instructions.

It Must Have Power

Computer devices crave power like an armband-wearing, social outcast, high
school hall monitor. The last thing you need to do, after plugging your computer components into the console, is to plug all those gizmos into the wall.

Plugging everything into a power strip

You may have noticed that the computer system has far more devices that
need to be plugged in than the number of available wall sockets. No problem!
That's why Thomas Edison invented power strips. The idea is to plug everything into a power strip and then plug that single power strip into the wall, as
illustrated in Figure 3-1.

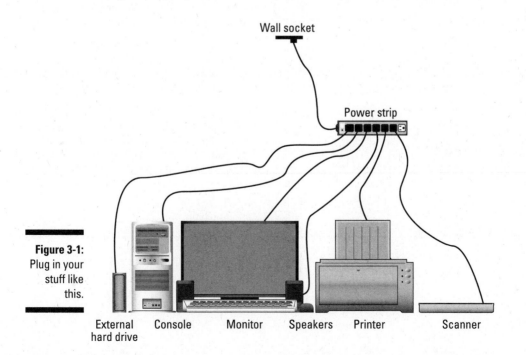

Figure 3-1:
Plug in your
stuff like
this.

External   Console   Monitor   Speakers   Printer   Scanner
hard drive

Follow these steps:

1. **Ensure that all your gizmos with on–off switches are in the Off position.**

   Don't worry if the device has a power button and you can't determine whether it's on or off. If it's not plugged in, it's off.

2. **Ensure that the power strip is in the Off position.**

3. **Plug everything into the power strip.**

4. **Turn your gizmos to the On position.**

To turn on the computer system, turn on the power strip. But not yet! The official on–off information is in Chapter 4. See that chapter for more information.

Surges, spikes, and lightning strikes

The power that comes from the wall socket into your computer isn't as pure as the wind-driven snow. Occasionally, it may be corrupted by some of the various electrical nasties that, every now and then, come uninvited into your home or office. Here's the lowdown:

Line noise: Interference on the power line, most commonly caused by an electric motor on the same circuit. For example, the radio turns to static when you use the blender. That's line noise.

Surge: A gradual increase in power.

Serge: Some guy from Europe.

Spike: A sudden increase in the power. Spikes happen when lightning strikes nearby.

Dip: The opposite of a surge; a decrease in power. Some electrical motors don't work, and room lights are dimmer than normal. A dip is also known as a *brownout*.

Power outage: An absence of power coming through the line. People in the 1960s called it a *blackout*.

A power strip with surge protection helps keep your electronics happy during a surge. If the power strip has noise filtering or line conditioning, it works even better.

The most expensive form of protection is spike protection, in which the power strip lays down its life by taking the full brunt of the spike and saving your computer equipment.

Because they're particularly nasty, spikes come through not only the power lines but also the phone and cable TV lines. So, if lightning strikes are a common occurrence in your area, use a power strip with phone line, cable, and maybe even network cable filters.

✔ Try to find a power strip with line noise filtering. Even better, pay more to buy a power strip that has line conditioning! That's super nice for your electronic goodies.

✔ I recommend the Kensington SmartSockets–brand power strips. Unlike cheaper power strips, the SmartSockets brand lines up its sockets in an arrangement that makes it easier to plug in bulky transformers.

✔ Most power strips have six sockets, which is plenty for a typical computer system. If not, buy a second power strip, plug it into its own wall socket, and use it for the rest of your computer devices. But:

✔ Don't plug one power strip into another power strip; it's electrically unsafe!

✔ Don't plug a laser printer into a power strip. The laser printer draws too much juice. Instead, you must plug the laser printer directly into the wall socket. (It says so in your laser printer's setup directions — if you ever get around to reading them.)

Taking advantage of a UPS

UPS stands for *uninterruptible power supply,* and it's the best thing to have for hooking up your computer system to the wall socket. Basically, a *UPS* is a power strip combined with a battery to keep your computer running when the power goes out.

Figure 3-2 illustrates the proper way to set up your computer system with a UPS and power strip. Not shown is a USB cable that connects the UPS to the console to alert the computer about a power outage.

The idea behind a UPS isn't to keep computing while the power is out. Instead, the UPS is designed to keep your basic computer components — the console and monitor — up and running just long enough for you to save your work and properly shut down the computer. That way, you never lose anything from an unexpected power outage.

✔ Ignore what it says on the box: A UPS gives you *maybe* five minutes of computer power. Most often, you get only two minutes of power.

✔ Some UPS systems also have non-battery-backed-up sockets so that you can plug everything into the UPS directly. Just be sure to plug the monitor and console into the battery-backed-up sockets.

✔ I also recommend plugging any external hard drives into the UPS's battery-backed-up sockets.

✔ Leave the UPS on all the time. Turn it off only when the power is out and the computer has been properly shut down.

✔ In addition to providing emergency power, a UPS provides higher levels of electrical protection for your equipment. Many models offer surge, spike, and dip protection, which keep your PC running smoothly despite any nasties the power company may throw your way.

✔ Also see Chapter 24 for information on having your computer shut down automatically when the power goes out.

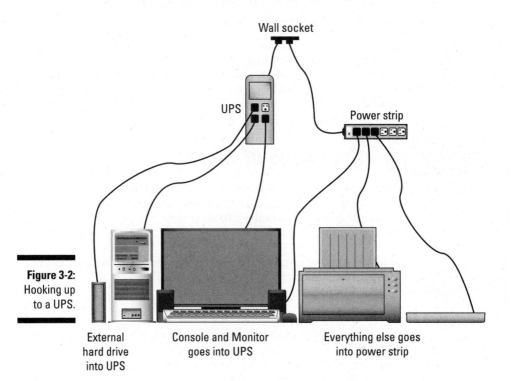

Wall socket

UPS

Power strip

Figure 3-2:
Hooking up
to a UPS.

External
hard drive
into UPS

Console and Monitor
goes into UPS

Everything else goes
into power strip

Using the UPS (a short play)

Interior upscale kitchen. A thunderclap is heard. The lights flicker and then go out. ROGER, 40ish and nerdy, is left sitting in the dark, his computer still on. The UPS beeps once every few seconds. *FELICIA rushes in. She is pretentious, but not insufferably so.*

FELICIA: The power is out! The brioche I put in the toaster oven is ruined! Did you lose that urgent doodle you were creating in Paint?

ROGER: No, darling, I'm still working on it. See? Our UPS has kept the computer console and monitor turned on despite the power outage.

FELICIA: Oh! That explains the beeping.

ROGER: Yes, the UPS beeps when the power has gone out. It does that just in case I failed to observe the pitch darkness.

FELICIA: Well, hurry up and print your doodle!

ROGER: Not now, sugarplum! Printing can wait, which is why I didn't connect the printer to the UPS. It's as powerless as the toaster oven.

FELICIA: What can you do? Hurry! The UPS battery won't last forever!

ROGER: Relax, gentle spouse. I shall save to the PC's main mass storage device, thus. (*He presses Ctrl+S on the keyboard.*) Now I may shut down the computer, assured with the knowledge that my urgent doodle is safely stored. There. (*He turns off the computer and monitor. He shuts off the UPS and the* beeping *ceases.*) Now we can weather the storm with peace of mind.

Two hours later, after the power is back on, FELICIA and ROGER are sipping wine.

FELICIA: Honey, you certainly demonstrated your Ivy League pedigree with the way you used that UPS.

ROGER: Well, I'm just thankful I read Dan Gookin's book *PCs For Dummies,* from Wiley Publishing, Inc. I think I shall buy more of his books.

FELICIA: Who knew that we could find such happiness, thanks to a computer book?

They canoodle.

Chapter 4

Both On and Off

*N*o doubt about it: Evil computers cannot be turned off. To prove it, I turn to the canon of *Star Trek,* Episode 53: When Scotty tried to turn off the malevolent M5 computer, it actually *killed* the red-shirted crewman trying to pull the plug. Nope, you just can't turn off an evil computer.

Your PC isn't evil. If it were, you could use Captain Kirk's infallible logic to reason the computer into committing suicide. I regret to tell you, however, that this book doesn't have information on arguing a computer to death. That's because your PC has a power button, which is used to turn the computer both on and off.

Turn On Your PC

You turn on the computer this way:

1. **Turn on everything but the console.**

   Everything includes only those items you intend to use — primarily, the monitor. If you're not using the scanner or printer, you don't need to turn them on until you need them.

2. **Turn on the console last.**

Or, if everything is plugged into a power strip, just turn on the power strip.

If the console and monitor are plugged into a UPS (which should remain turned on all the time) and everything else is plugged into a power strip, do this:

1. **Turn on the power strip, which turns on all the computer's external devices, or *peripherals*.**

2. **Press the monitor's power button to turn it on.**

3. **Press the console's power button to turn it on.**

Success is indicated by your computer system coming to life; you can hear the fan whine, and various lights on the console, keyboard, and other devices may flash their lamps. The scanner and printer may whirr and grind their servos. Your computing day begins.

- ✔ By turning on the console last, you allow time for the other devices in the computer system to initialize and get ready for work. That way, the console recognizes them faster than when those gizmos are turned on after the console is up and running.

- ✔ Not all computer devices have their own on–off switches. For example, some USB devices — scanners and external storage — use the USB port's power. You don't need to turn those devices on or off.

- ✔ Some devices can be left on all the time. For example, the printer may have an energy-saving mode that allows you to keep it on all the time. It's often better to keep these devices on than to turn them on or off several times a day.

- ✔ The largest button on the front of the monitor turns it on. Other monitors may have power buttons that aren't physical buttons at all but rather a sweet spot you tap. That sweet spot is often labeled with the universal power-button symbol, shown in the margin.

- ✔ When something doesn't turn on, check to see whether it's plugged in. Confirm that all the cables are properly connected, at both ends.

Ignore these alternative terms for starting a PC

Computers don't just start. They boot, cold start, cycle power, hard start, power on, power up, reboot, reset, restart, soft boot, or warm boot. Any of these terms is an acceptable replacement for "start," but avoid using them where your reputation is at risk.

Windows, Ahoy!

Starting a computer is a hardware thing, but it's the software that makes the computer useful. The software directly responsible for running the computer is called an *operating system*. On most PCs, that operating system is *Windows*. So, after starting your computer's hardware, the next thing you have to deal with is Windows.

The first step to using Windows is to identify yourself. That process is called signing in, logging in, or *loggin' on,* depending on the version of Windows installed and on which side of the Mississippi you live. The signing-in process is part of the computer's security. It's a good thing.

In Windows, you identify yourself by choosing your account picture or typing your account name or an email address. Then you type a password. Figure 4-1 illustrates the Windows 10 sign-in screen. Older versions of Windows look similar.

If your Windows 10 PC hosts multiple users and your account isn't the one shown center screen (refer to Figure 4-1), choose your user account from the list in the lower left corner of the screen. For other versions of Windows, if you don't see your account name listed, click the Switch User button.

If everything goes well, you're logged in! The next step is to start using your computer.

- ✔ To log in, you use an account name. Traditionally, the account name might be your own name, a nickname, some kind of computer superhero name, or something totally odd, like User117.

- ✔ In Windows 10, Microsoft prefers that you use an email address to sign in. If you do so, your account is coordinated to other Windows 10 computers you might own and use.

- ✔ The password is designed to ensure that you are who you say you are when you log in to the computer.

- ✔ Both the account name and password were set up when Windows was first configured on your computer. You probably forgot when you did that, but you did do it. If you're using Windows at a large, impersonal organization, the account setup and password were probably preset for you.

- ✔ When you goof up typing your password, try again.

- ✔ Mind the Caps Lock key on the keyboard! Your password is *case sensitive,* which means that the computer sees uppercase and lowercase letters differently.

User account
picture and name

Type password or PIN

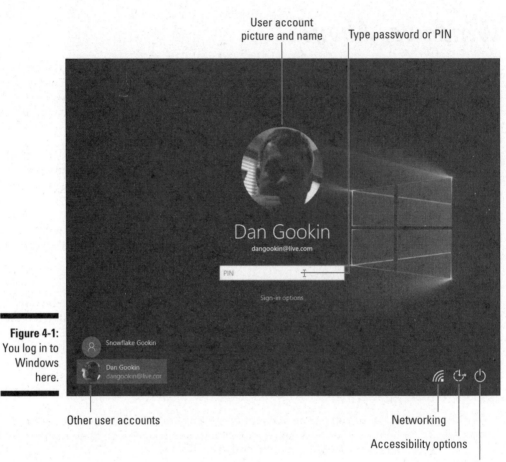

Figure 4-1:
You log in to
Windows
here.

Other user accounts

Networking

Accessibility options

Shutdown options

Turn Off the Computer

Nothing is more satisfying than turning off a computer by ripping its power
cord from the wall. I've done it several times myself. Each time is met with a
brief, mirthful smile. And although yanking out the cord works, it's not the
best way to turn off a computer.

Shutting down Windows

To shut down a PC, obey these directions:

1. Click the Windows button to summon the Start menu.

2. **In Windows 10, click Power.**

   The Power item is found on the left side of the Start menu, toward the bottom, as shown in Figure 4-2.

3. **Click Shutdown.**

   The computer turns itself off.

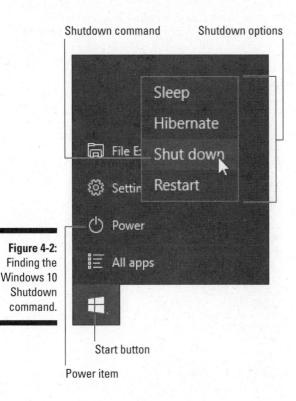

Shutdown command   Shutdown options

Sleep
Hibernate
File E Shut down
Settin Restart
Power
All apps

Figure 4-2:
Finding the
Windows 10
Shutdown
command.

Start button

Power item

If you have any open, unsaved documents or files, you're prompted to save them before the PC turns itself off. Or, occasionally, some program might suffer a catatonic fit and you'll have to click the Shut Down Now button to assist Windows with digital euthanasia and complete the shutdown process.

Putting Windows to sleep

Less drastic than shutting down the PC is to put it to sleep. In *Sleep mode,* Windows saves what you're doing and then puts the computer into a special low-power mode. The computer isn't exactly off, and it restores itself quickly, much faster than either hibernation or a complete shutdown.

To put the PC to sleep, follow these steps:

1. Click the Start button.

Up pops the Start menu.

2. In Windows 10, click Power; in Windows 7, click the Shutdown menu button.

The Windows 10 Power menu is shown in Figure 4-2. In Figure 4-3 you see the Shutdown menu button and the power items available in Windows 7.

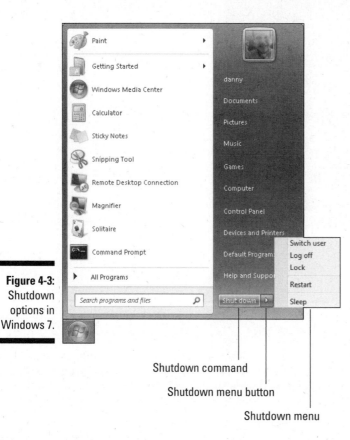

Figure 4-3: Shutdown options in Windows 7.

Shutdown command

Shutdown menu button

Shutdown menu

3. Click the Sleep command.

The computer readies itself for bed. Eventually the monitor times out, and the fan's whirr may soften. The PC snoozes.

To wake the computer from its slumber, you can wiggle the mouse or press a key on the keyboard. Be patient! Sometimes the PC takes a few seconds to wake up.

TECHNICAL STUFF

Regarding the PC's secret on–off button

Some PC cases have a true on–off switch in addition to a power button. You can find the on–off switch on the back of the console, usually near the place where the power cord connects to the PC's power supply. The switch is often labeled | and O, for on and off, respectively. Use this button rather than the power button only in times of dire emergency. Also note that the on–off switch must be in the On position for you to use the power button to turn on your computer.

✔ Sleep mode is part of the computer's power management features. See Chapter 24 for more information.

✔ The PC doesn't not snore while in Sleep mode.

Restarting the PC

You need to reset or restart your computer in two instances. First, Windows may direct you to restart after you install something new or change a setting. Second, restarting is a good idea whenever something strange happens. For some reason, a restart clears the computer's head like a good nose blow, and things return to normal.

The Restart command is found on the Power menu in Windows 10 and on the Shutdown menu in Windows 7. Refer to Figure 4-2 and 4-3, respectively. Choose that command to restart your PC.

✔ Windows may initiate a restart on its own, such as after an update. If you're lucky, a prompt is displayed, allowing you to click a button to restart the computer.

✔ See Chapter 22 for information on the Windows Update service, which may automatically restart Windows.

TIP

✔ Sometimes you don't need to restart to fix a problem. Instead, simply sign out. See the next section.

Signing out

Another option to end your computer day is to sign out. This option really makes sense only when the PC hosts multiple user accounts. For example, one for you, your partner, each of the kids, the dog, and so on. In that case, you can sign out and then have someone else sign in without having to restart the PC.

To sign out of Windows 10, follow these steps:

1. Click the Start button.

2. Click your account name, found at the top left of the Start menu.

Refer to Figure 4-4 for the location. When you click your account name, a menu appears.

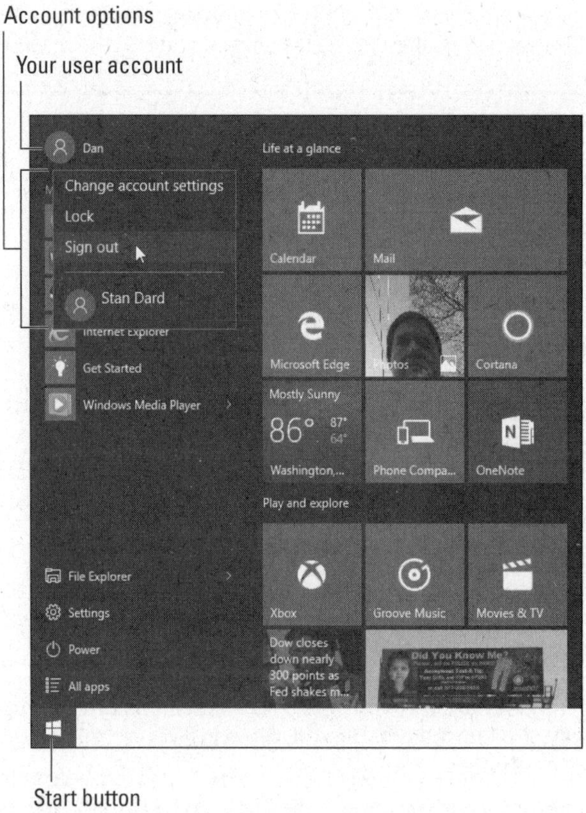

Account options

Your user account

Figure 4-4:
Windows 10
account
options.

Start button

3. Choose the Sign Out command.

Windows stops your programs, prompting you to save any unsaved documents. Eventually you see the main sign-in screen again.

In Windows 7, choose the Log Off command from the Shutdown menu, as illustrated in Figure 4-3.

Signing out of Windows does not turn off the PC.

Reviewing other shutdown options

Shut down. Sleep. Restart. Sign out. You would think that having four options for ending your computer day would be enough. But no! Windows features a few more options for releasing the helm.

Lock the computer: When you *lock* the computer, you're directing Windows to display the initial logon screen, similar to the one shown in Figure 4-1. You prevent anyone from seeing what you're doing, and you keep out anyone who doesn't have an account on your PC.

Switch users: When you switch users, you temporarily sign out of Windows so that another user on the same computer can log in. This option is faster than logging out, because it doesn't require you to save your stuff or close your programs. When you return (log in again), all your stuff is waiting for you, just as you left it.

Put the computer in hibernation: The most dramatic way to save power and not-quite-exactly turn off the PC is to use the Hibernate command. It saves all the computer's memory — everything the system is doing — and then turns off the computer. (It's turned off, not just sleeping.) When you turn on the computer again, things return to the way they were. So hibernation not only saves electricity but also provides a faster way to turn the computer off and then on again.

The commands to lock, switch users, or hibernate the PC are found on the Power, User Account, or Shutdown menus, as illustrated in Figures 4-2 through 4-4 and for the various releases of Windows.

✔ Lock the computer whenever you need to step away for a bit.

✔ The quick way to lock your PC is to press the Win+L key combination, where Win is the Windows key on the computer keyboard and L is the L key. I'm assuming that the L stands for *lock*.

✔ The Hibernation command may need to be activated before it's visible on the Power or Shutdown menu. See Chapter 24.

Should You Leave Mr. PC On All the Time?

I've been writing about computers since the 1920s, and this issue has yet to be settled: Should your computer — like the refrigerator or a lava lamp — be left on all the time? Does it waste electricity? Will we ever know *the truth?* Of course not! But people have opinions.

"I want to leave my computer off all the time"

It's an excellent solution, but one that renders nearly all of this book unnecessary.

"I want to leave my computer on all the time"

I say yes, but only when you use your computer often, such as for a home business. Also, if you find yourself turning the PC on and off several times during the day, just leave it on all the time.

The only time I ever turn off my computers is when I'll be away for longer than a weekend.

Does my method waste electricity? Perhaps, but computers have an energy-saving mode that keeps the power draw low when they're not in use. See Chapter 24 for details on implementing an energy-saving plan customized for how you use your PC.

Finally, computers do enjoy being on all the time. Having that fan whirring keeps the console's innards at a constant temperature, which avoids some of the problems that turning the system off (cooling) and on (heating) again cause.

- ✔ Keeping your PC on all the time doesn't raise your electric bill grotesquely, not like the Jacuzzi or the kids' Tesla coil does.

- ✔ If you use your PC only once a day (during the evening for email, chat, and the Internet, for example), turning it off for the rest of the day is fine. And if you're really that casual about your computer, consider replacing it with a tablet.

- ✔ Most businesses leave their computers on all the time, though medium-size businesses can save thousands of dollars a year by shutting down their computers overnight. Just a thought.

- ✔ If you leave your computer on all the time, don't put it under a dust cover. You'll suffocate the thing.

Part II
The Nerd's-Eye View

In this part . . .

- ✔ Explore mysteries of the PC console
- ✔ Discover memory and RAM
- ✔ Tame the disk drives and storage
- ✔ Behold monitors and PC graphics
- ✔ Understand input devices
- ✔ Review expansion options
- ✔ Train the PC's printer
- ✔ Control the PC's sound system

Chapter 5

Deep Inside the Console

● ●

In This Chapter

▶ Studying the console's insides

▶ Supplying the console with power

▶ Examining the motherboard

▶ Understanding the processor

▶ Checking your PC's processor

▶ Setting the time

● ●

*Y*ou have absolutely no reason to open up the computer console and peer inside. Just as you probably don't venture under the hood of your car or probe around the interior of the furnace or look inside a cat. You can find professionals who are better equipped to deal with such chores. Let them do it.

Then again, you may have a faint recollection of the terms *motherboard, processor, power supply,* and so on. It's possible to use your computer for eons and never really understand or relate to those terms. I'm guessing, however, that you want more from your PC investment than to simply gloss over such specifics. So although you may never venture inside of it, it still matters to you what's to be found deep inside the console.

Computer Guts

Science fiction television in the 1960s had a clever way to reveal that a character was, in fact, an android and not a human being. At some point in the episode, the character would open a conspicuous hatch on his belly. Revealed was a mess of wires and blinking lights. The visual effect was ominous and believable because, well, you figured a robot's guts would just be an impressive, complex, tangled nest of electronics no one could understand. If only computer guts were the same.

Looking under the hood

Buried in your PC's bosom is a maze of mysterious technology, from large metal boxes to tiny pointed, dangerous, raw electronics. There's no need to remove the case's cover to witness such madness. That's because in Figure 5-1 I provide a safe and lovely illustration of what you might see inside your PC's console.

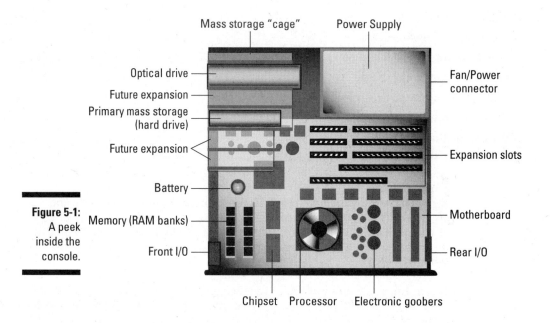

Figure 5-1: A peek inside the console.

To put things in perspective, Figure 5-1 illustrates the side view of a typical mini-tower PC console. The front of the computer is on the left. What you don't see in Figure 5-1 are the miles of cables that festoon the console's interior space like a spilled bowl of pasta. Also missing is a thin layer of dust and perhaps some pet hair.

Of all the things wonderful and terrifying inside the console's tummy, three are worthy in the big picture:

- ✔ The power supply
- ✔ The motherboard
- ✔ The mass storage cage

The *power supply* feeds the console all-important electricity.

The *motherboard* is the computer's main circuitry board. It's important, as are its many important residents, which include the processor and memory and stuff like that.

Finally, the *mass storage cage* is a contraption that houses internal storage devices, such as hard drives, SSDs, an optical drive, plus maybe a media card reader. The cage also has room for even more computer storage — the so-called future expansion — usually right behind some knockout panels on the console's front.

Even if your PC is the thinnest of thin tablets, it contains many of the parts illustrated in Figure 5-1. These include the power supply, processor, mass storage device, memory, and electronic goobers.

Powering Mr. Computer

Of all the goodies deep inside the console, one stands out as the least intelligent. That would be the PC's power supply. Although it may not be smart or fast, it is a necessary piece of equipment. The power supply does the following wonderful things for Mr. Computer:

- ✔ Brings in electricity from the wall socket and converts the electricity from wild, untamed, wishy-washy AC current into calm, collected DC current

- ✔ Provides electricity to the motherboard and everything living on it

- ✔ Provides juice to the internal mechanical disk drives

- ✔ Uses fans to help cool the inside of the console

The power supply is also designed to take the brunt of the damage if your computer ever suffers from electrical peril, such as a lightning strike or power surge. In those instances, the power supply is designed to die, sacrificing itself for the good of your PC. *Don't panic!* You can easily have the power supply replaced, at which point you might discover that the rest of your computer is still working fine.

Other curious and fun power supply facts:

- ✔ Thanks to the fan, the power supply is the noisiest part of any PC.

- ✔ Power supplies are rated in *watts*. The more internal hardware stuff your PC has — the more mechanical disk drives, memory, and expansion cards, for example — the greater the number of watts the power supply should provide. The typical PC has a power supply rated at 150 or 200 watts. More powerful systems may require a power supply upward of 750 watts.

✔ One way to keep your power supply — and your computer — from potentially going poof! (even in a lightning strike) is to invest in a surge protector, or UPS. Refer to Chapter 3 for details.

Lurking on the motherboard

The largest circuitry board inside the console is called the *motherboard*. It's a term of endearment. And, no, in Germany it's not known as the *fatherboard*.

The motherboard is where the computer's most important electronics dwell. It's home to the following essential PC components, some of which are illustrated in Figure 5-1:

✔ Processor

✔ Chipset

✔ Memory

✔ Battery

✔ Expansion slots

✔ I/O connectors

✔ Electronic goobers

Many of these items have their own sections elsewhere in this chapter. Refer to them for more information. Computer memory is a big deal, so it's covered exclusively in Chapter 6. Expansion slots are covered in Chapter 10.

The *I/O connectors* are simply places on the motherboard where various internal options plug in and communicate with the rest of the computer system. For example, on the motherboard, you find an I/O connector where the internal storage devices plug in and an I/O power connector for electricity from the power supply.

The electronic goobers are those miscellaneous pieces of technology that engineers put on the motherboard to justify their paychecks.

Corralling all the mass storage devices

To keep removable storage handy and other mass storage from jostling about the console, your PC's guts include a mass storage cage. This is nothing more than a series of slots into which storage components slide.

The chipset

Rather than refer to the tossed salad of computer chips on the PC's motherboard as The Tossed Salad of Computer Chips on the PC's Motherboard, computer scientists have devised a single descriptive term. All those chips constitute the chipset.

The *chipset* is what makes up your computer's personality. It contains instructions for operating the basic computer hardware: keyboard, mouse, networking interface, sound, video, and whatever else I can't think of right now.

Different chipsets are available, depending on which types of features the computer offers. For example, some motherboards contain advanced graphics in the chipset or maybe wireless networking. The chipset isn't anything you can change, but it is occasionally referenced in the computer's parts list.

An older term for the chipset, particularly the main ROM chip in a PC, is *BIOS,* which stands for Basic Input/Output System. There's a BIOS for the keyboard and mouse, one for the video system, one for the network, and so on. Altogether, they make up the *chipset.*

The primary mass storage device, a hard drive or SSD, inserts into one of the slots. If your PC sports an optical drive, it occupies a slot. A media card reader also squats in the cage. Some slots are accessible from the front of the console, and some lurk inside.

- Storage devices are anchored to the cage to keep them stable. Two cables wend their way from each device: a power cable and a data cable. The power cable finds the power supply; the data cable connects to the motherboard.

- The mass storage cage is traditionally known as the drive cage, or sometimes the disk drive cage. Because some PCs no longer come with disk drives, the term mass storage cage seems more apt.

- See Chapter 7 for more information about mass storage devices.

King Processor

It's a common mistake for folks to refer to the computer's processor as its *brain.* That's not true. Software is the brain in a computer; it controls all the hardware, which means that it also controls the processor.

- The processor is your PC's main chip. Just about everything else on the motherboard exists to serve the processor.

✔ Another term for a processor is CPU. *CPU* stands for *central processing unit.*

✔ Some people refer to the console as the CPU. These people are dorks.

✔ Processors run very hot and therefore require special cooling. If you ever look inside the PC console, you'll notice that the processor wears a tiny fan as a hat. That keeps the processor cool — and stylish.

Understanding the processor's role

Despite its importance, what the processor does is rather simple. It handles three basic tasks:

✔ First, it does simple math — addition, subtraction, multiplication, and division.

✔ Second, and most important, the processor can fetch and put information to and from memory.

✔ Finally, it can do input/output (I/O).

This list may not seem impressive, yet the key to the processor's success is that, unlike your typical brooding teenager, the processor does things *very fast.*

Try to imagine the processor as a combination adding machine and traffic cop, though the traffic is traveling 64 lanes wide and at the speed of light.

Naming PC processors

Once upon a time, computer processors were named after famous numbers, like 386 and 8088. The trend now is toward processor names, but not human names, like John or Mary, or even dog names like Rover or Abednego. No, now processors are named after potential science fiction heroes, pharmaceuticals, or sounds made by a baby rhinoceros in distress.

Seriously, the primary processor found in a typical PC is the Intel Core. It is commonly known as Core and has various last names, such as the Core i7. In fact, you can find a whole lineup of Core processors. Listing them all is pointless in that new variations come out all the time.

✔ Before the Intel Core, the most popular processor in a PC was named Pentium. Some people mistakenly refer to the Core processors as Pentium, but such a faux pas carries no social penalty.

✔ Intel (the company) developed the Intel Core (the processor). Other processor companies exist and make various Core-like processors with various, insignificant names. Truth be told, outside a courtroom, little difference exists between Intel and non-Intel processors. As far as your PC's software is concerned, the processor is the same no matter who made it.

Measuring processor speed

Beyond the name, the truly important yardstick used to judge a processor is its speed, measured in *gigahertz (GHz),* or billions of cycles per second. The higher that value, the faster the processor.

Typical processor speeds range between 2.0 GHz (slower) and 4.0 GHz (faster). Yep, faster processors cost more. Lots more.

Sadly, speed isn't a realistic gauge of how fast a processor does its processing. Speed is a relative measurement when it comes to computers. So although a Core i7 running at 3.4 GHz is technically slower than a Core i7 running at 4.0 GHz, you probably wouldn't notice any difference between the two.

Discovering your PC's processor

You may not know which processor spins busy inside your PCs thorax, but Windows does! The System window shows a technical inventory, similar to the one shown in Figure 5-2. To summon that window, press Win+Break on your keyboard. (That's the Windows key plus the key labeled Break or Pause Break.)

In Figure 5-2, the Windows 10 PC sports an Intel Core i7 processor, running at 3.4 GHz. The Windows 7 system uses a Core 2 Quad CPU. It runs at 2.40GHz.

Other information shown in the System window includes the total amount of memory (RAM) available in the computer. The computers shown in Figure 5-2 feature 8GB and 3GB of RAM, respectively. All that information jibes with what I paid for, so my dealer is off the hook.

✔ Not every System window displays information as complete as is shown in Figure 5-2. When Windows doesn't know, it may say something vague, as in *x86 Family.*

✔ See Chapter 6 for more information on computer memory.

✔ Windows comes in both 32-bit and 64-bit versions. The 64-bit version is best, but some software runs at only 32 bits. The System window (refer to Figure 5-2) also shows which version of Windows is installed. This setting is made when Windows is installed, although on some low-end computers only the 32-bit version of Windows can be chosen.

Memory

Processor

Memory

Processor

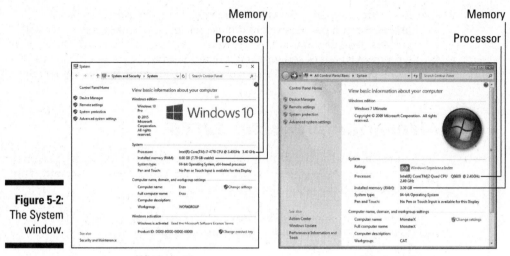

Memory

Processor

Figure 5-2:
The System
window.

Windows 10   Windows 7

Your Computer Is Also a Timepiece

All PCs come equipped with internal clocks. Don't look for a dial, and don't
bother leaning into the console to hear the thing going "tick-tock." Trust me:
The clock is in there. Specifically, clock circuitry exists somewhere on the
motherboard.

The amazing thing is that the PC keeps track of the time even when you
unplug it. That's because the motherboard sports a teensy battery (refer to
Figure 5-1). That battery helps the computer hardware keep track of the date
and time all the time.

- Computers, like humans, need clocks to keep track of time. Computers
  use clocks for scheduling, to timestamp information and events, and
  generally to prevent everything from happening all at once.

- Here's a secret: Computers make lousy clocks. A typical PC loses about
  a minute or two of time every day. Why? Who knows! Fortunately, the
  clock is set automatically when your computer is connected to the
  Internet. See the later section "Using the Internet to set the clock."

- On the positive side, the computer's clock is well aware of daylight sav-
  ings time: Windows automatically jumps the clock forward or backward,
  and does so without having to know the little ditty "Spring forward, fall
  back." Or is it the other way around? Whatever — the computer knows
  and obeys.

About the PC's battery

Your PC has an internal battery, which is found clinging to the motherboard. The battery's primary purpose is to help the PC's internal clock keep time even when the computer is turned off or unplugged. It's not the same as a laptop computer's battery.

A typical PC battery lasts for about six years, possibly more. You'll know when it dies because the computer's date and time go screwy, or perhaps the PC even has a message telling you that the motherboard's battery needs replacing.

Viewing the date and time

Windows reads the PC's hardware clock and displays a software clock for you. You can see the date and time displayed on the lock screen. Otherwise, the date-and-time display shows up in the notification area on the desktop, usually in the lower right corner of the screen.

To see a pop-up clock and calendar, click the time display on the taskbar.

Using the Internet to set the clock

One way to tame the wild computer clock is to have the computer itself automatically synchronize the time with one of the many worldwide time servers. A *time server* is a computer designed to cough up accurate time information for any computer that checks in on the Internet.

Your PC should be configured to automatically set itself to Internet time. To confirm that option, or to set up Internet time, follow these steps in Windows 10:

1. **Right-click the mouse on the date-and-time display in the taskbar's notification area.**

2. **Choose the command Adjust Date/Time from the pop-up menu.**

    The Settings app appears with the Date and Time area of the window displayed and ready for action.

3. **Ensure that the toggle beneath the heading Set Time Automatically is in the On position.**

    Click the toggle thingy if it reads Off instead of On.

In more antique versions of Windows, follow these steps to ensure that the PC's clock is set to Internet time:

1. **Right-click the time display in the notification area on the taskbar, and choose the command Adjust Date/Time.**

   The Date and Time dialog box appears.

2. **Click the Internet Time tab in the Date and Time Properties dialog box.**

   If you see the text telling you that the computer is set to automatically synchronize on a scheduled basis, you're set. Skip to Step 7.

3. **Click the Change Settings button.**

   The Internet Time Settings dialog box appears.

4. **Click to place a check mark by the option Synchronize with an Internet Time Server.**

5. **Click the Update Now button to ensure that everything works.**

   When a problem occurs, choose another time server from the Server drop-down list and try again.

6. **Click OK to close the Internet Time Settings dialog box.**

7. **Click OK to close the Date and Time dialog box.**

When Internet time isn't set you can manually adjust the clock. Yes, this process is a pain because, again, PCs make lousy clocks.

In Windows 10, adjust the clock in the Settings app. Choose Time and Language, and then click the Change button to set the current date and time.

In Windows 7, set the date and time in the Date and Time Properties dialog box: Manipulate the onscreen controls to the current date and time.

On Internet time, Windows automatically adjusts the PC's clock whenever you're connected to the Internet. There's nothing else you need to do — ever!

Chapter 6

PC Memory

*M*emories, like a PC full of RAM . . .

With plenty of memory installed in the console, your PC has ample elbow room to handle a variety of tasks easily and swiftly. When the computer lacks a sufficient amount of memory, things get cramped worse than a tour bus overflowing with sweaty-drunk PhDs returning from a binge at an all-you-can-eat kimchi bar. But I digress. When it comes to PC memory, more is better.

What Is Computer Memory?

If your computer were a sport, memory would be the field on which competition would take place. Memory is where the action is.

Your computer needs memory because the processor has no storage. Well, it has *some* storage, but not a lot. Basically, the processor works like an old-fashioned calculator but without the paper tape. Computer memory acts like that paper tape to help the processor store information and work on data.

Computer memory is often referred to as *temporary* storage. That's because the memory chips require electricity to maintain their information. So, when you're done creating something in memory, you must *save* that information to long-term storage in the PC's mass storage system. But for working on things, creating stuff, and engaging in general computer activity, memory is where it's at.

- ✔ All computers need memory.
- ✔ Memory is where the processor saves and stores its work.
- ✔ The more memory in your PC, the better. With more computer memory on hand, you can work on larger documents, work graphics programs without interminable delays, play games faster, edit video, and boast to your friends about your PC having all that memory.
- ✔ The term *RAM* is used interchangeably with the word *memory*. They're the same thing.
- ✔ RAM stands for *random access memory,* in case you have been working any crossword puzzles lately.
- ✔ Incidentally, more acronyms exist for computer memory types than I care to mention.

- ✔ Turning off the power makes the *contents* of memory go bye-bye. The memory chips themselves aren't destroyed, but without electricity to maintain their contents, the information stored on the chips is lost.
- ✔ Computer memory is *fast.* The processor can scan millions of bytes of memory — the equivalent of Shakespeare's entire folio — in fractions of a second, which is far less time than it took you to trudge through *Hamlet* in the 11th grade.
- ✔ The PC's mass storage system is for long-term storage. See Chapter 7.
- ✔ Memory is reusable. After you create something and save it, the computer allows that memory to be used again for something else.

- ✔ Yes, Mr. Smartypants, some types of computer memory do not require electricity to maintain information. The problem is that this type of memory isn't fast enough. Only fast RAM, which requires electricity, is best used as temporary storage in your PC.

Tasty Chocolate Memory Chips

Physically, memory dwells on the PC's motherboard, sitting very close to the processor for fast access and ready dispatch. The memory itself resides on a tiny memory expansion card, or *DIMM*. On the DIMM, you find the actual memory chips.

DIMM stands for dual inline memory module, and it's pronounced "jaga-da-wawa."

No, I'm kidding. It's pronounced "dim."

A typical DIMM is illustrated in Figure 6-1, although in real life you'll find chips on both sides. That's why it's a DIMM and not a SIMM, or single inline memory module.

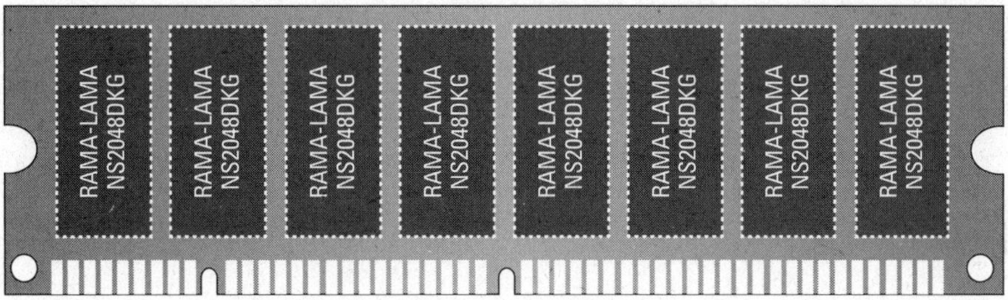

Figure 6-1:
A
semisweet
DIMM.

Each DIMM contains a given chunk of RAM, measured in megabytes or gigabytes using one of the magical memory quantities of 1, 2, 4, 8, 16, 32, 64, 128, 256, or 512. See the later section "Memory, One Byte at a Time" for information on megabytes and gigabytes.

Boring details on RAM, ROM, and flash memory

RAM, or *random access memory,* refers to memory that the processor can read from and write to. When you create something in memory, it's created in RAM. RAM is memory, and vice versa.

ROM stands for *read-only memory:* The processor can read from ROM, but it cannot write to it or modify it. ROM is permanent, like some members of Congress. ROM chips contain special instructions or other information that the computer uses — important stuff that never changes. For example, the chipset on the motherboard is in ROM (refer to Chapter 5). The processor can access information stored on a ROM chip, but unlike with RAM, the processor cannot change that information.

Flash memory is a special type of memory that works like both RAM and ROM. Information can be written to flash memory, like RAM, but like ROM the information isn't erased when the power is turned off. Sadly, flash memory isn't as fast as RAM, so don't expect it to replace standard computer memory any time soon.

A DIMM is plugged into a slot on the motherboard, where it forms a *bank* of memory. So, a PC with 2GB of RAM may have four banks of 512MB DIMMs installed or two banks of 1GB DIMMs. That's all trivial, however. The only time you need to give a rip is when you want to upgrade memory. I'll write more about that task later in this chapter.

- ✔ The most common type of memory chip installed in a PC is the DRAM, which stands for *dynamic random access memory*. It's pronounced "dee-ram."

- ✔ It's gigabyte, not giggle-byte.

- ✔ Other types of memory chips exist, each with a name similar to DRAM, such as EDORAM or BATTERINGRAM or DODGERAM. And then there's DDR3 and WRAM and RAMA LAMA DING DONG. Most of these are merely marketing terms, designed to make one type of memory sound spiffier than another.

Memory, One Byte at a Time

Computer memory is measured by the byte. So what is a byte?

A *byte* is a very tiny storage unit, like a small box. Into that box fits a single character. For example, the word *cerumen* is seven letters (characters) long, so it requires seven bytes of storage. That's seven bytes of computer memory, which isn't a lot these days, thanks to inflation.

Individual bytes aren't very useful. It's only when you have lots of bytes that you can store interesting and wonderful things.

Back in the 1970s, having a few thousand bytes of computer storage was *really something!* The Apollo lunar module computer had 2,048 bytes of memory. Today's PCs demand *millions* of bytes just to run the operating system. That works because today's PCs typically have *billions* of bytes of storage available.

Because the words *million* and *billion* represent values too large for the human mind to comprehend, and to keep things lively, computer scientists use special terms to reference large quantities of computer storage. That jargon is shown in Table 6-1.

Table 6-1		Memory Quantities	
Term	*Abbreviation*	*About*	*Actual*
Byte		1 byte	1 byte
Kilobyte	K or KB	1 thousand bytes	1,024 bytes
Megabyte	M or MB	1 million bytes	1,048,576 bytes
Gigabyte	G or GB	1 billion bytes	1,073,741,824 bytes
Terabyte	T or TB	1 trillion bytes	1,099,511,627,776 bytes

Although it's handy to say "kilobyte" rather than mouth out "1,024 bytes," it's difficult to visualize how much data that is. For comparison, think of a kilobyte (KB) as a page of text from a novel. That's about 1,000 characters.

One *megabyte* (MB) of information is required to store one minute of music in your computer, a medium-resolution photograph, or as much text information as in a complete encyclopedia.

The *gigabyte* (GB) is a huge amount of storage — 1 billion bytes. You can store about 30 minutes of high-quality video in a gigabyte.

The *terabyte* (TB) is 1 trillion bytes, or enough RAM to dim the lights when you start the PC. Although I can think of no individual item that requires 1TB of storage, lots of 1GB items abound that fit happily into that 1TB of storage, which is why the term is needed.

A *trilobite* is an extinct arthropod that flourished in the oceans during the Paleozoic era. It has nothing to do with computer memory.

Other trivia:

- ✔ The term *giga* is Greek and means *giant*.
- ✔ The term *tera* is also Greek. It means *monster!*
- ✔ Your computer's long-term mass storage media is also measured in bytes; see Chapter 7.
- ✔ A PC running the 32-bit version of Windows 10 requires at least 1GB of memory to work well. Windows 10 64-bit requires 2GB of memory. Having at least 4GB of RAM is considered optimum.

- ✔ The PC's processor can access and manipulate trillions and trillions of bytes of memory. Even so, because of various hardware and software limitations, your computer can access only a given amount of RAM. The exact value depends on the motherboard design as well as on the version of Windows.

The holy numbers of computing

Computer memory comes in given sizes. You see the same numbers over and over:

1, 2, 4, 8, 16, 32, 64, 128, 256, 512, 1024, 2048, 4096, and so on

Each of these values represents a *power of two* — a scary mathematical concept that you can avoid while still enjoying a fruitful life. To quickly review: $2^0 = 1$, $2^1 = 2$, $2^2 = 4$, $2^3 = 8$, and up to $2^{10} = 1024$ and more, until you get a nosebleed.

These specific values happen because computers count by twos — 1s and 0s — the old binary counting base from medieval times. So, computer memory, which is a binary-like thing, is measured in those same powers of two. RAM chips come in quantities such as 512MB, 1GB, 2GB, and so on.

Note that, starting with 1024, the values take on a predictable pattern: 1024 bytes is really 1K; 1024K is really 1M; and 1024M is 1G. So, really, only the first ten values, 1 through 512, are the magical ones.

Enough of that.

Memory Q&A

It doesn't matter where I am — greeting people at church, gesturing to my fellow drivers on the freeway, or leaving detox — folks stop and ask me questions about computer memory. Over the years, I've collected the questions and distilled the answers in this section. They should help clear up any random access thoughts you may have about computer memory.

"How much memory is in my PC right now?"

You may not know how much RAM resides in your PC's carcass, but the computer knows! Summon the System window to find out: Press Win+Break on the computer keyboard to behold the System window.

The amount of memory (RAM) appears right below the type of processor that lives in your PC. Looking at the value is about all you can do in the System window, so close that window when you've had enough.

"Do I have enough memory?"

If you have to keep asking this question, the answer is no.

"Does my PC have enough memory?"

Knowing how much memory is in your PC is one thing, but knowing whether that amount is sufficient is entirely different.

The amount of memory your PC needs depends on two things. The first, and most important, is the memory requirement of the computer's software. Some programs, such as video editing programs, require lots of memory. Just check the software's hardware requirements to see how much memory is needed. For example, the Adobe Premier Pro video editing program demands at least 2GB of RAM to run properly.

✔ Not enough memory? You can upgrade! See the upcoming section "Can I add memory to my PC?"

✔ Here's one sure sign that your PC needs more memory: It slows to a crawl, especially during memory-intensive operations, such as working with graphics or switching between running programs. See the next section.

"Can I test whether my PC has enough memory?"

Your computer is designed to function even when it lacks a sufficient amount of memory. To test whether your PC has enough memory installed, make the computer *very* busy, by loading and running several programs simultaneously. I'm talking about *big* programs, such as Photoshop and Word and Excel. While all those programs are running, switch between them by pressing the Alt+Esc key combination.

If you can use Alt+Esc to easily switch between several running programs, your PC most likely has plenty of memory. When you press Alt+Esc and the system slows down, the mass-storage lamp flashes, and it takes a bit of time for the next program's window to appear, your PC could use more memory.

Close any programs you have opened.

"Can I add memory to my PC?"

You bet! The best thing you can do for your PC is to add memory. It's like putting garlic in a salad. *Bam!* More memory provides an instant boost to the system.

Adding memory to your computer is LEGO-block simple. Well, if LEGOs cost a few hundred dollars each and required electricity, then it would be LEGO-block simple. Knowing how much memory and which type to buy is the tough part. Because of that, I highly recommend that you have a dealer or computer expert do the work for you.

If you opt to perform your own PC memory upgrade, I can recommend Crucial at `www.crucial.com`. The website uses special software to determine which type of memory you need and how much. You can then buy the memory directly from the site.

"Will the computer ever run out of memory?"

Nope. Unlike mass storage, which can fill up just like a closet full of shoes and hats, your PC's memory can never truly get full. At one time, back in the dark ages of computing, the "memory full" error was common. That doesn't happen now, thanks to something called virtual memory.

"What is virtual memory?"

Virtual memory is a fake-out. It lets the computer pretend that it has much more memory than it has physical RAM.

To make the scheme work, Windows swaps out chunks of memory to mass storage. Because Windows manages both memory and mass storage, it keeps track of things quite well: Chunks of data are swapped back and forth between memory and mass storage. *Et, voilà!* — you never see an "out of memory" error, thanks to virtual storage.

Alas, there's trouble in paradise. One problem with virtual memory is that the swapping action slows things down. Although the swapping can happen quickly and often without your noticing, when memory gets tight, virtual memory takes over and things start moving more slowly.

✔ The solution to avoiding the use of virtual memory is to pack your PC with as much RAM as it can hold.

✔ Windows never says that it's "out of memory." No, you just notice that the hard drive is churning frequently as the memory is swapped into and out of mass storage. Oh, and things tend to slow down dramatically.

✔ You have no reason to mess with the virtual memory settings in your computer. Windows does an excellent job of managing them for you.

"What is video memory?"

Memory used by your PC's video system is known as *video memory*. Specifically, memory chips live on the display adapter expansion card. Those memory chips are used for the computer's video output and help you see higher resolutions, more colors, 3D graphics, bigger and uglier aliens, and girlie pictures that your husband downloads from the Internet late at night but says that he doesn't.

As with regular computer memory, you can upgrade video memory if your PC's display adapter has room. See Chapter 8 for more information on display adapters.

"What about shared video memory?"

Shared video memory is used on some computers to save money. What happens is that the PC lacks true video memory and instead borrows some main memory for use in displaying graphics. This strategy is fine for simple home computers but not nearly good enough to play cutting-edge games or to use photo editing software.

Chapter 7

The Mass Storage System

*Y*our PC uses mass storage to keep digital stuff for the long haul. It's the equivalent of your closet, basement, garage, or any cubbyhole or cranny where you store your personal stuff. The big difference is that everything put into mass storage on a computer dwells within the digital realm.

The PC's Mass Storage System

The PC's mass storage system is far more interesting than computer memory. Face it: RAM is like dry toast. The mass storage system, on the other hand, is like a Cobb salad or beef stew. It's a single item with many separate components, all of which do the same thing: store information for the long run.

Mass storage is the home for the computer's operating system, programs, and all the stuff you create and use on the PC. It's a big deal. All PCs — all computers and computer-like devices — include some form of mass storage.

✔ You might refer to mass storage by its discrete names based on storage type or media. These names include hard drive (or hard disk), thumb drive, media card, and others. All those devices fall under the main category, mass storage.

✔ Mass storage might also be referred to as *memory*. Though it's a type of memory (long-term), it's not the same as RAM, or the PC's short-term memory, as covered in Chapter 6.

✔ As with computer memory, mass storage is measured in bytes. Chapter 6 offers a clever and interesting explanation on how bytes measure storage capacity.

✔ In the olden days, the PC's mass storage was referred to by one term: disk drive. Today's PC uses more than disk drives for storage, so the whole kit and caboodle is called *mass storage*.

Surveying the mass storage landscape

Your computer plays host to several forms of storage media. These devices all work together to form the PC's mass storage system.

The various storage devices fall into two broad categories: fixed and removable.

Fixed storage: This type of storage is located inside the PC's console. It's not "fixed" in the sense that it was ever broken; it's fixed in the sense that it's not removable. The two types of fixed media are the traditional hard drive and the newer solid-state drive, or SSD.

Removable storage: This storage category includes just about every type of storage media: the media card, thumb drive, optical drive (CD or DVD drive), external hard drive, and even the old floppy drive.

These two categories also reflect the media's location. Fixed storage is always located inside the console. Removable storage is external to the console. The oddball is the optical drive, which is internal, but its media (the discs) are removable.

✔ Removable storage most often uses the USB interface. See Chapter 10 for details on USB stuff.

✔ It's possible to expand your PC's storage system by adding more internal storage, such as a second hard drive or SSD. Depending on the size of the console, you may be able to add one or several — or none, for small-format PCs and laptops.

✔ The hard drive is also known as a hard disk drive or, sometimes, hard disk. See the nearby sidebar, "Mass storage technical terms to ignore."

✔ An SSD is essentially a large-capacity media card. SSDs are fast, but because of their higher cost, they're not as common as traditional hard drives.

✔ You use removable media such as optical discs, media cards, and thumb drives for a variety of purposes. Some common tasks include transferring files between computers and portable electronic gizmos and backing up important information.

✔ At one time, optical drives were the PC's primary removable storage device. Because the optical disc capacity hasn't increased over time, media cards now serve as the primary removable storage media.

✔ If your PC didn't come with an optical drive and you desperately want one, you can obtain an external, USB optical drive.

Identifying the primary storage device

Of all the storage media available to your PC, one has to be the head honcho, the big cheese, the A-number-one. That media is known as the PC's primary storage device.

The PC uses the primary storage device to start the computer and load the operating system. The primary storage device is also home to all the programs installed on the computer, and to your own personal storage area, and it's where programs prefer to save the stuff you create.

✔ Your PC's primary storage media is either a hard drive or SSD.

✔ The primary storage device is always fixed storage located inside the console.

✔ An SSD is like a giant media card, but with a capacity high enough that it can be used as the PC's primary mass storage device. Because the SSD is fully electronic, it's very fast.

✔ The PC's primary storage media is known as *Drive C* or *the C drive.* See the section "Handing out drive letters," later in this chapter, for an explanation.

✔ The primary storage media is also known as the *boot disk.* The PC's firmware looks to that location for the operating system when the computer first starts. The operating system could also be loaded from another source, such as an optical disc or thumb drive. If that source is available, a prompt appears when the computer first starts, inquiring whether you want to use the media as the boot device.

Mass storage technical terms to ignore

The following terms may rear their ugly heads when dealing with mass storage. You have no sane reason to know this stuff:

Disk: The disk is the part of a disk drive that holds information. It's the media upon which the bits and bytes are written. It really is a disk, too: round media with a hole in the middle.

Drive: The drive is the mechanism that reads the media. For a disk drive, the drive spins the disk upon which information is written to and read from. For a media card, the drive is the gizmo that accesses the information stored on the media card's flash memory chip. As an example, a media card requires a card reader (drive). A thumb drive contains both the media and the drive.

Interface: The interface refers to both the hardware and software that transfers information between the storage media and the rest of the computer. The current interface standard for hard drives, optical drives, and SSDs is called *SATA,* which stands for Serial Advanced Technology Attachment. For external storage, the interface standards include USB, IEEE, and eSATA. Chapter 10 offers scintillating details.

Media: The media is where information is recorded. Media is the disk in a disk drive or the CD or DVD in an optical drive. For a media card, media is the card itself, though some humans may insist that it's the *flash memory* inside the media card. Nerds.

Finding mass storage devices

Of the two types of mass storage devices — fixed and removable — removable is easier to locate and identify. After all, a thumb drive sticking out of the console like some tiny diving board is pretty obvious. External hard drives are obnoxiously present, thanks to their multitude of cables. Internally, however, fixed storage is more difficult to ID.

The primary storage device might be evident by a drive lamp on the console. This lamp flickers when the device is accessed. The lamp isn't as common a feature as it once was. In fact, the lamp was once part of the physical drive itself, the front part of which was exposed in the standard PC console. Today, it's just a lamp.

An optical drive is fixed in the console, but its media (the discs) are removable. Therefore, the drive requires exposure so that you can insert and remove the discs. Figure 7-1 illustrates the typical optical drive interface. It may be readily apparent on the front of the console or hidden behind a door.

The key elements of an optical drive are the disc tray, which slides out to accept a disc, and the Eject button, which pops out the tray. Some optical drives use a slot instead of a tray, in which case the drive appears as a mysterious slit and not festooned with the fancy features shown in Figure 7-1.

If the PC sports a media card reader, its drive also appears on the console. Figure 7-2 illustrates the standard 19-in-1 media card reader, which contains slits and slots for all types of media cards.

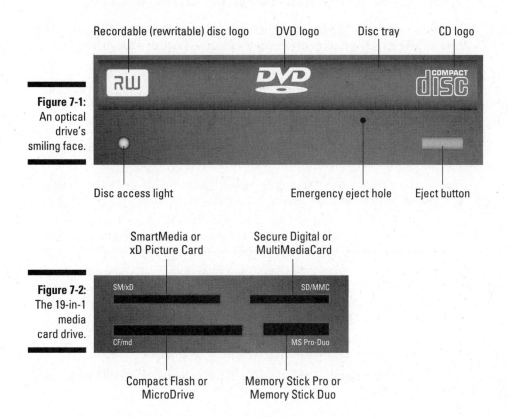

Recordable (rewritable) disc logo   DVD logo   Disc tray   CD logo

Figure 7-1:
An optical
drive's
smiling face.

Disc access light   Emergency eject hole   Eject button

SmartMedia or
xD Picture Card

Secure Digital or
MultiMediaCard

Figure 7-2:
The 19-in-1
media
card drive.

Compact Flash or
MicroDrive

Memory Stick Pro or
Memory Stick Duo

Some PCs may sport only a single media card slot — typically, for a Secure Digital (SD) card. Otherwise, whatever the media card type, you can jam it into one of the available holes on the 19-in-1 card interface.

✔ PCs with multiple internal hard drives still sport only one hard drive lamp on the console. Is it really a hard drive lamp? I think it's just a signal for when the hard drive manufacturer's stock price jumps.

✔ An important feature of the optical drive is the emergency eject hole (refer to Figure 7-1). If a disc becomes stuck or the computer is off, jab an unbent paperclip into the hole to pop out the tray. This feature explains why nerds keep unbent paperclips by their computers. The nerds most definitely don't use the paperclips to clean their ears.

✔ If your PC lacks an internal media card reader, you can buy a USB media card reader. Curiously, the media card reader is cheaper than the price of a typical media card.

Inserting a media card or thumb drive

The term *removable* implies the ability to both insert and remove storage media. You attach a thumb drive, insert a media card, or slide in a DVD. Then, when you're done using the storage, you eject the media.

Once inserted, the removable media is accessed on your computer system just like any other mass storage. It's given a drive letter, and the files and whatnot on that media are made instantly available for use.

✔ See the later section "Handing out drive letters" for information on the drive letter assigned to removable media.

✔ Also see the section "Accessing removable media" to see what you can do with media after it's added to the PC's storage system.

✔ Media cards are inserted label side up — unless the card reader is mounted vertically. Regardless of the drive's orientation, the card goes in only one way.

✔ To connect a thumb drive to your PC, plug the thumb drive into an available USB port. The drive plugs in only one way, and the odds are pretty good that your first attempt will be wrong, so just flip over the thumb drive and try again.

✔ The USB connector on some thumb drives is hidden. You must remove a cover or press a slide switch to reveal the connector.

✔ Don't force a media card into a slot! If the media card doesn't fit into one slot, try another.

Inserting an optical disc

An optical disc is inserted label side up — unless the drive is mounted vertically, such as in an all-in-one PC. In that case, the label faces you.

If the optical drive uses a tray to hold the disc, press the drive's Eject button. Out pops the tray. Drop the disc into the tray, label side up. Gently nudge the tray back into the computer. The tray slides back in the rest of the way on its own.

For the slot type of optical drive, push the disc into the slot. A gremlin inside the drive eventually grabs the disc and pulls it in all the way.

What happens after you insert the disc depends on the disc's content. You may see a prompt to install software, play a movie, or play or import music — or sometimes you don't see anything. In that case, to discover what to do next, you must heed whatever paltry directions came with the optical disc.

Ejecting media

You cannot just yank media out of a computer. Although nothing prevents you from being naughty and doing so, you run the risk of damaging the information stored on the media, not to mention having to endure a nasty warning message from Windows. That's the worst part.

Follow these steps to properly and politely remove media:

1. **Ensure that you're done using the storage media.**

   Close any open files on the media, which may imply closing whatever program you used to access those files.

2. **Summon a File Explorer window.**

   Press the Win+E keyboard shortcut. The File Explorer window appears.

3. **In Windows 10, choose This PC from the list on the left side of the window.**

   The File Explorer window lists your PC's mass storage devices, including removable media, similar to what's shown in Figure 7-3.

4. **Click to select the removable media's drive icon.**

   Just click once; you want to select the icon, not open it.

   It's not always obvious which icon in the window represents a media card or thumb drive. Sometimes, you can tell because the name below the icon is something other than Removable Disk.

5. **In Windows 10, click the Drive Tools Manage tab.**

   Refer to Figure 7-3 for its location.

6. **Click the Eject button.**

   Optical drives spit out the disc automatically. Otherwise, you see a notification explaining that the media can be removed.

7. **Remove the media.**

Store the media in a safe location when you're not using it.

Manage tab   Eject button

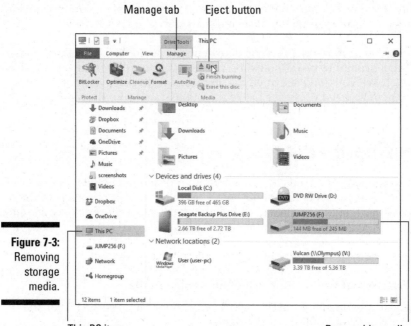

Figure 7-3:
Removing
storage
media.

This PC item   Removable media

Avoid temptation! Do not simply yank out a thumb drive or pinch free a
media card. Never punch the Eject button on the front of the optical drive.
If the media is in use, you witness an ugly, embarrassing, and potentially
career-ending error message.

Adding more storage

You can increase your PC's mass storage by adding more drives and media,
either internally or externally. The external choice is easier: You can connect
an external USB hard drive, media card reader, optical drive, and so on. Plug
in the drive and the storage is available.

Internally, you can add another hard drive, SSD, or optical drive to the PC —
as long as that room is available inside the console. You can do this operation yourself, although I recommend having a dealer, computer repair place,
or suitably nerdy teenager do the installation and setup for you.

✔ Many external hard drives require a power source, which makes for two
cables total: USB and power. Unlike in the movies, real-life computers
have way too many cables.

✔ If your PC uses a UPS, plug the external hard drive into the UPS to ensure that the storage doesn't go offline during a power dip or outage. See Chapter 3 for details.

The Mass Storage Alphabet

To keep your mass storage devices honest, the PC's operating system requires three forms of ID: a drive letter, an icon, and a name. Also in the mix is information about the media's capacity and how much of that capacity is being ravenously consumed. Then there's the media's superhero identity, which for national security reasons isn't disclosed in this book.

Handing out drive letters

Of all the forms of mass storage ID, the drive letter is the most important. Windows assigns each individual storage gizmo a drive letter. As you might suspect, these letters follow the Latin alphabet, which optimally ascends from A to Z. I assume that the drive letters go from A to Я in Russian, and the range is probably A to Ω in Greek. To access the media, you must know its drive letter.

Using logic found only in the computer industry, Windows assigns the most important letter to the PC's primary storage device. That letter is C.

Additional storage devices are assigned letters alphabetically, with internal storage coming next (Drive D and up). External media is assigned drive letters as the media is attached, although a media card reader may use preset drive letters.

Bottom line: Beyond drive C, the primary storage device, the drive letters used by storage media in your PC could be anything. And just because the optical drive on your computer is Drive D doesn't mean that it's Drive D on all PCs.

To overview all the storage devices available to your computer, follow these steps:

1. **Press the Win+E keyboard shortcut.**

   A File Explorer window appears.

2. **In Windows 10, choose This PC from the items listed on the left side of the window.**

   You see a window, either This PC (Windows 10) or Computer (earlier, cruder versions of Windows). Storage devices are listed, along with their assigned drive letters, as illustrated in Figure 7-4.

Folders group is collapsed   Primary storage device   Optical drive

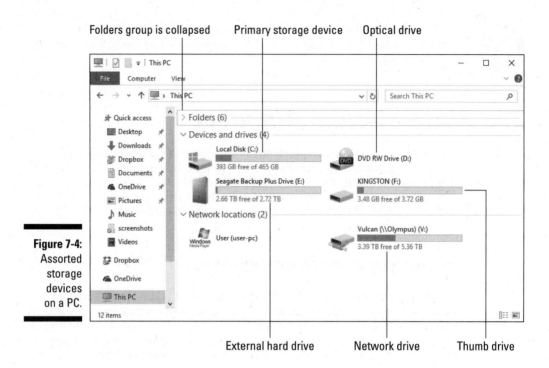

Figure 7-4:
Assorted
storage
devices
on a PC.

External hard drive   Network drive   Thumb drive

In Figure 7-4, the PC's storage media is assigned drive letters in this manner:

> Drive C is the primary hard drive, named Local Disk.
>
> Drive D is an optical drive (with no media).
>
> Drive E is an external hard drive.
>
> Drive F is a thumb drive.
>
> Drive V is a mapped network drive.

The letter assignments you see on your PC can be different, with only Drive C the constant.

✔ Beyond Drive C, the drive letters used on one PC may not be the same for another PC. To know which letters are which, you have to view the This PC window or the Computer window, as described in this section.

✔ Drive V in Figure 7-4 is known as a *mapped* network drive. It exists on a network server (or another computer on the network) and is referenced locally by using drive letter V. See Chapter 17 for details on mapping network drives.

✔ The optical drive is represented by a single drive letter and icon in Windows. Similarly, each hole in the media card reader is represented by a drive letter. That letter stays the same no matter which media you place into the drive.

- ✔ Rumor has it that the letter *C* was chosen for the primary storage device because it was Bill Gates' college grade average.

- ✔ Here's a weird thing: If you attach a USB floppy disk drive to your PC, it's assigned drive letter A. See the nearby sidebar, "Crazy drive-letter rules."

- ✔ The issue I have with the Windows drive-lettering scheme is that it divides all mass storage by device. It's far more convenient for all mass storage to exist in a single structure and be referenced from a central starting point. The fact that the drive letter scheme is inconsistent from computer to computer further compounds the problem.

Exploring drive icons and names

To keep you entertained, and in addition to drive letters, Windows uses icons and names to help identify storage devices. Both are shown in Figure 7-4 and also appear on your own PC in the This PC window or Computer window.

The icons are pulled from an assortment stored within Windows. They typically represent an image of the storage device or what Windows believes the storage device might look like. The primary storage device features a Windows logo; in Figure 7-4, the Windows 10 logo is shown affixed to Drive C.

The device names are a joke. They appear by the drive icons, as shown in Figure 7-4. The names are rather dull, such as Local Disk and Seagate Backup Plus Drive. That's okay because nothing I know of uses the name, other than the name of the primary storage device, and even that can be changed.

- ✔ You can change a drive name just as you can rename any file: Click the drive icon and press the F2 key. Type in a new name. Change the name Thumb Drive to the name This Is Not Where I Keep My Porn or something even more exciting.

- ✔ See Chapter 15 for official information on renaming files.

- ✔ You need Administrator privileges to change the name of the primary storage device. This is supposedly some type of security, although nothing catastrophic happens when you change the name.

- ✔ Some versions of Windows categorize the storage devices as internal, external, and network. These categories are shown in the Computer window. Otherwise, you have no visual clue to where a storage device is physically located.

- ✔ I recommend changing the name of removable media, simply to keep the devices organized. For example, all your thumb drives might be named KINGSTON (refer to Figure 7-4). Changing the name may help you recognize the thumb drive and its contents.

Crazy drive-letter rules

Windows uses a storage media lettering scheme that is rife with confusion, mostly because it's buried in a tradition that dates back to 1981 and the original IBM PC. Back then, mass storage devices were a rare commodity on a personal computer.

The original IBM PC came with one or two floppy drives, named A and B. When the IBM PC XT model was introduced, it sported a whopping 10MB hard drive, which was given drive letter C. Since then, the first, or primary, storage device in all PCs is given drive letter C, with letters A and B reserved for floppy drives, if available.

Any additional internal storage after the primary hard drive is assigned the next letter of the alphabet after *C.* So, if you have a second internal hard drive, it becomes Drive D. A third internal hard drive would be Drive E. The

internal optical drive is given the next drive letter after the last internal hard drive. Any additional internal optical drives are given the next letter (or letters) of the alphabet.

After the optical drive, any internal media card readers are given the next few drive letters, one for each media card slot.

After all internal storage has been assigned letters, Windows begins assigning letters to external storage devices in the order in which they're found when the PC was first turned on or when the drives were attached. Each new storage device is given the next letter in the alphabet.

Network drives are assigned, or *mapped,* to drive letters. So you can pick any available letter of the alphabet to use for a mapped network drive.

✔ The optical drive icon changes to reflect the media. When you insert a music CD, the icon turns into a music CD icon. Windows also uses a DVD movie icon, and programs installed from an optical disc also sport their own fun and non-offensive icons.

Checking drive capacity

One vital storage information tidbit is the media's capacity. Specifically, you want to ensure that free storage space on a device doesn't get too low. If it does, the PC starts acting sluggish and might even refuse to install new software or save files. As with feeding peas to a 3-year-old, it's a situation you want to avoid.

In Figure 7-4, you see storage capacity shown by each device. A thermometer bar graphically indicates how much storage is used and how much is available. A better way to gauge capacity is to check the storage device's Properties icon. Follow these steps:

1. **Bring up a File Explorer window.**

   Press the Win+E keyboard shortcut.

2. **In Windows 10, choose This PC on the left side of the window.**

3. **Right-click a storage device icon and choose Properties from the shortcut menu.**

   The device's Properties dialog box appears, similar to what's shown in Figure 7-5.

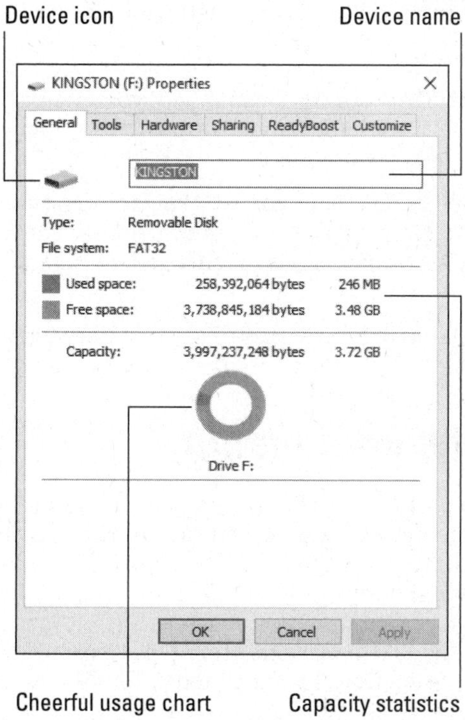

Device icon   Device name

KINGSTON (F:) Properties   ✕

General   Tools   Hardware   Sharing   ReadyBoost   Customize

KINGSTON

Type: Removable Disk
File system: FAT32

Used space: 258,392,064 bytes   246 MB
Free space: 3,738,845,184 bytes   3.48 GB

Capacity: 3,997,237,248 bytes   3.72 GB

Drive F:

OK   Cancel   Apply

Figure 7-5:
Checking
storage
device info.

Cheerful usage chart   Capacity statistics

The information shown in the dialog box is unique to the storage device. Shown are the device's name, type of storage, cryptic file system info, as well as used and free space. A handy chart illustrates storage capacity graphically, as shown in Figure 7-5.

4. **Close the Properties dialog box when you're done gawking.**

When a device's storage nears capacity, Windows displays a warning. Your job is to free space on the storage device or begin using another storage device. See Chapter 24 for details.

Although watching capacity is a good thing to do, be aware that optical drives are always shown at full capacity. Unless you're creating (burning) your own optical disc, the media appears to be full. This situation isn't a problem.

Using mass storage

All mass storage available to the computer is available for your use. You can use a File Explorer window to manage files directly. You also use Open and Save As dialog boxes to access media for retrieving and saving items, respectively.

- ✔ Anytime you use the Save As or Save command, you're putting information into mass storage. That information is transferred from computer memory (RAM) to long-term storage.

- ✔ When you use the Open command, you're taking information out of long-term storage and copying it to computer memory. That's because information can only be examined, used, changed, or created in computer memory.

- ✔ The Open and Save As dialog boxes are covered in Chapter 15.

Accessing removable media

The key to using external storage is to first insert the media card or thumb drive, or attach the storage device. After the storage device is available, you can start using it. How do you know the device is available? Its icon appears in the This PC or Computer window.

- ✔ The key to stopping the use of external storage is to properly eject it, which is covered in the section "Ejecting media," earlier in this chapter.

- ✔ After inserting a media card, a thumb drive, or an optical disc, you may see a flurry of activity in Windows. A notification might appear (explaining that drivers are being installed), an AutoPlay message might pop in, a prompt to install software may show up, music can start playing, or any number of wild and exciting things can happen. Refer to Chapter 19 for information on AutoPlay.

- ✔ Another term for adding storage to a computer is *mount*. For example, you mount an external hard drive. Only fully confessed nerds should use the term *mount*.

Chapter 8

Merry Monitor Mayhem

- -

In This Chapter

▶ Discovering the monitor

▶ Understanding the display adapter

▶ Setting up a PC monitor

▶ Adjusting the resolution

▶ Adding a second monitor

▶ Setting monitor orientation

- -

Contrary to what Hollywood may have led you to believe, text makes no noise when it appears on a computer screen. Text also appears rather quickly, not one letter at a time. If you really want a noisy computer, you need to return to the deafening days of the teletype, which served as the main input-and-output gizmo for the ancient, steam-powered mainframe computers of the 1960s. Things today are much better, and quieter.

The PC's Graphics System

Your PC's graphics system is composed of two parts. The pretty part, the one that the hackers don't see when they're hunched over the keyboard, is the monitor. It's what most normal people stare at while they use a computer.

The second part of the PC's graphics system is the brains of the operation. It's the display adapter, which dwells inside the console. Its circuitry is either part of the motherboard's chipset or, for more powerful display adapters, held on an expansion card.

Figure 8-1 illustrates the PC graphics system, showing both the monitor and the display adapter.

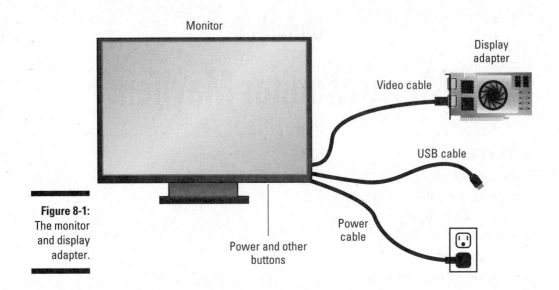

Figure 8-1:
The monitor
and display
adapter.

A video cable connects the two parts of the PC's graphics system, as illustrated in the figure. Not to come up short on cables, the monitor also features a power cable. Touchscreen monitors require an additional cable, which plugs into a USB port on the console. That connection is required for the PC to interpret how you smear, smudge, and poke your fingers at the touchscreen.

Not shown in Figure 8-1 is the software that controls the video hardware. The software, called a *video driver* or *graphics driver,* is part of Windows. It tells the display adapter what kind of graphical goodness to toss up on the monitor.

- ✔ That's correct: The monitor is the dumb part. All it does is display information.

- ✔ The monitor is the PC's primary output device.

- ✔ The display adapter is the heart of the PC's display system. It tells the monitor what to display and where, plus how many colors to use and the overall resolution of the image. The display adapter determines your PC's graphics potential.

- ✔ The monitor and the display adapter are two separate things — even on an all-in-one PC.

- ✔ The display adapter is also known as a *video card.*

- ✔ The term *integrated video* describes a display adapter that's part of the motherboard, not a separate expansion card.

- ✔ You can have more than one monitor attached to your PC. See the section "Adding a second monitor," later in this chapter.

Minding the monitor

The most common type of PC monitor is the LCD monitor, where LCD stands for *liquid crystal display,* not a hallucinogenic.

LCD monitors are flat. They're also thin, and they don't use much power, which keeps the bearded, sandal-wearing Seattle crowd happy.

A special type of LCD monitor is the touchscreen. It works like any other monitor, but it also has the capability to read locations where you physically touch the screen. This type of monitor might also be referred to as a *multitouch* monitor.

✔ Windows 10 takes advantage of touchscreen monitors, although it works just as well without touchscreen input. In fact, touchscreen input is used primarily on tablet PCs and laptops.

✔ It's popular, and often economical, to use an HDTV as your PC's monitor. In fact, many large-format TVs feature a computer input, into which you can plug the console's monitor cable. Gamers love the big screens, but that might just be the Red Bull talking.

✔ You don't need to have the same brand of computer and monitor. You can mix and match. You can even keep your old PC's monitor for use with a new console — as long as the monitor is in good shape, why not?

✔ Before LCD monitors took over the world, computers used bulky, hot, power-hogging, glass-faced *CRT* monitors. CRT stands for *cathode ray tube,* not *catheter* ray tube.

Monitor-screen-display jargon

Where does text appear? Is it on the monitor? On the screen? What is the display? Sadly, several confusing terms are often used interchangeably to refer to the stuff the computer displays. Here's the handy lexicon for you:

The *monitor* is the box.

The *screen* is the part of the monitor on which information is displayed.

The *display* is the information that appears on the screen.

These are the terms as I use them. Other folks, manuals, and web pages mix and match them to mean whatever. In this book, however, I pretend to use these terms consistently.

Discovering the display adapter

The smarter and most important half of the PC's display system is the graphics hardware itself, known as the *display adapter*. This circuitry runs the monitor and controls the image that the monitor displays.

Of all the deadly electronics on the display adapter, two items stand out as important: the GPU and the graphics memory.

GPU: Display adapters feature their own processor, a second processor to the computer's main processor. This *graphics processing unit*, or GPU, is specially geared toward graphical operations. It allows the display adapter to handle all that ugly graphics math, which means that images appear with more pep and vigor than if the PC's main processor were burdened with the graphics task.

Graphics memory: PC graphics require special memory that's separate from the computer's main memory. This memory is known as *video RAM,* or VRAM. The more video memory, the more colors and high resolutions and fancier tricks the display adapter is capable of.

Think of these two items in general terms. Say out loud: "My PC's video system features a display adapter, on which I'll find a GPU and lots of graphics memory." That's all you need to acknowledge. That's because, of all the oddball jargon in the realm of computers, display adapters feature the most confusing names, numbers, terms, and acronyms.

✔ The more video memory the display adapter has, the higher the resolutions it can support and the more colors it can display at those higher resolutions.

✔ Display adapters can have from 0M (no memory) to several gigabytes of memory. Oodles of graphics memory is necessary only when applications — especially games and photo editing software — demand more memory.

✔ Some video adapters share memory with main memory. These adapters show 0MB of video memory. This configuration isn't the best way to play games or work with graphics on a PC. But fret not! You can always add or replace the PC's display adapter.

✔ Refer to Chapter 10 for more information on expansion slots, which is how the display adapter attaches to the PC's motherboard.

✔ See Chapter 6 for more information on computer memory.

✔ Touchscreen monitors don't use the display adapter to interpret touch input. The monitor's USB cable feeds that information directly to the console (refer to Figure 8-1).

✔ Many display adapters are advertised as supporting 3D graphics or having a physics engine. Note that these features work only if your software supports them.

Show Me What Ya Got

Despite all its glorious graphical goodness, your PC's monitor is merely a peripheral. Yes, it's an important peripheral, but like the keyboard, printer, and teleporter, it's simply another gizmo you control to get something done when you use your computer.

Measuring a monitor

Because all computer monitors sold today are of the LCD type, the differences in the variety lie with the monitor's size and aspect ratio and whether the monitor features a touchscreen.

A computer monitor, like a TV set, is measured on the diagonal. This measurement can be misleading, because a 24-inch monitor may be less than 24 inches wide. That's trigonometry in action, which is something you successfully avoided in high school and, thankfully, can continue to avoid when using a computer.

Another descriptive characteristic of a monitor is its *aspect ratio,* or the relationship between the monitor's width to its height. Traditionally, computer monitors used the Academy Standard aspect ratio of 4:3. That's 4 units of width for 3 units of height. Today's monitors are widescreen, sporting a ratio of 16:9; the screen is 16 units wide for every 9 units in height.

Figure 8-2 illustrates how monitors are measured diagonally and compares the aspect ratios of a widescreen monitor to the traditional computer monitor.

Touchscreen monitors are judged by how many places you can poke the screen at one time and not drive the thing nuts. For example, a monitor that can read ten touches is called a *10-point monitor.* Windows 10 needs at least a 5-point multitouch monitor.

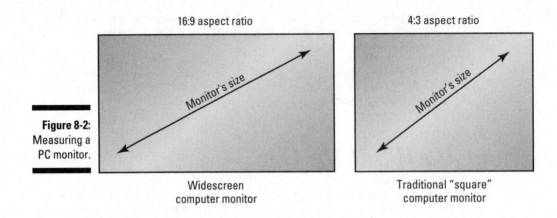

16:9 aspect ratio   4:3 aspect ratio

Monitor's size   Monitor's size

Figure 8-2:
Measuring a
PC monitor.

Widescreen   Traditional "square"
computer monitor   computer monitor

Other features that have found their way onto modern PC monitors include integrated stereo speakers and webcams. Generally, these devices are adequate, but better options for speakers and PC video exist.

Connecting the monitor to the PC

Your monitor may use only one cable, but it probably has options for several different cable types. If you look closely, you may see the back of the monitor dotted with different connectors. Likewise, your PC may sport multiple monitor connectors. Here's the lot:

DVI: The most common connector, a DVI connector is white and rectangular and the best way to connect an LCD monitor to a display adapter.

Mini-DV: This is a tiny version of the DVI interface, usually found on laptops and other small-footprint PCs.

HDMI: This connector allows you to use a high-end HDTV as a monitor. It's the same connector used to attach other gizmos (Blu-ray players and video game consoles, for example) to big-screen TVs.

VGA: The oldest of the video connectors, VGA uses a D-shaped connector with 15 holes. On many consoles, the connector is colored cyan or blue.

To make the connection, you choose the proper cable type, plug one end into the monitor, and plug the other end into the console.

If given the choice, use the DVI connection.

Reading monitor messages

Your computer monitor is capable of displaying its own messages, separate from the PC. The most common message is usually something like No Signal or Power Save Mode. This message appears when the console isn't on or the display adapter has shut down to save power.

Other monitor messages appear from time to time. Most common are the onscreen menus that appear when you use the monitor's buttons to adjust the display.

Working the monitor's controls

Tuning a computer monitor isn't the chore it once was. Today's LCD monitors are pretty much ready to go right out of the box. If you desire to mess with monitor settings, such as color temperature or some other setting, that option is available to you. The only ordeal is knowing how to use the secret buttons to work the silly monitor menu.

Some monitor buttons are obvious, such as the Power button. Near that button, or hidden along the monitor's side or bottom, are other buttons. These buttons manipulate the monitor's onscreen menu. Which button is which? No one knows. If the buttons are labeled at all, they're usually simple symbols or numbers. Don't expect anything useful to pop out at you.

Typically, one button displays the onscreen menu. Two buttons move left and right or up and down through the menu items. One button may choose an item. Another button causes the cat to look at the ceiling in an alarming manner.

The most wonderful news is that you rarely, if ever, need to manipulate the buttons.

✔ The power button may be a touch-sensitive button right there on the front of the monitor. It may be illuminated with the universal On/Off graphic, shown in the margin. Tap the button to turn on the monitor; tap it again to turn off the monitor.

✔ Some onscreen monitor menus disappear after a while. Others require you to select an Exit command. If the onscreen menu lingers like that one guy who refuses to leave the party even though you've put on your pajamas, just turn off the monitor and turn it on again.

Windows Controls What You See

The supreme lord of your PC's graphics system isn't the display adapter, and it most certainly isn't the monitor. Sitting in the driver's seat for all things graphical is the PC's operating system, Windows. To control the graphics system, you use Windows.

- ✔ Some display adapters come with special software that offers additional graphical control, such as the NVIDIA Control Panel program. These programs are accessed from the notifications area; click on the wee Graphics Adapter icon to pop up the program.

- ✔ The specific software that controls the display is something called the *video driver.* It is not a computer car simulator.

Setting resolution

The monitor's physical dimensions cannot change, but you can control the amount of stuff you see on the screen by adjusting the screen *resolution.* That's the number of dots, or *pixels,* the monitor displays, measuring horizontally by vertically.

To change the screen's resolution in Windows 10, heed these directions:

1. **Right-click the desktop and choose Display Settings from the pop-up menu.**

    The Settings app opens, showing information about the display.

2. **Click the Advanced Display Settings link.**

3. **Use the Resolution menu button to choose a new resolution.**

    For example, choose 1024-by-768 to see how computer users in 1998 saw the digital world.

4. **Click the apply button to see a preview of how that resolution appears on your PC's monitor.**

5. **Click the Keep Changes button to set the new resolution, or click the Revert button to return to the current resolution.**

In Windows 7, follow these steps to reset the screen resolution:

1. **Right-click the desktop and choose Screen Resolution from the pop-up menu.**

2. **Click the Resolution menu button.**

3. **Use the slider gizmo to choose a resolution.**

4. **Click the Apply button to try out the new resolution.**

5. **Click OK or Keep Changes to accept the new resolution.**

One of the resolution items is marked Recommended. That setting is the optimal resolution for your PC's graphics hardware. You don't have to choose that setting, but it's what works best.

- ✔ Higher resolutions display more information, but the items on the screen appear smaller. Likewise, lower resolutions display less information, but the items on the screen appear larger.

- ✔ The dots measured in screen resolution are pixels. *Pixel* is a contraction of *pic*ture *el*ement.

- ✔ Some computer games reset the monitor's resolution. This change is okay, and the resolution returns to normal after you quit the game.

Adding a second monitor

If your PC sports two graphics ports, the system can handle two monitors. It would be like if your body had two necks, you could go shopping for a second head. Hat sales would go through the roof!

The second monitor expands the desktop real estate, allowing you to get more work done! Or to see more stuff at once, if you loathe work.

Connecting the second monitor works just like connecting the first: Plug it in, to both the graphics adapter and the power supply. Windows should recognize the second monitor at once. Your job is to configure how the monitor is used. For most folks, the second monitor works as an extension to the first monitor.

In Windows 10, the monitor is instantly recognized and the desktop extended, assuming that the second monitor sits to the right of the main monitor. To adjust the second monitor's position, resolution, or other settings in Windows 10, follow these steps:

1. **Right-click the mouse on the desktop.**

2. **Choose the Display Settings command.**

   The Settings app opens, showing a preview of both displays, similar to what's shown in Figure 8-3.

3. **If you need to extend the desktop to the second display, from the Multiple Displays menu choose the option Extend These Displays.**

   The option is shown in Figure 8-3.

4. **Drag the preview icon to position the second monitor.**

   Where you place the second monitor's Preview icon determines how it interacts with the first monitor.

5. **If you need to set the second monitor's resolution, scroll down the right side of the Settings window (see Figure 8-3) and click the link Advanced Display Settings.**

   Refer to the preceding section for information on setting the second monitor's resolution: Click the monitor before choosing a resolution.

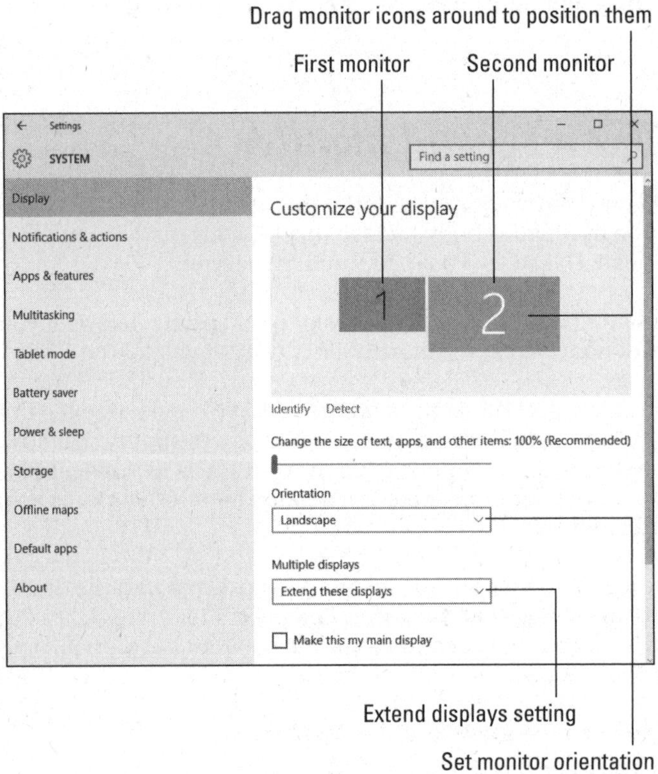

Figure 8-3:
Working
with dual
monitors.

6. **Click the Apply button to preview your changes.**

7. **If you need to make adjustments, keep repeating Steps 4 through 6.**

8. **Close the Settings app window when you're done configuring the second monitor.**

In Windows 10, the first monitor features the taskbar notifications, date, and time. Also, the Action Center slides in only on the first monitor. Both monitors show the Start button and pinned icons, plus buttons showing any open window.

In Windows 7, connect the second monitor, and then follow these steps to configure the monitor:

1. **Right-click the mouse on the desktop and choose Screen Resolution from the pop-up menu.**

2. **Click the menu button next to Multiple Displays and choose the Extend These Displays option.**

3. **Use the mouse to adjust the two monitor preview icons so that they line up onscreen as they do in the real world.**

4. **Click OK.**

In Windows 7, the taskbar stays on only the main monitor. Otherwise, you can use both monitors in Windows as though your PC had one, huge monitor.

- ✔ The dual-monitor trick works only when the display adapter features two monitor connectors, such as two white DVI connectors.

- ✔ If the adapter features a single DVI and then an HDMI, it might not work for two monitors. That's because DVI splitter cables are available and you might be able to use one to pull off the dual-monitor trick.

- ✔ Some versions of Windows may not support dual monitors.

- ✔ Graphics memory is the limiting factor for the success or failure of a single PC running two monitors. When graphics memory is plentiful, the trick works well. When graphics memory is low, you may see video performance suffer. In that case, lower both monitors' resolution, to see whether that helps.

Orienting the monitor

Nothing says that a widescreen PC monitor needs to be oriented like a movie screen. Some people like *portrait,* or tall, orientation, especially when dealing with spreadsheets or other listy items.

The first step to changing the monitor's orientation is to physically rotate the monitor. Some monitor stands allow for free rotation. For other monitors, you may need a special stand or wall mount.

After setting the monitor in an up-down orientation, you must direct Windows to reset the display's presentation.

In Windows 10, follow these steps to reorient the PC's monitor:

1. **Right-click the mouse on the desktop and choose Display Settings.**

2. **If multiple monitors are present, click the one you want to reorient.**

3. **From the Orientation menu, choose Portrait.**

   Other options include Landscape, which is the normal monitor orientation, but also two Flipped settings. The Flipped settings work for monitors reflected on a mirrored surface, which is weird, but it's an option.

4. **Click the Apply button to check out the arrangement.**

   You may also need to adjust the monitor's positions, as described in the preceding section, especially if one monitor is in portrait orientation and the other is in landscape.

In Windows 7, follow these steps to change the orientation of one or two monitors:

1. **Right-click the mouse on the desktop.**

2. **Choose the Screen Resolution command from the pop-up menu.**

3. **Click to select the display you want to set in portrait orientation.**

4. **From the Orientation button menu, choose Portrait.**

5. **Click the Apply button to preview.**

6. **Click OK.**

If you're setting two monitors to portrait orientation, you must apply that setting to each monitor, one after the other.

Chapter 9

Input This!

*J*ust like yin and yang, input and output on a computer must balance. One needs the other. Output may get all the attention, thanks to fancy graphics and stereo sound. Input is no less important. The PC's primary input device is the keyboard, followed closely by the mouse. If a computer system sports a multitouch monitor, then perfect balance is attained because that peripheral provides both input and output. Om.

Meet Mr. Keyboard

It may be a subtle thing, and it takes a lot of blame for your typos, but the humble computer keyboard comes from a violent past. It's the offspring of a shotgun marriage between the electric typewriter and the calculator. The feud was settled. And eventually the clans agreed upon 12 function keys instead of 10. That's good news. No more killing. And we have amiable, if not toothless, grinning all around the table.

Attaching a keyboard

The PC keyboard plugs into a USB port on the console.

✔ The keyboard can be attached or detached at any time, although Windows complains when a keyboard isn't attached.

✔ Wireless keyboards don't use a USB port. The wireless receiver may attach to a USB port, but the keyboard itself is wild and free to wander.

✔ Older PC keyboards plugged into a specific keyboard port. If your PC uses one of these older keyboards, do not attach or detach the keyboard while the computer is turned on. Doing so will damage the system.

Examining the typical PC keyboard

There's no such thing as a typical PC keyboard. Each manufacturer likes to customize things a tad. Some keyboards have extra buttons for playing media or browsing the web. If there was a typical PC keyboard, it would look like the example illustrated in Figure 9-1.

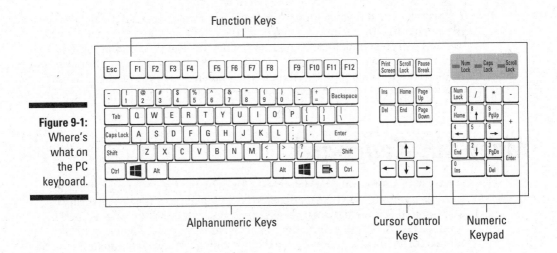

Figure 9-1: Where's what on the PC keyboard.

You can safely divide the typical PC keyboard into four areas, as shown in Figure 9-1:

Function keys: These keys are positioned near the top of the keyboard. They're labeled F1, F2, F3, and so on, up to F12. They're also called *F-keys*, where F stands for *function*, not anything naughty.

Alphanumeric keys: These keys include letters, numbers, and punctuation symbols. They might also be called the *typewriter* keys by humans old enough to remember typewriters.

Cursor control keys: Also called *arrow keys,* this clutch of keys is used primarily for text editing.

Numeric keypad: Borrowing a lot from a calculator, the numeric keyboard makes entering numbers quick and easy.

These four areas are common to all PC keyboards. The keyboard resting before your PC's monitor may have more keys with custom functions. Such variations are mentioned elsewhere in this chapter.

- ✔ The *cursor* is the blinking goober on the screen that shows you where the characters you type appear. The vertical blinking cursor is referred to as the *insertion pointer.*

- ✔ The term *cursor* comes from the Latin word for *runner.* The term *insertion pointer* has its roots in proctology.

- ✔ If you're really old — and I mean ancient — you must remember that a computer keyboard has 1 and 0 keys. Don't type a lowercase *l* to represent the numeral 1 or a capital letter *O* for the numeral 0.

"Must I learn to type to use a computer?"

The short answer: No, you don't need to touch-type to use a computer. Plenty of computer users hunt and peck. In fact, most programmers don't know how to type, but that brings up an interesting story: A computer software developer once halted all development and had his programmers learn to touch-type. It took two whole weeks, but afterward, they all got their work done much faster and had more time available to break away and play those all-important computer games.

As a bonus to owning a computer, you can have it teach you how to type. The Mavis Beacon Teaches Typing software package does just that. Other packages are available, but I personally enjoy saying the name Mavis Beacon.

Using modifier keys

Four keys on the computer keyboard qualify as shift keys, though only one is labeled Shift. The other three are Ctrl, Alt, and Win. Rather than call them all *shift keys,* the term *modifier keys* seems more appropriate.

A modifier key works in combination with other keys: You hold down a modifier key and then press another key on the keyboard. What happens then depends on the keys you press and how the program you're using reacts to the key combination.

You use modifier keys thus:

1. **Press and hold down the modifier key, such as Shift.**
2. **Tap the key it's modifying, such as the 8 key.**

   Shift+8 generates the * character.
3. **Release the modifier key.**

You can substitute any modifier key for Shift in Step 1: Ctrl, Alt, or Win. For example, you hold down the Alt key and press the F4 key, written as Alt+F4.

- The Shift key helps generate capital letters, punctuation, and other symbols on the number keys and other keys. That's how you can create the %@#^ characters that come in handy for cursing in comic strips.

- Ctrl is pronounced "control." It's the *control* key.

- Alt is the *alternate* key.

- Win is the Windows key, adorned with the Windows logo.

- Most of the time, pressing the Shift or Ctrl key by itself does nothing. Pressing the Win key displays the Start menu. Pressing the Alt key by itself activates keyboard shortcuts in some programs.

- Keyboard shortcuts are written using capital letters. So even though you may see Ctrl+S or Alt+S with a capital *S,* for example, it doesn't mean that you must press Ctrl+Shift+S or Alt+Shift+S. The *S* is written in upper-case simply because Ctrl+s looks like a typesetting error.

- Multiple modifier keys are used together, as in Shift+Ctrl+F6 and Ctrl+Shift+Alt+C. Just remember to press and hold down both modifier keys first and then tap the other key. Release all the keys together.

- Some technical manuals use the notation ^Y rather than Ctrl+Y. This term means the same thing: Hold down the Ctrl key, press Y, and release the Ctrl key. The ^ symbol is the traditional computer symbol for the Control key.

Strange keyboard abbreviations

The key caps are only so big, so some key names have to be scrunched down to fit. Here's your guide to some of the more oddly named keys and what they mean:

✔ Print Screen is also known as PrtSc, PrScr, or Print Scrn.

✔ Scr Lk is the Scroll Lock key.

✔ Page Up and Page Down are sometimes written as PgUp and PgDn on the numeric keypad.

✔ Insert and Delete may appear as Ins and Del on the numeric keypad.

✔ SysRq means System Request, and it has no purpose.

Changing keyboard behavior keys

Three keys change how certain parts of the PC keyboard behave. I call them the Lock keys. Behold:

Caps Lock: This key works like holding down the Shift key, but it affects only the letter keys. (Think *Caps* as in *capital* letters.) Press Caps Lock again, and the letters return to their normal, lowercase state.

Num Lock: This key controls the behavior of the numeric keypad. Press the key to activate the Num Lock state, and the numeric keypad produces numbers. Press this key again to deactivate Num Lock, and you can use the numeric keypad to move the cursor.

Scroll Lock: This key has no purpose. Well, some spreadsheets use it to reverse the function of the cursor keys (which move the spreadsheet rather than the cell highlight), but that doesn't count.

When a lock key is on, a corresponding light appears on the keyboard. The light may be on the keyboard or on the key itself. The light is your clue that a lock key's feature is turned on.

✔ Caps Lock affects only the keys A through Z; it doesn't affect any other keys.

✔ If you type This Text Looks Like A Ransom Note and it appears as tHIS tEXT lOOKS lIKE a rANSOM nOTE, the Caps Lock key is inadvertently turned on. Press it once and then try typing your stuff again.

✔ If you press the Shift key while Caps Lock is on, the letter keys return to normal. (Shift cancels out Caps Lock.)

Touring some useful keys

All keys are created equal, but some keys are more equal than others. I find the following to be the most useful keys on the keyboard.

 You'll find two Enter keys on the typical PC keyboard. They're duplicates. You press the Enter key to accept input, to end a paragraph in a word processor, to open a highlighted icon, or to "click" the OK button in a dialog box.

 The Escape key is labeled Esc, but it means Escape. Pressing the key doesn't immediately take you to some luscious tropical locale complete with refreshing beverage. Nope — pressing the Esc key is the same as clicking Cancel in a dialog box.

 Don't bother looking on the keyboard: It has no Help key. Instead, whenever you need help in Windows, whack the F1 key. F1 equals help. Commit that to memory.

 The Tab key is used in two ways on your computer, neither of which generates the diet cola beverage. In a word processor, the Tab key is used to indent paragraphs or line up text. In a dialog box, the Tab key moves the focus between the various graphical gizmos.

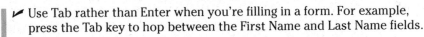

- Use Tab rather than Enter when you're filling in a form. For example, press the Tab key to hop between the First Name and Last Name fields.

- The Tab key often has two arrows on it, left and right. These arrows may be in addition to the word *Tab,* or they may appear by themselves.

- The arrows on the Tab key go both ways because Shift+Tab is a valid key combination. For example, pressing Shift+Tab in a dialog box moves you "backward" through the options.

- PC keyboards use the Enter key. Macintosh keyboards have the Return key. The difference depends on which side of the aisle the manufacturer sat during the keyboard's shotgun wedding: Enter comes from the calculator; Return comes from the electric typewriter.

Understanding strange keys

Arguably, all keys on a computer keyboard are strange. I mean, how many times do you use the { and } characters when you type? Beyond the weirdo character keys, some keys may have you really scratching your head. Here's the list:

Break The Break key shares a keycap with the Pause key. It's not used any more, which is good because it should have been spelled *Brake* in the first place.

Pause Some games may use the Pause key to temporarily suspend the action, but it's not a consistent thing.

**** The backslash (\\) leans to the left. Don't confuse it with the forward slash key, which leans to the right (/). That other symbol on the backslash key? That's the vertical-bar character, also called the *pipe*.

Print Screen The Print Screen key, also named PrtSc, takes a snapshot of the Windows desktop, saving the image in the Windows Clipboard. You can then paste that image into any program that lets you paste a graphical image. The key has nothing to do with the computer printer. (Well, not any more.)

AltGr The AltGr, or Alt Graph, key is used on non–U.S. keyboards to help non-English–speaking humans access characters specific to their non-English language.

$ € 4 Some international keyboards sport the euro currency symbol, often found sharing the 4 key with the dollar sign. That key will be a collector's item in a few years.

SysRq The System Request key shares its roost with the Print Screen key. It does nothing.

⊟ This booger is the Context key. It resides between the Windows and Ctrl keys to the right of the spacebar. Pressing this key displays the shortcut menu for whatever item is selected on the screen — the same as right-clicking the mouse when something is selected. No one in recorded computer history has ever used this key.

Any No "Any" key appears on the keyboard. When you're prompted to "Press any key," do what I do: Press the spacebar.

Understanding keys for math

No matter how hard you look, you won't find a × or ÷ key on the computer keyboard. That's because computer math doesn't involve multiplication or division.

Just kidding. Computers take advantage of character symbols to carry out various mathematical operations. To help you remember the symbols, the keyboard designers clustered them on the numeric keypad, where most of the math stuff takes place anyway. Here's the list:

+ is for addition.

– is for subtraction.

* is for multiplication.

/ is for division.

You use the asterisk (*), not the lowercase *x,* for multiplication.

Controlling the keyboard in Windows

If you plan to write a lot of fast-paced theatrical drama on your computer, you'll probably write the word *Aaaaaaaaaaaaaaa* a lot. To do so, you press and hold the A key. After a delay, the A key repeats itself, spewing out the letter *A* like water from a fire hose. You can control both the delay and how fast the character repeats itself by using the Keyboard Properties dialog box in Windows, shown in Figure 9-2.

To open the Keyboard Properties dialog box, follow these steps:

1. **Open the Control Panel window.**

   In Windows 10, press Win+X to summon the super-secret menu and choose the Control Panel command. In Windows 7, choose Control Panel from the Start menu.

2. **On the View By menu, near the upper-right corner of the window, choose Large Icons.**

   You need to revert to Icon view in the Control Panel because a direct link to the Keyboard Properties dialog box isn't available otherwise.

3. **Click the Keyboard icon to display the Keyboard Properties dialog box.**

4. **Use the mouse to manipulate the sliders in the dialog box to set the rates.**

   As you adjust the sliders, type in the box, illustrated in Figure 9-2. Press a key, and check the delay and then the repeat rate.

5. **Click the OK button only when you're happy.**

6. **Close the Control Panel window when you're done.**

Adjust sliders

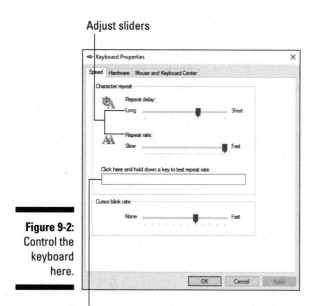

Figure 9-2:
Control the
keyboard
here.

Test keyboard here

You might want to change Control Panel view back to Category view before you close its window. And check out Chapter 13 if you need more information on the Control Panel.

Say "Eeek!" to the Mouse

As the PC's primary input device, the keyboard can do almost anything. In the graphical realm that is Windows, however, you need a mouse. And not just any mouse, but a computer mouse. Those real rodents have a tendency not to stay put.

Connecting the mouse

The computer mouse can be wired or wireless. A wired mouse uses a USB cable, which you fit snugly into a USB port on the PC's console. A wireless mouse uses telepathy to communicate with the console, although a USB gizmo generally plugs into the console, which provides wireless reception.

The mouse usually rests to the right of the keyboard, with its tail pointing back to the computer. The flat part of the mouse goes on the bottom.

You need space to roll the mouse around, usually a swath of desktop real estate about the size of this book. Or the size of a mouse pad, which is why mouse pads are popular.

- ✔ You can also set the mouse on the left side of the keyboard if you're left-handed. See the section "Use the mouse left-handed," later in this chapter.

- ✔ Older PCs used a specific mouse port, into which the mouse plugged. This port looks similar to the keyboard port, also found on older PCs, but the two ports are different. As with the old keyboard port, the PC must be turned off when you attach or detach the mouse.

Reviewing basic mouse parts

A typical computer mouse is shown in Figure 9-3, where the basic and important mouse features are illustrated.

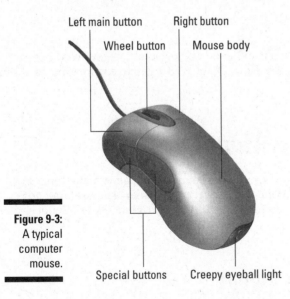

Left main button   Right button

Wheel button   Mouse body

Figure 9-3:
A typical
computer
mouse.

Special buttons   Creepy eyeball light

Mouse body: The mouse is about the size of a bar of soap. You rest your palm on its body and use your fingers to manipulate the mouse buttons.

Left (main) button: The left button, which falls under your right hand's index finger, is the *main* button. That's the button you click the most.

Wheel button: The center, or wheel, button can be pressed like the left and right buttons, and it can be rolled back and forth. Some wheels can even be tilted from side to side.

Right button: The right button is used for special operations, although right-clicking mostly pops up a shortcut menu.

Special buttons: Some mice come with special buttons, which can be used for Internet navigation or assigned specific functions by using special software. (See "Changing mouse settings," later in this chapter.)

On the mouse's belly, you find its method of motion detection, which is either a light or a laser. The light reflects off the desktop to track the mouse's movements, although it won't work on a shiny surface.

Exploring mouse species

The variety of computer mice seems endless. They have different styles and shapes, special buttons, and unique features designed to drive the mildest of nerds into a technogeek frenzy.

A popular mouse variation is the *trackball,* which is like an upside-down mouse. Rather than roll the mouse around, you use your thumb or index finger to roll a ball on top of the mouse. The whole contraption stays stationary, so it doesn't need nearly as much room and its cord never gets tangled. This type of mouse is preferred by graphical artists because it's often more precise than the traditional "soap-on-a-rope" mouse.

Another mouse mutation enjoyed by the artistic type is the digital stylus, which is classified as an input device and not a mouse. The *digital stylus* looks like a pen and draws on a special pad or right on the screen. Tablet PCs feature a digital stylus as an input device option.

Moving the mouse

 The computer's mouse controls a graphical mouse pointer on the screen, as shown in the margin. Roll the mouse around on your desktop, and the pointer on the screen moves in a similar manner. Roll the mouse left, and the pointer moves left; roll it in circles, and the pointer mimics that action. Tickle the mouse, the pointer laughs.

Moving the mouse and clicking the buttons are how the mouse works with the computer. Specific names are given to those actions. Here's a list:

Point: When you're told to "point the mouse," you move the mouse on the desktop, which moves the mouse pointer on the screen to point at something interesting (or not).

Click: A *click* is a press of the main (left) mouse button — press and release. It makes a clicking sound.

Right-click: This action is the same as a click, but with the right mouse button.

Double-click: A double-click is two clicks of the mouse in a row without moving the mouse. The clicks don't need to be *really* fast, and you can adjust the click time, as covered later in this chapter, in the "Fix double-click" section.

Drag: The drag operation is a multistep process. Point the mouse at the thing you want to move, a graphical object or an icon. Press and hold down the mouse's button, and then move the mouse to relocate the object on the screen. Keep the mouse button down until you're finished moving the mouse. Release the mouse button to "drop" whatever you moved.

Right-drag: This action is the same as a drag, but the mouse's right button is used instead.

Ctrl+drag: This action is the same as a drag, though you also press the Ctrl key on the keyboard while you drag around a graphical doodad.

Shift+drag: This action is just like a Ctrl+drag, but the Shift key is used instead.

The best way to learn how to use a computer mouse is to play a computer game. The Solitaire game was included with Windows for years so that people could hone their mouse skills.

The mouse pointer is also known as the mouse cursor. I use the term mouse pointer so as not to cause confusion between the cursor where text appears and the mouse pointer.

Changing mouse settings

In Windows, you use the Mouse Properties dialog box to control, manipulate, and tease the mouse. To visit this dialog box, heed these directions:

1. **Open the Control Panel.**

   In Windows 10, press Win+X and then choose Control Panel from the super-secret menu. In Windows 7, choose Control Panel from the Start menu.

2. **Choose Hardware and Sound.**

3. **Click the Mouse link, found under the Devices and Printers heading.**

   Lo and behold: the Mouse Properties dialog box.

The Mouse Properties dialog box controls the mouse's look and behavior. It may also feature custom tabs that deal with special features particular to your mouse.

The following sections assume that the Mouse Properties dialog box is open on the screen.

Make the pointer easier to find

To help you locate a wayward mouse pointer, use the Pointer Options tab in the Mouse Properties dialog box. The options in the Visibility area, near the bottom of the dialog box, can come in handy, especially on larger screens or when the display is particularly busy. Other items worthy of note include:

Snap To: This option jumps the mouse pointer to the main button in any dialog box that appears.

Display Pointer Trails: This option spawns a comet trail of mouse pointers as you move the mouse about. Jiggling or circling the mouse makes lots of visual racket, which allows you to quickly locate the mouse pointer.

Show Location/Ctrl Key: This option allows you to find the mouse pointer by tapping the keyboard's Ctrl key. When you do, a radar-like circle appears, by zeroing in on the cursor's location.

Another way to make the pointer more visible is to choose a more visible mouse pointer: Click the Pointers tab in the Mouse Properties dialog box. Use the options there to choose a different look or size for the mouse pointer.

Fix double-click

If you can't seem to double-click, one of two things is happening: You're moving the mouse pointer a little between clicks or the double-click rate is set too fast for human fingers to manage.

The *double-click rate* is set in the Mouse Properties dialog box, on the Buttons tab, in the Double-Click Speed area. Practice your double-clicking on the tiny folder icon off to the right. Use the Slow-Fast slider to adjust the double-click speed to better match your click-click timing.

Use the mouse left-handed

In Windows, you can adjust the mouse for southpaw use on the Buttons tab. Put a check mark by the box labeled Switch Primary and Secondary Buttons. That way, the main mouse button is under your left index finger.

This book and all computer documentation assume that the left mouse button is the main button. *Right-clicks* are clicks of the right mouse button. If you tell Windows to use the left-handed mouse, these buttons are reversed. A right-click is then a left-click.

Left-handed mice are available, designed to fit your left hand better than all those biased, right-hand-oriented mice on the market.

Touchscreen Input

It's not a necessary input device for a desktop PC, but for a laptop and especially for a tablet PC, touchscreen input is handy. You can use your finger, or a digital stylus, to manipulate items on the screen. You can even summon an onscreen keyboard to type, which helps when the tablet PC lacks a physical keyboard.

Using basic touchscreen techniques

The following actions describe common ways to manipulate items displayed on a touchscreen monitor.

Touch: The simplest way to manipulate the touchscreen is to touch it. You touch an object, an icon, a control, a menu item, a doodad, and so on. The touch operation is similar to a mouse click. It may also be referred to as a *tap* or *press*.

Double-tap: Touch the screen twice in the same location. Double-tapping is used to zoom in on an image or a map, but it can also zoom out. Because of the double-tap's dual nature, I recommend using the *pinch* or *spread* operation instead when you want to zoom.

Long-press: A long-press occurs when you touch part of the screen and hold your finger down. Depending on what you're doing, a pop-up menu may appear, or the item you're long-pressing may get "picked up" so that you can drag (move) it around after a long-press. *Long-press* might also be referred to as *touch and hold*. In many programs or apps, the long-press is a substitute for a right-click of the mouse.

Swipe: To swipe, you touch your finger on one spot and then drag it to another spot. Swipes can go up, down, left, or right, which moves the touchscreen content in the direction you swipe your finger. A swipe can be fast or slow, and it can also involve more than a single finger. It's also called a *flick* or *slide*.

Drag: In a combination of long-press and swipe, you first long-press an item then, keeping your finger down, swipe your finger. The drag technique moves items on the screen.

Pinch: A pinch involves two fingers, which start out separated and then are brought together. The effect is used to *zoom out,* to reduce the size of an image or see more of a map.

Spread: The opposite of *pinch* is *spread.* You start out with your fingers together and then spread them. The spread is used to *zoom in,* to enlarge an image or see more detail on a map.

Rotate: A few apps let you rotate an image on the screen by touching with two fingers and twisting them around a center point. Think of turning a combination lock on a safe, and you get the rotate operation.

You can't manipulate the touchscreen while wearing gloves unless they're gloves specially designed for using electronic touchscreens, such as the gloves that Batman wears.

Typing on a touchscreen

When text input is demanded and a physical keyboard is unavailable, Windows displays a touchscreen keyboard. You use the keyboard on a touchscreen monitor to type text in a sluggish and uncomfortable manner.

Figure 9-4 illustrates the Windows 10 touchscreen keyboard. It provides basic alphabet key input. To access other keys on the touchscreen keyboard, tap or click the special symbols key, as illustrated in the figure.

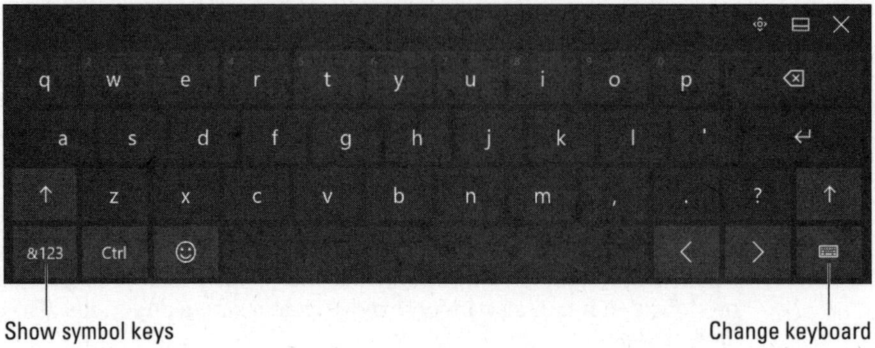

Figure 9-4:
A touch-
screen
keyboard.

Show symbol keys   Change keyboard

To type on the touchscreen keyboard, tap a key. That letter is produced. If
you don't find the key you need, tap the &123 key to peruse available symbols. You can also tap the Change Keyboard icon (refer to Figure 9-4) to
select another keyboard layout.

Tap the X button to dismiss the touchscreen keyboard.

Chapter 10

System Expansion

- -

- -

*I*t's relatively easy for a human being to expand. I'm expanding all the time! Of course, the expansion I'm experiencing doesn't add new options or features to my system, at least not new features I'm eager to have. With a PC, however, such expansion is both possible and desirable. Indeed, you have at your disposal many beneficial ways to expand your computer system, none of which involves adult beverages, donuts, or pizza.

It's a Port

Your PC is adorned with various connectors. These connectors are known by various technical names, though they're commonly called *holes, jacks,* and *ports.* Of those terms, *port* is the best.

A port is more than a hole. It defines the shape of the hole and its connector, the type of devices that can be plugged in, and all sorts of technology required to control the device being connected. It's a big deal.

The PC's console features a host of ports into which a variety of devices can be attached. The goal is to expand the computer system.

✔ Officially, a *port* is a place on the computer where information can be sent or received or both. It's also a dessert wine.

✔ In the past, PCs had specific ports for specific tasks, such as a keyboard port, modem port, and printer port. Those various ports have been eliminated over the years, replaced with the more versatile USB port.

The Versatile USB Port

The most popular and useful port on your PC is the USB port, where the *U* stands for *universal* and means that this port can be used to *plug* in an entire universe of peripherals. I could also make up that the *S* in USB stands for cinchy, but cinchy is spelled with a *C,* so that one won't fly.

Since I brought it up, USB stands for Universal Serial Bus. Pronounce it letters-only: "yoo-ess-bee."

The variety of USB devices is legion: printers, speakers, headsets, joysticks, scanners, digital cameras, video cameras, webcams, hard drives, media storage, keyboards, networking gizmos, pointing devices, tiny fans, lamps, tanning beds, time machines — the list goes on and on. More and more USB devices are appearing every day.

The best news about USB? It's *easy.* Just plug in the gizmo. Often, that's all you need to do!

✔ USB ports, as well as USB devices, sport the USB symbol, shown in the margin.

✔ The most popular USB standard is 2.0. USB 3.0 devices are available, which are many times faster. If your PC has USB 3.0, do yourself a favor and find some USB 3.0 gizmos — and some USB cables. Otherwise, most USB 3.0 devices can be used on older USB ports, although they don't run as fast.

Understanding USB cables

Some USB devices, such as a USB thumb drive, attach directly to the computer. For the rest, a cable is necessary. The name of the cable is, surprisingly, *USB cable.*

USB cables are judged by their length and the type of connector on each end.

As far as length goes, you can get a USB cable up to 3 or 4 meters long. Any longer and you'd probably want me to specify the length in feet instead of meters. But seriously, the signal may be compromised after about 15 feet or so.

A standard USB cable has two different ends, dubbed A and B. As USB has evolved, different A and B ends have appeared. Table 10-1 lists the lot.

Table 10-1	USB Cable Ends
End Type	*Appearance*
USB A	
USB A 3.0	
USB B	
USB B 3.0	
USB micro B	
USB micro B 3.0	
USB mini B	
USB Type C	

Generally speaking, the A end of the cable plugs into the console or a USB hub. The B end, the weird one, plugs into the peripheral.

Some devices, such as keyboards and mice, have only an A end on their USB cable. The other end is the device itself.

New on the block is the USB Type C connector. It works up or down, so the connection is perfect the first time you try.

USB 3.0 connectors and ports feature a blue tongue. This differs from the older connectors, which use a black or gray tongue.

Connecting a USB device

One reason that the USB port took over the world is that it's smart. Dumb things never take over the world. That's why you don't see any cheese-flavored gelato. But I digress.

To add a USB device to your computer, just plug it in. You don't need to turn off the computer first, and most of the time you don't need to install special software. When you plug in a USB device, Windows instantly recognizes it and configures the device for you.

Of course, it pays to read the directions! Some USB gizmos require that you first install software before connecting the device. The only way to tell is to read the quick-setup guide or the manual that came with the USB device.

There may be some onscreen activity when you attach a USB device. You might see a pop-up window or information saying that a driver is being installed. The *driver* is the software Windows uses to interface with the device. It's installed automatically.

For USB storage devices, you see an AutoPlay notice. Refer to Chapter 19 for information on AutoPlay.

Working with USB-powered gizmos

Quite a few USB gizmos don't require separate power cords. Instead, they use the power supplied by the USB port, making them *USB-powered* devices. The issue is that these devices can be connected only to USB-powered ports.

You'll find USB-powered ports in two locations. The first is the console. The second is a USB-powered hub. See the section "Using hubs to expand the USB universe."

- ✔ A USB-powered gizmo plugged into a non-USB-powered hub won't work properly.

- ✔ Don't worry about turning off a USB-powered peripheral. You can't! It's fine to leave the device on, as long as you keep the computer on. But, if you really, *really* want to turn the gizmo off, simply unplug the USB cable.

- ✔ USB devices that require lots of power, such as printers and certain external storage devices, use their own power cords.

Removing a USB device

Removing a USB device is cinchy: Just unplug it. That's it!

Well, that's it unless that device is storage media, such as an external hard drive or a thumb drive. In that case, you must officially *unmount* the gizmo before you unplug it. Here's how:

1. **Press Win+E to bring up a File Explorer window.**

2. **In Windows 10, choose This PC from the items listed on the left side of the Window.**

   You see a list of all your PC's storage devices, plus maybe some network locations.

3. **Right-click the external storage device's icon.**

4. **From the pop-up menu, choose the Eject or Safely Remove command.**

   Windows displays a message (in the notification area), informing you that the device can be safely removed.

5. **Disconnect the external storage device.**

 If the Eject or Safely Remove item doesn't appear, a different approach is required: Look for the Safely Remove USB icon in the taskbar's notification area, as shown in the margin. Click that item to see a list of attached devices, similar to what's shown in Figure 10-1.

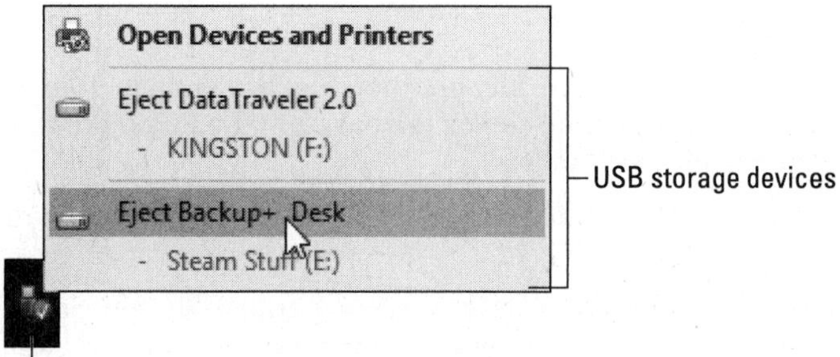

Figure 10-1: Safely removing external storage.

> 🖨 **Open Devices and Printers**
> 💾 Eject DataTraveler 2.0
>   - KINGSTON (F:)
> 💾 Eject Backup+ Desk
>   - Steam Stuff (E:)

USB storage devices

Safely Remove USB notification icon

Choose a device to remove from the list, such as the Backup+hard drive, shown in Figure 10-1. When Windows tells you it's okay to remove the device, detach its USB cable.

Using hubs to expand the USB universe

There never seem to be enough USB ports. Fortunately, when you need more USB ports, you can quickly add them by plugging a USB hub into your PC.

A USB *hub* allows you to greatly expand your PC's USB universe. A typical expansion hub, shown in Figure 10-2, connects to the console's USB port. When you add such a USB hub, you increase the number of USB gizmos you can attach to the computer system.

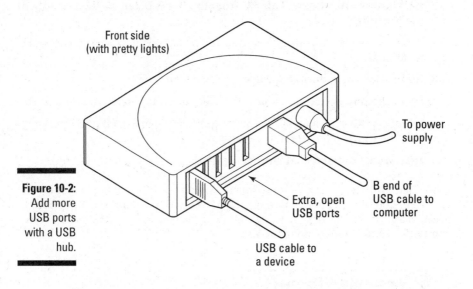

Front side
(with pretty lights)

To power
supply

Figure 10-2:
Add more
USB ports
with a USB
hub.

Extra, open
USB ports

B end of
USB cable to
computer

USB cable to
a device

✔ If one hub isn't enough, buy another! You can connect hubs to hubs, if you like. As long as the cables fan out from the PC and nothing loops back on itself, it all works.

✔ You can also add a hub to the console internally by installing a USB expansion card.

✔ Sometimes, you don't have to buy a separate USB hub. Some USB devices act as their own hubs, providing connectors for plugging in additional USB devices.

✔ Your PC's USB universe has a maximum limit of 127 USB devices. You'll probably run out of desk space before then.

✔ A hub that also plugs into the wall socket is known as a *powered* USB hub. This type of hub is necessary for some USB devices to operate. See the earlier section "Working with USB-powered gizmos."

✔ The console is a powered USB hub.

Other ports, weird and rare

Some high-end PCs sport additional ports, some of which are really fast and super-duper, but uncommon. Two terms you may see are IEEE 1394 and eSATA.

The IEEE 1394 port, which is also the name of the technical standard, is more commonly known as the FireWire port on a Macintosh. It works similarly to the USB port in that IEEE devices can be plugged and unplugged at any time. You can find IEEE hubs, just as you can find USB hubs. Sadly, IEEE never caught on as well as USB.

Another rare port you may see listed is eSATA. *SATA* is the standard for connecting mass storage devices inside the console to the PC's motherboard. *eSATA* is an external version of that standard, allowing you to connect eSATA storage devices to your PC. To properly pronounce eSATA, say "ee-SAY-tuh."

✔ An example of an unpowered hub is a keyboard that has USB ports on it. Those ports are designed to connect non-USB-powered devices, such as mice.

✔ The first hub (your PC) is the *root* hub.

Expansion Slots

The internal way to expand your PC is by adding new circuitry directly to the motherboard. Believe it or not, it's possible for you to do such a thing without wielding a soldering iron. No, this trick works thanks to the motherboard's *expansion slots*. Into those expansion slots, you plug *expansion cards*.

Shopping for expansion cards

At one time, installing expansion cards into your PC was a necessity. That's because older PC motherboards didn't house a lot of hardware, including memory. To add memory, or even something basic like a printer port, you needed to install an expansion card.

Today, the variety of expansion cards is pretty limited, mostly because PCs come supplied with enough hardware. Still, options are available for adding more robust graphics, improved audio, additional USB ports, video capture hardware, and other interesting if not esoteric upgrades.

Expansion cards are available at computer stores and online. Depending on what you're adding, the cost can be modest, although some high-end video cards can cost more than a house payment.

- ✔ All PCs sport a single expansion card standard, called PCI Express and abbreviated PCIe. Because this is the only standard, you don't need to hunt for this or that type of expansion card. If it's a PC expansion card, it'll work in your computer. However:

- ✔ Not every PC offers internal expansion slots. The availability of slots is determined by the console's size as well as by the motherboard's design. Mini-tower PCs have expansion slots. All-in-ones, tablet PCs, laptops, and mini-desktop systems lack expansion slots.

- ✔ It's tempting for me to prattle on about the history of PC expansion cards and riff all the names and changing standards, but I won't. Today, everything is PCI Express. Oh, and PCI stands for Peripheral Component Interconnect.

Adding an expansion card

Buying an expansion card is easy. Installing it is not so easy. I strongly recommend you have your dealer or a competent and fully insured 12-year-old do the work for you.

To thrust an expansion card into your PC's bosom, follow these general steps:

1. **Turn off the PC and unplug it.**

2. **Remove the PC's case.**

   Stop here if this concept chills you into a catatonic state.

3. **Locate an unoccupied expansion slot.**

   You may need to move around — or even disconnect — various cables or other internal items to freely access the expansion slot.

4. **Gingerly cram the new expansion card into the available expansion slot.**

   The card's rump sticks out the back of the PC.

5. **Close 'er up.**

   Redo what you undid in Steps 2 and 3. Plug it in. Turn it on. Pray that it works.

The backsides of expansion cards stick out the console's rear. For a majority of expansion cards, that's how you access the card's features. The ports or jacks or whatever abilities are added when the card is installed.

The Bluetooth Thing

Bluetooth refers to a wireless standard for connecting computer peripherals. Just as wireless computer networking involves more setup than the wired kind of network, connecting Bluetooth peripherals involves a bit more effort than connecting wired peripherals.

✔ Bluetooth peripherals include printers, keyboards, speakers, mice, monitors, robot butlers, and cell phones.

✔ Wireless peripherals use batteries. Specifically, wireless keyboard and mice need batteries to send and receive their signals.

✔ Not all wireless peripherals use the Bluetooth standard. Most wireless keyboards and mice use a proprietary radio, which doesn't require the same configuration overhead as Bluetooth.

✔ Perhaps the greatest advantage of Bluetooth is that it lets you connect to a variety of peripherals without having to use a separate wireless adapter for each peripheral.

✔ Bluetooth began its existence as a wireless replacement for the PC's serial or RS-232 port, which was common on PCs in the 1980s and 1990s.

Checking for Bluetooth

PCs don't traditionally come supplied with Bluetooth wireless radios. Some laptops do, but most computers don't.

To be certain that your PC sports a Bluetooth wireless radio, look on the taskbar for a Bluetooth notification icon, similar to what's shown in the margin. If you find that icon, the PC features Bluetooth.

If you desire to use a Bluetooth peripheral, and your PC lacks a Bluetooth wireless radio, you can easily add one: Obtain a USB Bluetooth adapter. The teensy gizmo, which is small enough to smuggle through customs in your nostril, plugs directly into a USB port. Windows automatically installs the Bluetooth software the second you install the gizmo.

✔ USB Bluetooth adapters are cheap! Even so, there's no need to get one if you don't plan on using any Bluetooth peripherals.

✔ Bluetooth peripherals frequently feature the Bluetooth logo. For example, a Bluetooth printer features the logo, which means that you could configure your PC to wirelessly use that printer.

Controlling Bluetooth in Windows

When Bluetooth is available and configured, you see the Bluetooth logo as an icon in the desktop's notification area on the right end of the taskbar. You click that icon to view a pop-up menu, as shown in Figure 10-3. Use the menu to control Bluetooth gizmos from your PC.

The pop-up menu you see on your computer may look slightly different from the one shown in Figure 10-3. Most of the important menu items are there no matter what you see.

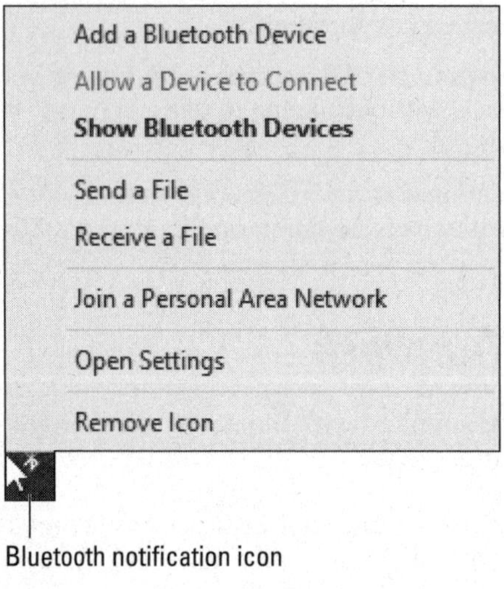

Add a Bluetooth Device

Allow a Device to Connect

Show Bluetooth Devices

Send a File

Receive a File

Join a Personal Area Network

Figure 10-3:
Bluetooth
control in
Windows.

Open Settings

Remove Icon

Bluetooth notification icon

Pairing a Bluetooth peripheral

The whole point of Bluetooth is to allow your PC to connect with peripherals and other devices without the burden of wires. Unlike the TV remote, however, you can't just point-and-click to get the job done. Instead, the devices must be paired.

These steps are specific to pairing with a Bluetooth mouse, although they can generically be applied to any Bluetooth peripheral:

1. **Ensure that the Bluetooth peripheral is discoverable.**

   The Bluetooth device must broadcast its availability. For a mouse, simply turn on the mouse, although you may have to press a special Bluetooth button. The device's documentation offers the specifics.

2. **On your PC, click the Bluetooth icon in the notification area and choose the command Add a Bluetooth Device.**

   The command might read Add a Device instead.

   A window or screen appears, listing any available Bluetooth devices. If you're lucky, the one you want to pair with appears in that list.

3. **Choose the device from the list.**

4. **In Windows 10, click the Pair button.**

5. **Obey the directions on your computer screen or on the Bluetooth device.**

   Time is ticking, so be quick! For a Bluetooth mouse, you may only have to click a mouse button. For a Bluetooth keyboard, you must type in a code.

6. **Continue obeying directions on the screen.**

   Eventually, the device is paired and you can begin using it.

The good news is that after you initially pair the device, there's no need to pair it again. Anytime the computer is on and the Bluetooth device is on, they automatically reconnect.

✔ Unlike the long arm of the law, the Bluetooth wireless connection goes only so far. In the United States, that distance is about 20 feet. In Europe, the distance is far less, just over 6 meters.

✔ The reason for pairing the devices is so that some other Bluetooth device doesn't steal away the peripheral. That can happen only if you unpair the devices, which is covered in the later section "Unpairing a Bluetooth device."

✔ Bluetooth devices are discoverable for only a brief amount of time, usually 2 minutes. If the connection fails during that time, you need to try again.

Reviewing paired devices

To check up on the status of connected Bluetooth devices, follow these steps:

1. Click on the Bluetooth icon in the taskbar's notification area.

2. Choose the Show Bluetooth Devices command.

You see a window that lists all paired Bluetooth devices. Some devices may be active, which means that they're on and connected. Other devices may be listed as inactive, which means they're turned off, out of range, or temporarily insane.

Don't let some of the oddball peripheral names frighten you. As far as you're concerned, the device is a Bluetooth mouse. Don't be alarmed when Windows calls it an M26A2.

Unpairing a Bluetooth device

Normally, there's no need to unpair a Bluetooth peripheral. If you want to stop using the device, simply turn it off. The connection is broken when the device is off.

Oh. You're being insistent? Well, then: The only time you truly need to unpair a Bluetooth device is when you want to use the device with another Bluetooth computer at the same location. In that case, follow these steps:

1. Click the Bluetooth icon in the notification area.

2. Choose the Show Bluetooth Devices command.

3. Click to select the paired Bluetooth device.

4. Click the Remove Device button.

5. Confirm your choice; click the Yes button.

   The device is no longer connected to your PC.

After the device is unpaired, you're free to pair it with another Bluetooth computer. Or you can again pair the device with your PC. Bluetooth gizmos have low standards and loose morals and really don't care what they're paired with, as long as they're paired with something.

Chapter 11

P Is for Printer

*T*his chapter is brought to you by the letter *P*. *P* stands for *PC*. It also stands for *peripheral*. One of the PC's preferred peripherals is the printer. *Printer* starts with *P*. PCs prefer printers, specifically for producing output on paper. The printer makes it possible.

The Printer, the Paper, the Document Maker

Printers are a necessary peripheral in any computer system. That's because dragging the PC around and showing everyone what's on the monitor is just too much of a chore. No, it's much better to *print* your stuff on paper, to create a *hard copy* of your data, documents, and doodles.

Surveying the printer landscape

Computer printers come in all shapes and sizes, some with just the bare bones and others with features galore. When you strip that all away, you find only two types of printers, categorized by how the ink gets thrown on the paper. Those two types are inkjet and laser.

Inkjet: The inkjet printer creates its image by spewing tiny balls of ink directly on the paper. That jet-of-ink action gives this printer category its name. The inkjet printer is the most common type of computer printer.

Laser: Laser printers are found primarily in the office environment, where they deftly handle high workloads. The printer uses a laser beam to create the image, which somehow helps fuse toner powder (ink) onto the paper. The result is crisp and fast output, but at a premium price over standard inkjet printers.

All inkjet printers are color printers. Laser printers come in both mono-chrome and color varieties.

All-in-one printers combine a basic inkjet printer with a fax machine, scanner, and copier. This type of printer is popular in home and small offices because it replaces four devices.

- You can print a color image or document on a monochrome printer; the printout will just be in black-and-white.

- Black-and-white. Monochrome. Grayscale. It's all the same thing.

- Inkjet printers are by no means messy. The ink is dry on the paper by the time the paper comes flopping out of the printer.

- Higher-priced printers offer a higher-quality output, faster speed, more printing options, the capability to print on larger sheets of paper, and other superhero features. Low-priced printers are good but print more slowly. And besides, the manufacturers makes up the cost difference on the prices they charge you for the ink.

Touring the typical printer

Take a moment to examine the PC's printer to look for some specific items. Use Figure 11-1 as your guide.

Power button: Like other devices electronic, the printer features a power button, although some printers may have a traditional On-Off switch. Press the power button to turn on the printer or to turn it off.

Control panel: The control panel is where you set printer options and make settings. Refer to the next section for the details.

Paper feed: The paper feed is where you store the paper on which the printer eventually prints. For more information, see the section "Eating paper," later in this chapter.

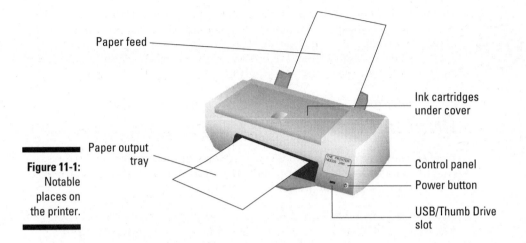

Paper feed

Ink cartridges
under cover

Paper output
tray

Figure 11-1:
Notable
places on
the printer.

Control panel

Power button

USB/Thumb Drive
slot

Manual/envelope feeder: The printer may have a special slot, tray, or foldout-thing for feeding special papers or envelopes. It may be hidden on your printer, and it's not shown in Figure 11-1, so rummage around a bit to see whether your printer has such a deal.

Ink/toner replacement: Printers don't go on printing forever. At some point, you need to feed the thing more ink. Be sure that you know how to open the printer to find where the ink goes. See the later section "Drinking ink."

USB port or media card reader: I doubt anyone uses this feature, but if you desire, you can attach a thumb drive or memory card directly to certain printers. Use the printer's control panel to select and print images.

Paper output tray: The printed paper comes out and is stacked in the output tray.

Using the printer's control panel

Every printer has a control panel somewhere on its body. The fancy models have touchscreens that work like cell phone touchscreens for input. Less fancy printers may have only a couple of buttons or lights.

The primary function for the control panel is to set options, eject paper, clear printer jams, and cancel print jobs run amok. Simple printers offer only those basic features. All-in-one printers have a slate of options, including faxing, making copies, scanning images, and, of course, printing.

The more advanced the printer, the more options available on the control panel. Most of these printers have a Help setting. The most helpful feature of the Help setting is an option that actually prints out the printer's manual. If not the whole manual, then the option prints out basic printer commands and tips. Look for that option on your PC's printer.

Drinking ink

The Chinese invented ink over 3,000 years ago, but it's still basically the same stuff used today in a computer printer. The type of ink and how it's stored depend on which type of printer you're using.

Inkjet printers use *ink cartridges*. A black cartridge, and then three color cartridges: cyan, magenta, and yellow. Inkjet printers customized for printing photos may feature two additional ink cartridges: light cyan and light magenta.

Laser printers use *toner,* a powdery ink substance that also comes in a cartridge.

All laser printers use black ink or toner. Color printers also use black ink plus color inks: cyan, magenta, and yellow.

Replacing the ink in your printer works differently for each printer. Instructions are usually found on the inside of the lid or compartment where the ink or toner cartridges reside. Overall advice: Be careful! Spill the ink and you've got a serious mess.

- ✔ The printer has a drinking problem. Printer manufacturers take advantage of that dependency by selling ink at a very high price. It's the old "Give away the razor and sell them the blade" concept all over again.

- ✔ Some manufacturers sell their cartridges with return envelopes so that you can send the old cartridge back to the factory for recycling or proper disposal. Also check at your local office supply store, which may assist in recycling ink cartridges.

- ✔ Make sure that you don't breathe in the dust from a laser toner cartridge or else you'll die.

- ✔ Make a note of which type of inkjet cartridges your printer uses. Keep the catalog number somewhere handy, such as taped to your printer's case or as a note in your cell phone, so that you can reorder the proper cartridge.

- ✔ Always follow carefully the instructions for changing cartridges. Old cartridges can leak and spread messy ink all over. Use rubber gloves, or simple household cleaning gloves, and wear them when changing the ink or toner cartridge. I also suggest having paper towels handy.

✔ When a laser printer first warns you with its `Toner [is] low` message, you can squeeze a few more pages from it by gently rocking the toner cartridge: Remove the cartridge and rock it back and forth the short way (not from end to end), which helps redistribute the toner dust.

✔ Rather than buy new cartridges, consider getting ink cartridge refills or recharged toner cartridges. Be sure that you deal with a reputable company; not every type of ink or toner cartridge can be reused successfully.

✔ Never let your printer cartridges go dry. You may think that squeezing every last drop of ink saves you money, but it's not good for the printer.

Eating paper

Next to drinking ink, printers eat paper. Fortunately, paper isn't as expensive as ink, so it doesn't bankrupt you to churn through a ream or two. The only issue is where to feed in the paper. Like feeding a baby, there's a right end and a wrong end.

The paper goes into a feeder tray either near the printer's bottom or sticking out the top.

Some laser printers require you to fill a cartridge with paper, similar to the way a copy machine works. Slide the cartridge all the way into the printer after it's loaded.

When printing on letterhead or a check, you need to ensure that the paper is set in the right direction, either face down or face up, and you need to know which side is the top. Most printers feature Paper Feed icons that tell you how the paper goes into the printer. Here's how those symbols translate into English:

✔ The paper goes in face down, top side up.

✔ The paper goes in face down, top side down.

✔ The paper goes in face up, top side up.

✔ The paper goes in face up, top side down.

If the printer doesn't tell you which way is up, write *Top* on a sheet of paper and run it through the printer. Then draw your own icon, similar to those just shown, to help orient the pages you manually insert into the printer.

Always make sure that you have enough printer paper. Buying too much isn't a sin.

Choosing the proper paper

There's really no such thing as a typical sheet of paper. Paper comes in different sizes, weights (degrees of thickness), colors, styles, textures, and I assume, flavors.

The best general-purpose paper for computer printing is standard photocopier paper. If you want better results from your inkjet printer, getting specific inkjet paper works best, although you pay more for that paper. The higher-quality (and spendy) inkjet paper is good for printing colors because it is designed to absorb the ink.

At the high end of the spectrum are specialty papers, such as photographic papers that come in smooth or glossy finishes, transparencies, and iron-on T-shirt transfers. Just ensure that the paper you get is made for your type of printer — inkjet or laser.

- ✔ Some printers are capable of handling larger-size paper, such as legal or tabloid size. If so, make sure that you load the paper properly and tell your application that it's printing on a different paper size. See the later section "Printer Operation" for more information.

- ✔ Avoid thick papers, because they get jammed inside the printer.

- ✔ Avoid using erasable bond and other fancy dusted papers in your printer. The powder coating on these papers gums up the works.

Where the Printer Meets the PC

As with all other computer peripherals, the PC-printer relationship has a courting phase. It involves an introduction, some dating, and finally, a full-on-marriage. You'll be grateful that the entire operation is much faster and far more successful than in human relationships.

Connecting the printer

Printers are really their own computers, containing a processor, memory, networking, and sometimes mass storage. Getting the printer and computer connected is too routine to be considered a miracle, yet I'm constantly surprised when the operation meets with success.

The printer can connect with your computer either directly or over the network. Years ago, the direct connection was most popular. Today, it's the network connection.

To directly connect a printer to your PC, you use a standard USB cable, just like the cable that doesn't come with the printer. That's right: Printers don't come with cables.

The network connection involves plugging the printer into a network cable and then attaching that cable to the network's gateway. Many printers also offer wireless networking. In that case, you use the printer's control panel to select the Wi-Fi network and type in the password.

When the printer is connected, Windows instantly installs its software. The printer is made available and ready for use.

TIP

 ✔ Always read the printer's setup information before you connect the printer. Occasionally, the printer demands that special software be installed before the printer is connected to the PC.

 ✔ You can connect a number of printers to a single computer. In fact, networked PCs have access to multiple network printers.

 ✔ It's okay to leave the printer on all the time. The printer automatically slips into a low-power mode when it's no longer needed.

 ✔ See Chapter 17 for more information on PC networking.

Finding printers in Windows

You'll find the various printers available to your PC in a central spot in Windows. Windows 10 offers the Printers and Scanners part of the Settings app, but a better view is provided in the Devices and Printers window, shown in Figure 11-2.

To visit the Devices and Printers window, obey these steps:

1. **Summon the Control Panel.**

   In Windows 10, press the Win+X keyboard shortcut and choose Control Panel from the super-secret menu. In Windows 7, choose Control Panel from the Start menu.

2. **Click the View Devices and Printers link, found below the Hardware and Sound heading.**

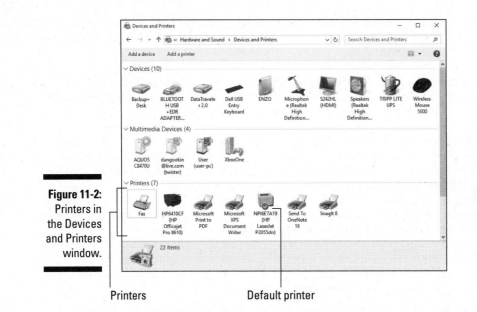

Figure 11-2:
Printers in
the Devices
and Printers
window.

Printers   Default printer

Icons shown in the Devices and Printers window represent various gizmos connected to your PC, including the monitor, the keyboard, external storage, and so on, as shown in Figure 11-2. You'll find a Printers category, under which all available printers are listed, including network printers.

One printer in the list is known as the *default* printer, shown by the green check mark (refer to Figure 11-2). The default printer is identified as your computer's primary printer. A default printer is handy, especially when your PC has multiple printers and you don't want to waste time choosing one every time you print.

Setting the default printer

When you set a default printer, you're ensuring that Windows uses that printer as your favorite. That way, when you do a quick print, you don't need to select a specific printer. Follow these steps to set a default printer:

1. **Open the Devices and Printers window.**

   Refer to the preceding section for specific directions.

2. **Right-click the printer you plan to use most often.**

3. **Choose Set As Default Printer from the pop-up menu.**

   The green check mark on the printer's icon confirms that you've speci-fied the default printer.

4. **Close the Devices and Printers window.**

You can change the default printer at any time by repeating these steps. To choose any printer for a particular print job, you can use the Print dialog box, as described in the next section.

Printer Operation

On a computer, the final act of creating something is to print it. Ink on paper provides that hard copy, the physical evidence that you actually use your computer to make something and not just check Facebook dozens of times a day.

✔ The paperless office never really came to full fruition. Though lots of drafts are no longer printed — and that's good — eventually, items are printed.

✔ I haven't printed text from a book in over 20 years. This book's text is sent electronically to my editors and stays in that form until it's finally printed. That's a good example of the paperless office in action.

Printing something

The key to printing in any Windows program is to use the Print command and summon the Print dialog box. You'll find a Print command nestled on the File menu, or you can use the handy — and surprisingly memorable — keyboard shortcut, Ctrl+P.

The standard Print dialog box is shown in Figure 11-3. In some programs, a Print screen replaces this dialog box, but all the elements remain the same, as illustrated in the figure.

To print the entire document on the default printer, just click the Print button. In fact, to print quickly, press Ctrl+P and then Enter. That's it.

If you want to change what's printing or how it's printed, here are some common Print dialog box tasks:

Print to a specific printer. If you want to use a printer other than the default, such as that nice color laser printer that Edward hogs in his office, choose it from the list of printers.

Print only a specific page or range of pages. To print only pages 1 through 5, choose Pages in the Page Range part of the Print dialog box (refer to Figure 11-3), and type **1-5** in the text box. To print pages 4 and 8, type **8,4**. Or, to print only select text, choose Selection.

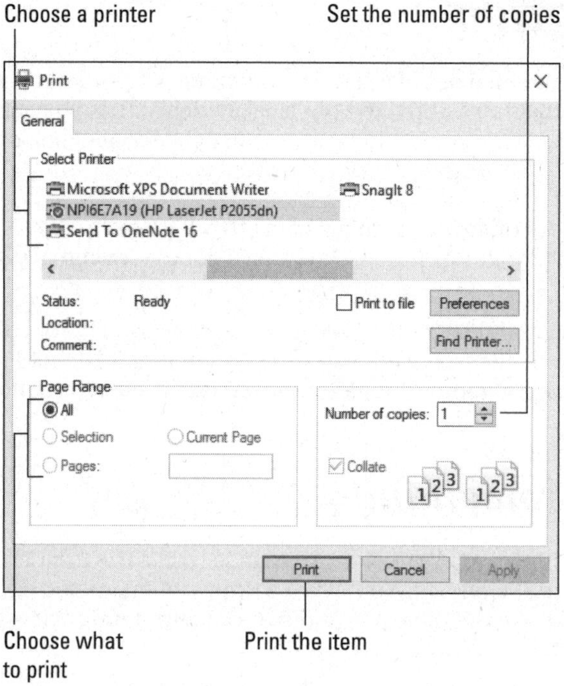

Choose a printer   Set the number of copies

Figure 11-3:
The Print
dialog box.

Choose what   Print the item
to print

Print multiple copies. Set a value other than 1 by the Number of Copies field to print several copies of your work. If you want the copies to print page by page, such as 7 copies of page 1 and then 7 copies of page 2, uncheck the Collate option.

Click the Print button after making your choices to print your document. Or, you can click Cancel or press the Esc key to not print anything.

✔ Use the Print command only *once*. When the printer seems unbearably slow, just wait a while before thinking that you goofed up and choosing the Print command again. Otherwise, you print a copy of the document for every time you use the Print command.

✔ Some printer options, such as paper size and orientation, are set in the Page Setup dialog box. To get there, you must choose the Page Setup command from the File menu. You might also try the Preferences button in the Print dialog box and, if you're fortunate, locate page orientation settings there.

✔ Rather than waste paper, preview the document before you print. Some Print dialog boxes feature a print preview window. If not, look for the Print Preview command, usually found on the File menu.

Stopping a printer run amok

The fastest, bestest way to stop printing is to look for a Cancel button on the printer's control panel. Press that button, and all printing stops.

If printing doesn't stop after pressing the Cancel button, be patient and wait. Printers have RAM, just like a computer, so some of the pages may be buffered and continue to print.

Another, more technical way to stop printing involves opening the printer's window and manually canceling the print job. The problem with this technique is that the printer is simply too fast; by the time you find and open the printer's window, the document has finished printing. If you're up for it, however, follow these steps:

1. **Locate the printer's notification icon on the taskbar.**

   The icon appears similar to the one shown in the margin.

2. **Right-click the printer's notification icon.**

   Up pops a menu. The bottom item is the printer's name.

3. **Choose the printer's name from the pop-up menu.**

   The printer's window appears, which lists current printing jobs.

4. **Select the job(s) you want to terminate.**

5. **Choose Document⇨Cancel.**

6. **If prompted, confirm that you want to cancel the print jobs.**

7. **Close the printer's window.**

If you see the document or job disappear in the printer's window, it's too late to cancel. That's okay, because it means the document is probably short and won't waste that much paper.

To pause a printing job, follow Steps 1 through 4 and choose Document ⇨ Pause in Step 5. To resume printing, choose Document ⇨ Resume.

Chapter 12

PC Audio Abilities

*O*riginally, a computer's audio was a simple bell. *Ding!* When the first microcomputers came out in the 1970s, they had small, tinny speakers to emulate the bell. *Beep.* Your computer's audio system has moved far beyond that primitive beep. Built into the chipset on the PC's motherboard is specialized sound circuitry, including a complete music synthesizer. *[Insert symphony sound here.]* The computer can talk, sing, and even ding like a bell. It can also listen to your utterances.

The Noisy PC

All PCs include sound-generation hardware on the motherboard. This hardware can process and play digitally recorded sounds, play music from external media (such as a CD), generate music using the onboard synthesizer, and record sounds. That's a lot of capability, yet it's so common on a PC that the manufacturers seldom boast about it.

> ✔ When you're really into audio, you can use an audio expansion card to add more advanced sound hardware to your PC. This type of upgrade is necessary only for diehard audiophiles, people who are composing

their own music, or professionals who use their PCs as the heart of an audio studio.

✔ If your PC lacks expansion slots or you have a laptop with limited audio, you can upgrade by adding an external USB sound device, such as the Sound Blaster Audigy system.

Setting up speakers

The PC console has always come with a pitiful, internal speaker. Beyond that, your PC most likely has a standard set of stereo (left-right) speakers. That's fine for basic sound, but the PC is capable of so much more.

The next step up from the basic speaker set is to add a *subwoofer*. It's a speaker box designed for low-frequency sounds, which gives oomph to the bass in music or adds emphasis to the sounds in games.

Typically, the subwoofer sits on the floor beneath your PC. It plugs directly into the PC's speakers jack, and the stereo speakers plug into the subwoofer.

The final step up the audio ladder is to go with surround sound, similar to the sound setup for a home theater. In that configuration, multiple speakers cluster around the computer, depending on the implementation of surround sound hardware used.

Figure 12-1 illustrates all possible locations for speakers in a surround sound setup. You'd be nuts to have *all* those speakers connected at one time, but it's possible. Table 12-1 lists the options for surround sound.

✔ Left and right speakers are positioned on the left and right sides of the monitor as you're facing it.

✔ Some monitors come with built-in speakers, though they're generally terrible.

✔ I recommend getting speakers that have a volume control, on either the left or right speaker. A bonus is a Mute button on the speaker. Note that some high-end speaker systems have the Volume and Mute buttons on a control (wired or remote).

✔ The *.x* part of a surround sound specification refers to the presence of a subwoofer: .0 means no subwoofer; .1 means one subwoofer; .2 means two subwoofers.

✔ If you have an audio expansion card on your PC, plug the speakers into the back of that card.

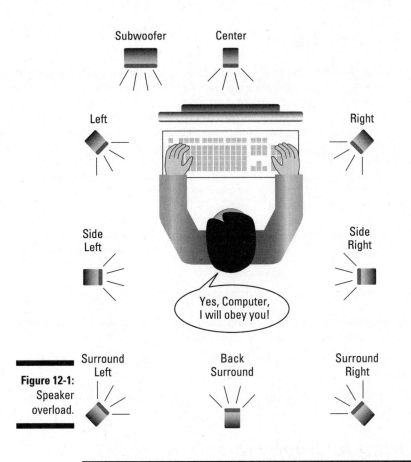

Figure 12-1:
Speaker
overload.

Table 12-1	Surround Sound Speaker Options
Surround Sound Version	*Speakers Used*
3.0	Left, right, back surround
4.0	Left, right, surround left, surround right
4.1	Left, right, surround left, surround right, subwoofer
5.1	Left, right, center, surround left, surround right, subwoofer
6.1	Left, right, center, side left, side right, back surround, subwoofer
7.1	Left, right, center, side left, side right, surround left, surround right, subwoofer

Using headphones

Rather than startle everyone in the room when you launch artillery in a computer game, consider using headphones with your PC instead of an external sound system. A good set of headphones can truly emulate a sound environment beyond what the traditional stereo speakers offer. In fact, some high-end gaming headphones can cost more than the standard home-theater surround sound system. They're worth it.

Beyond headphones you can get a headset, which includes a microphone. This configuration is ideal not only for playing computer games but also for online chat, Skype, and dictation.

To use the headphones, plug them into the PC's speaker jack. If the PC features a headphone jack, use it instead. This jack is color-coded green or lime.

For a headset, plug the pink microphone connector into the mic jack.

- Good headphones come with a volume control and maybe even a Mute button on the same wire that connects the headphones to the PC.

- The audio jacks on the front of the console are designed for a headphone or headset.

- Look for headphones that are comfy on your ears, with big, puffy "cans."

Exploring microphone options

Any cheesy microphone works on a PC. If sound quality is important to you and you're using your PC as a digital audio studio, you have to spend money on microphones and mixers and all that. But if that's not you, any old microphone does the trick.

The microphone plugs into the PC's audio input or mic jack. This jack is color-coded pink.

- The best-quality microphones use a USB connection, not the PC's mic input jack.

- If you plan to use voice over the Internet or dictation, get a headset. See the preceding section.

Sound Control in Windows

Being a hardware thing, the computer's audio system serves subject to the PC's potentate, the operating system. Windows exercises its dictatorial control in a place called the Sound dialog box, beautifully illustrated in Figure 12-2.

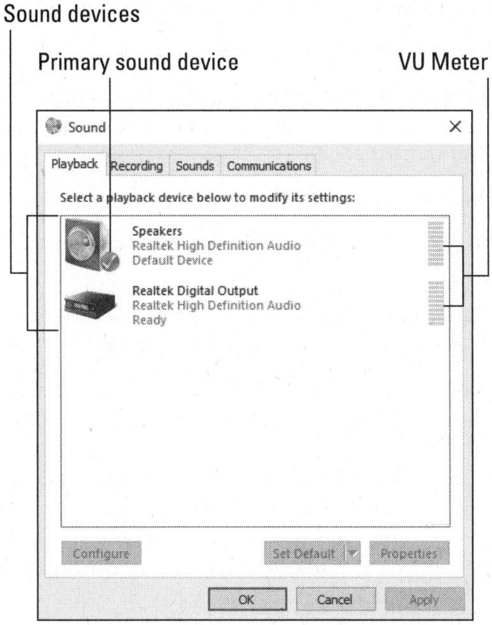

Sound devices

Primary sound device   VU Meter

Figure 12-2:
Sound control happens here.

To display the Sound dialog box, follow these steps:

1. **Open the Control Panel.**

   In Windows 10, press Win+X to display the super-secret menu, and then choose Control Panel. In Windows 7, choose Control Panel from the Start menu.

2. **Choose Hardware and Sound.**

3. **Click the Sound heading.**

   The Sound dialog box appears. You'd think the computer would play a sound or "Ta-da!" when the Sound dialog box appears, but no.

Later sections in this chapter discuss various things you can do with the Sound dialog box.

Configuring the speakers

To adjust the PC's speakers in Windows, follow these steps:

1. **Summon the Sound dialog box.**

   Refer to the steps in the preceding section.

2. **If necessary, click the Playback tab in the Sound dialog box.**

3. **Choose the primary playback device.**

   The Sound dialog box lists all sound output devices, some of which you may not use. The primary device features a green Check Mark button, as illustrated earlier, in Figure 12-2.

4. **Click the Configure button.**

   If the Configure button is unavailable (dimmed), there's nothing to configure; you're done.

5. **Work through the Speaker Setup Wizard to ensure that your speakers are set up properly and that everything is working.**

   A Test button appears in the wizard, which you click to preview sounds. Or you can click on the wee Speaker icons to test an individual speaker.

You can close the Sound dialog box after working through the Speaker Setup Wizard, or simply move on to configure the PC's microphone.

To set the default playback device, click to select a playback gizmo and then click the Set Default button in the Sound dialog box.

Configuring the microphone

To set up your PC's microphone, follow these steps:

1. **Conjure forth the Sounds dialog box.**

   Refer to the earlier section "Sound Control in Windows" for details on hunting down and displaying the Sound dialog box.

2. **Click the Recording tab.**

3. **Choose the primary recording device.**

   It may be the only item in the list; otherwise, look for the device adorned with the green Check Mark icon.

4. **Click the Configure button.**

   The Speech Recognition window appears, which is one of the Windows Ease of Access features.

5. **Click the Set Up Microphone link.**

6. **Work through the Microphone Setup Wizard to properly configure the microphone attached to your PC.**

If you're having trouble getting the microphone to work, ensure that it's connected to the proper input jack, that it's not muted, and that the cat hasn't chewed through the cord.

Enabling the microphone

In Windows 10, the microphone is controlled not only as an audio input device but also as a privacy device. To make the microphone work, you must enable its use in specific apps. Follow these steps:

1. **Open the Settings app.**

   The keyboard shortcut is Win+I.

2. **Click the Privacy button.**

3. **Choose Microphone from the list of items on the left side of the screen.**

4. **Set to the On position the toggle below the item Let Apps Use My Microphone.**

5. **Ensure that the apps listed on the right side of the screen are enabled to access the PC's microphone.**

   Set their toggle gizmos to the On position.

You may not have to enable the microphone for computer games or older Windows programs. But if you use a newer app and it tells you that the microphone isn't enabled, follow the steps in this section to address the issue.

Adjusting the volume

The volume control gizmo on the taskbar offers you ultimate and final control over how loud or soft any sound plays anywhere in Windows. To become Master of Sound on the PC, click the Volume Control icon once. Up pops a volume control slider, as shown in Figure 12-3. Use the mouse to slide the gizmo louder or quieter, or to mute sound as illustrated in the figure.

If you click the control's slider, the Windows beep sounds, clueing you in to the actual volume level.

Before you don your Master of Sound robes and don that nifty hat, know that individual apps can override the Windows volume setting. Games, specifically, use their own volume controls. YouTube on the Internet, as well as other web media, also features its own volume control. If you mute the sound in Windows, however, all sounds are muted.

> ✔ The PC's stereo speakers may contain volume settings. You can use those settings in addition to the volume control in Windows, though I recommend adjusting the Windows volume control first.

> ✔ Volume control keys are found on some of the swankier PC keyboards.

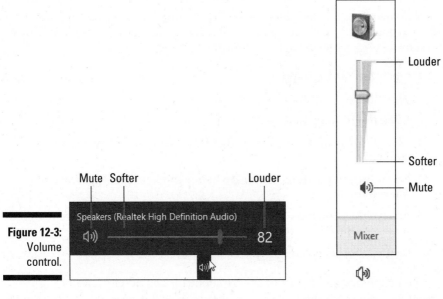

Figure 12-3: Volume control.

Windows 10 volume control

Windows 7 volume control

Windows Goes Bleep

That old bell from the early computers wasn't used purely for entertainment value. It was an alert, an alarm. *Ding!* That meant you had to pay attention. The computer was angry. Well, maybe not angry, but the bell wasn't to be ignored.

Your PC still uses sound to alert you to various situations serious and trivial. Windows again proves to be the master of selecting and setting those audio alerts. To see how the alert sounds are set, follow these steps:

1. **Right-click the speaker icon in the taskbar's notification area.**

2. **Choose the Sounds command from the pop-up menu.**

   The Sound dialog box appears with the Sounds tab front and center. The scrolling Program Events list highlights various and sundry actions and situations. The Speaker icon next to an event means that a sound is associated with that event.

3. **Select an event to assign a sound to it.**

   For example, in Windows 10 select Notification, which is the sound that plays when a new notification floats in.

4. **Click the Test button to hear the current sound.**

   Not every event has a sound, so the Test button is disabled when no sound has been assigned.

5. **Choose a new sound from the Sounds menu.**

   Ho, boy! I see a lot of sounds.

6. **Click the Test button to preview the sound you selected.**

7. **Click the OK button when you've finished assigning sounds.**

You can assign any sound found on your PC to an event. To do so, choose the event (refer to Step 3) and click the Browse button. Use the Browse dialog box to search for sound files.

✔ To remove a sound from an event, choose (None) from the top of the Sounds button menu.

✔ The best source for sounds is the Internet, where you can find web page libraries full of sound samples. To find them, search for *Windows WAV file sounds*.

✔ You can also use sounds that you record yourself, assigning them to specific events in Windows. See the later section "Recording your own sounds."

✔ Windows is also capable of speaking, using an accessibility tool called the Narrator. I'd go into more detail, but the Narrator can get very annoying after a while because it reads *everything* on the screen, not just alert messages.

It Listens

Don't get your hopes up. The days of talking casually to the computer are still *far* in the future. In fact, I doubt that we'll ever just bark orders at a PC, mostly because the Windows interface isn't designed for vocal interaction. Still, it's possible, in a crude way. Also possible is the art of recording your own sounds, including the sound of your voice.

Recording your own sounds

Windows comes with a voice recording app or program. In Windows 10, it's the Voice Recorder app. In older versions of Windows, the app is named Sound Recorder.

To run the Voice Recorder app in Windows 10, follow these steps:

1. **Press the Win key to pop up the Start menu.**
2. **Type** Voice **to search for the Voice Recorder app.**

   Programs matching the word *Voice* appear in a list.
3. **Choose Voice Recorder.**

The Voice Recorder app starts. Click the Microphone icon to begin recording your voice. When you're done, click the Stop button, as illustrated in Figure 12-4.

The Voice Recorder app saves your audio recordings in the `Documents\ Sound Recordings` folder, located in your home folder on the PC.

In Windows 7, you can use the Sound Recorder program to record your voice. Follow these steps:

1. **Press the Win+R keyboard shortcut to summon the Run dialog box.**
2. **Type** Soundrecorder **(all one word) and press the Enter key.**

   Just type **Soundrecorder** with no space between *Sound* and *recorder*.

   Upon success, the Sound Recorder app starts.
3. **Click the Start Recording button.**
4. **Talk: "blah blah blah."**
5. **Click the Stop Recording button when you're done.**
6. **Use the Save As dialog box to save your audio recording.**
7. **Close the Sound Recorder window.**

Previous recordings   Play current recording

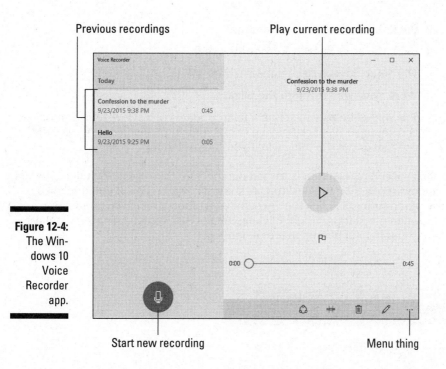

Figure 12-4:
The Win-
dows 10
Voice
Recorder
app.

Start new recording   Menu thing

You can use the Voice Recorder or Sound Recorder to capture audio from
any sound-producing gizmo attached to your PC, such as a turntable or VCR.
Simply connect the gizmo to the proper line-in audio jack on the console, and
then follow the same steps for recording your voice.

Dictating to the PC

Blabbing to your PC isn't perfect, but it has come a long way from the days
when you had to spend hours (up to 20) to train the computer to understand
your voice. Man, that was tiring, not to mention the cottonmouth you'd get
from talking for such long stretches! Things are better today.

To get started with speech recognition in Windows, you need a microphone
or, preferably, a headset. The next stop is the Control Panel to set up the
microphone. Follow these steps:

1. **Open the Control Panel.**

   In Windows 10, press the Win+X keyboard shortcut and choose the
   Control Panel command from the super-secret pop-up menu. In
   Windows 7, choose Control Panel from the Start menu.

2. **Click the Ease of Access heading.**

3. **Click the Start Speech Recognition link.**

   The Setup Speech Recognition Wizard starts.

4. **Work your way through the wizard.**

   The wizard helps you set up a microphone; you review some options and settings. Just keep saying "Next" and you'll be fine. Or do as I did and bail out of the thing when you tire of training.

 When speech recognition is turned on, the Speech Recognition microphone window appears on the desktop, as shown in Figure 12-5. If you don't see the window, double-click the Speech Recognition icon in the notification area (shown in the margin). Right-clicking the Speech Recognition icon displays a handy and helpful pop-up menu of options.

Figure 12-5:
The Speech
Recognition
microphone
window.

Activate Speech Recognition

To activate speech recognition, say "Listen" or click the big Microphone button in the window (refer to Figure 12-5). To turn off speech recognition, say, "Stop listening."

Many Windows commands can be uttered while speech recognition is on, such as Open, Save, Print, Close, and Undo.

To test out speech recognition, dictate the following paragraph:

Open WordPad. Hello, period. I am trying out the dictation feature in Windows period. This is really neat period. I hope the results are not too embarrassing period. Save document no I mean save period. Save this. Save this document. What's the command to save the document? Aw, forget it.

I hope you meet with better success.

Part III
Basic Computing

KINGSTON (F:) Properties   ✕

| General | Tools | Hardware | Sharing | ReadyBoost | Customize |

KINGSTON

Type:	Removable Disk
File system:	FAT32

	Used space:	258,392,064 bytes	246 MB
	Free space:	3,738,845,184 bytes	3.48 GB

| | Capacity: | 3,997,237,248 bytes | 3.72 GB |

Drive F:

OK   Cancel   Apply

Discover tricks and tips for using file shortcuts at www.dummies.com/
extras/pcs.

In this part . . .

- ✔ Find important locations in Windows
- ✔ Discover where programs are kept
- ✔ Manage files and folders
- ✔ Explore cloud storage
- ✔ Manage the network

Chapter 13

Relevant Parts of Windows

- -

In This Chapter

▶ Understanding operating systems

▶ Checking out the desktop

▶ Finding the taskbar

▶ Getting at the Start menu

▶ Working with notifications

▶ Opening the Settings app

▶ Accessing the Control Panel

- -

This book's topic is primarily hardware, the clunky stuff. To make that clunky stuff work, you must interact with software. The chief piece of software in a computer is the operating system. On a PC, that operating system is Microsoft Windows. Frequently, you'll find Windows rubbing into the PC's various hardware parts.

What's an Operating System?

As the top bird on the PC software totem pole, the operating system has several duties:

Control the computer's hardware: Hardware does nothing without software to tell it what to do, and the operating system *is* that software.

Manage all the computer programs: The operating system isn't the only software in your computer, but it is the software in charge of all the other software.

Organize the storage system: The operating system is in charge of the computer's memory, both long-term or mass storage, and short-term or memory. With the mass storage system, Windows is in charge of, organizes, and maintains all the files created and stored on the PC.

Interface with you: As its final task, the operating system deigns to interact with you, the human. There is no requirement that this duty be a pleasant one.

All these tasks are important, but for this book the first task is key: The operating system controls the hardware. The mass storage system also plays a role, which is covered in Chapter 7.

✔ The operating system is the most important piece of software in your computer. It's in charge.

✔ The operating system comes with the PC when you buy it. Though you're free to buy another operating system, you won't.

✔ Other operating systems are available for the PC, but Windows defeated them all in a bloody battle involving treachery, betrayal, and sweeping romantic drama that only high school computer nerds would appreciate.

Windows and Its Gooey, Glorious Graphical Interface

One of an operating system's duties is to interface with you, the human. Windows does that by presenting itself graphically. You use hardware to make it all work: the keyboard, mouse, and the computer monitor.

Windows itself employs various means and methods for you to interact with and control your PC hardware. It's important to know where these items are located and how to use each one.

✔ This book is updated to cover Windows 10, but Windows 7 is also mentioned kindly. Windows 8 is deliberately ignored.

✔ Windows sports a graphical user interface, or GUI. It's pronounced "gooey." Seriously.

Starting at the desktop

Windows 10 blessedly returns all your computer action to a central location called the desktop, illustrated in Figure 13-1. If the screen is overburdened with windows or other detritus, press the Win+D keyboard shortcut to whisk yourself instantly to the desktop.

Icons   Mouse pointer   Window

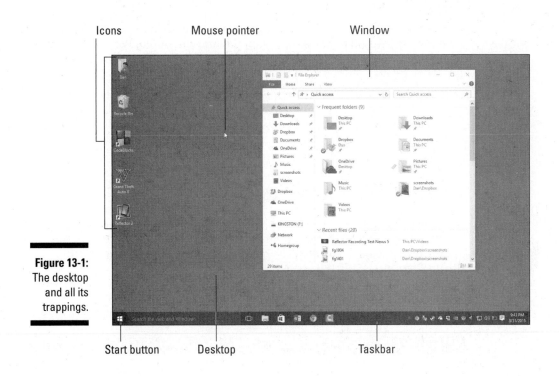

Figure 13-1:
The desktop
and all its
trappings.

Start button   Desktop   Taskbar

About the desktop you'll find a fun festival of interesting goobers, as labeled in Figure 13-1. Other sections in this chapter offer details on the more useful items.

Of all the distractions, the *desktop* is the place where the actual windows appear. These windows contain your programs, games, and other fun computer whatnot. The windows can show up smaller than the desktop, but can also be unfurled to cover the entire screen.

Icons affixed directly to the desktop represent programs, files, and folders. Double-click an icon to open it. Programs run. Files open inside the program that created them, or inside the one used to view the file's data. Double-click a folder to view its contents.

- ✓ It's possible to run Windows 10 in Tablet mode, in which case the desktop is eschewed in favor of a full-screen approach to using all your programs and other Windows features. The Tablet mode button is found in the Action Center, covered elsewhere in this chapter.

- ✓ The desktop background is called the *wallpaper*. It can be a fancy image or picture, or a slide show, or dull and gray, as shown in Figure 13-1.

✔ Windows 7 featured desktop widgets, which displayed interesting information right on the desktop. Upon the introduction of Windows 10, these widgets were taken to a landfill in the Arizona desert and haven't been heard from since.

✔ The desktop is called a *desktop* for traditional reasons. Early graphical operating systems featured a desktop that really did look like a desktop, complete with paper pad, clock, glue, scissors, and other desktop-y things.

Working the taskbar

The action in Windows takes place on the desktop, but that action starts at the taskbar. The taskbar is optimally found lurking at the bottom of the screen, as shown in Figure 13-2. Here are some fun things to identify on the taskbar:

Figure 13-2:
The
Windows
taskbar.

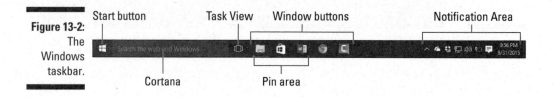

Start button   Task View   Window buttons   Notification Area

Cortana   Pin area

Start button: This button is where you start programs and control Windows. See the next section.

Cortana: A feature unique to Windows 10, Cortana can be used to search the PC or Internet or to bark out commands.

Pin area: Use the icons on this part of the taskbar to quickly start programs or perform common tasks in Windows. The Task View icon helps manage windows on the desktop.

Window buttons: A button appears on the taskbar for each window or program running in Windows. Those things are called *tasks,* which is why the taskbar is called the taskbar and not the candy bar. They appear along with the icons pinned to the taskbar.

Notification area: This part of the taskbar shows tiny icons that help you run your computer or alert you to certain things going on.

The taskbar is locked into position, held at the bottom of the desktop by digital bolts made of the strongest bits. Still, the taskbar can be unlocked and moved wantonly to any screen edge. Further, the taskbar can hide itself, so it may not appear at all.

Accessing the Start menu

On the left end of the taskbar, you'll find the Start button — assuming that the taskbar is docked at its usual spot at the bottom of the screen. As its name suggests, the Start button is used to start things in Windows. What kinds of things? Trouble!

Seriously, click the Start button to display the Start menu, shown in Figure 13-3. It's from that menu that you can start just about any program or activity in Windows.

Frequently-used programs

Your account icon

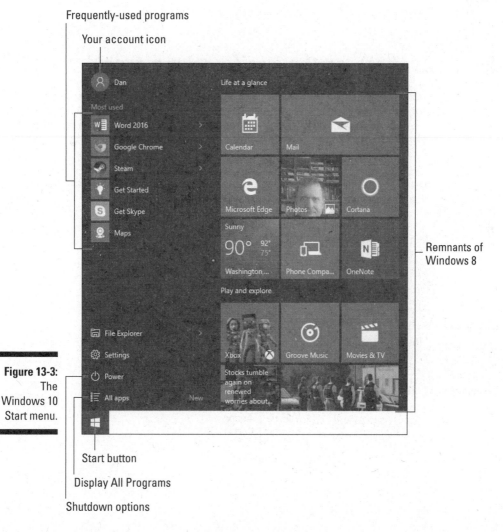

Remnants of Windows 8

Figure 13-3:
The Windows 10 Start menu.

Start button

Display All Programs

Shutdown options

To view all programs installed on your PC, click the All Apps item, shown in the figure. In earlier versions of Windows, the item is titled All Programs. Choose a program to start from the list that's displayed. Some programs are found in folders on the All Apps list: Open the folder, and then click the icon to start a program.

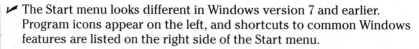

- ✔ The Start menu looks different in Windows version 7 and earlier. Program icons appear on the left, and shortcuts to common Windows features are listed on the right side of the Start menu.

- ✔ A quick way to pop up the Start button menu is to press the Win key on your computer's keyboard.

- ✔ Press the Esc key to dismiss the Start menu.

Looking at the notifications area

Those teensy icons on the far right side of the taskbar aren't just sitting around, waiting for a bus. Nope, they are part of a thing called the *notification area*. The icons, along with the current date and time, allow you to control various things in Windows, check in on running programs, adjust the volume, and perform other miscellaneous chores.

Figure 13-4 illustrates some of the more common icons. To see the full lot, click the upward chevron, as illustrated in the figure.

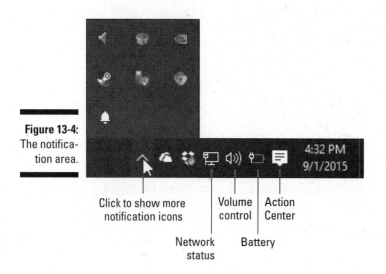

Figure 13-4: The notifica-tion area.

Click to show more notification icons

Volume control

Action Center

Network status

Battery

As with just about everything in Windows, the notifications area can be customized. You can see a lot of icons there, a few, or none. Also, icons may come or go. Follow these steps:

1. **Right-click the time display on the taskbar.**

2. **Choose the Properties command from the shortcut menu.**

3. **In Windows 10, click the link Select Which Icons Appear on the Taskbar.**

   In earlier versions of Windows, click the Customize Notification Icons link to set how other items come and go in the notifications area.

Don't let the random nature of the notifications area perturb you. I set all my PCs to show all the icons all the time, which works great on a widescreen monitor.

✔ You can see more information about the special programs by clicking, right-clicking, or double-clicking the wee icons. Windows is inconsistent on the action required, so try all three: click, right-click, and then double-click.

✔ Some icons display pop-up bubbles with messages in them as various things happen in Windows. Click the X in the pop-up bubble to dismiss the message.

Summoning the Action Center

The Windows 10 method for imparting important system information is to slide a notification in from the right edge of the screen. You can click that notification banner or display the Action Center to view all Windows 10 notifications.

Press the Win+A keyboard shortcut to summon the Action Center, shown in Figure 13-5. The top part contains notifications, updates, and alerts. The bottom part lists Quick Settings, which you can click or tap to turn a PC feature on or off.

✔ If your PC, laptop, or tablet features a touchscreen, swipe inward from the right edge of the screen to view the Action Center.

✔ You can also display the Action Center by clicking the Action Center notification icon, shown in the margin.

✔ Windows also sports a security screen called the Action Center. It's easily accessible in Windows 7, but buried in the Control Panel for Windows 8 and 10. That Action Center provides a quick summary of the PC's security settings. See Chapter 22.

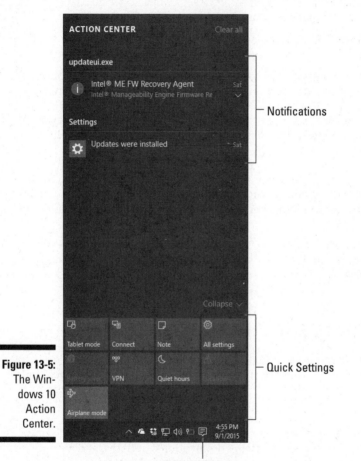

Figure 13-5: The Windows 10 Action Center.

Action Center icon

Settings and Controls

To control various PC hardware settings, you'll find yourself visiting one of two key locations in Windows. The first location, introduced in Windows 8, is the Settings app. The second location, common in all versions of Windows but hidden in Windows 10, is the Control Panel.

Using the Settings app

Apparently, it's the desire of our Microsoft overlords to use the Settings app to control all aspects of Windows. This approach works for the most part, although the Control Panel remains as a backup.

To activate the Settings app, choose Settings from the Start menu. The keyboard shortcut is Win+I. Why the letter *I?* I dunno.

The Settings app window lists nine major categories, as shown in Figure 13-6. Choose a category, and then select a more specific subcategory from the items shown on the left side of the screen. Details appear on the right, as illustrated in the figure.

Categories   Sub-categories   Specifics

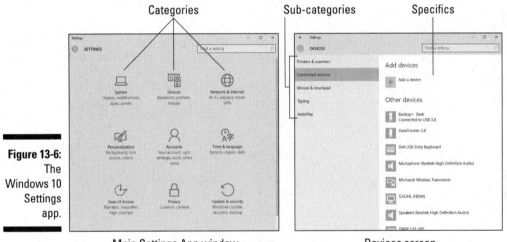

Figure 13-6: The Windows 10 Settings app.

Main Settings App window   Devices screen

After you've changed or checked a setting, close the Settings app: Click the X button in the upper right corner of the window.

✔ Use the Quick Settings area of the Action Center to quickly change many PC settings — for example, the Connect setting used to access a Wi-Fi network.

✔ Because the Settings app is an app (as opposed to a program), it's designed for both mouse and touch input. That explains why its appearance is large and friendly as opposed to more traditional Windows programs, which are tiny and intimidating.

✔ The Settings app may eventually lead you to the Control Panel. See the next section.

Visiting the Control Panel

For generations, the Control Panel has been the go-to spot for adjusting PC hardware and changing Windows settings. Until now.

Windows 8 eschewed the Control Panel for the Settings app, and Windows 10 gladly extends that tradition. The Control Panel isn't gone, but it's being shown the exit.

To summon the Control Panel in Windows 10, right-click the lower left corner of the screen. Up pops what I call the super-secret menu. Choose the Control Panel command from that menu.

In earlier versions of Windows, to display the Control Panel, click the Start button and click the Control Panel menu item on the right side of the Start menu.

The Control Panel is shown in Figure 13-7. Choose a category or link to make a setting. Sometimes, you have to click a few links to get down to the specific spot you need to access.

Change view

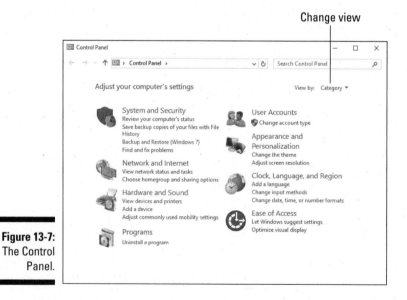

Figure 13-7:
The Control
Panel.

For example, to view a list of hardware devices available to your PC, open the Control Panel. Below the heading Hardware and Sound, click the View Devices and Printers link.

Close the Control Panel window when you're done messing around.

✔ The Control Panel originally displayed its categories as a slate of icons. To restore that mode, click the View By menu and choose either Large Icons or Small Icons from the menu. Many Windows old-timers find this method faster than using Category view, although most documentation refers to Category view.

✔ According to the nerds, eventually the Control Panel will be replaced by the Settings app in future Windows updates.

Chapter 14

Programs On Your PC

*T*he PC is a lovely piece of computer hardware, but without the proper software, that hardware just sits pretty and consumes electricity. Obviously, software is important to the PC. In fact, beyond the operating system, the software consists of those programs you use to make the computer a useful and productive tool.

Software Nomenclature

The term *software* generally refers to computer programs. So if it's a program, it's software. And if someone is talking about software, they're pretty much talking about one or more computer programs.

Software exists in many forms, which makes it a broad topic. For example, the programs encoded on the chips inside your PC help the computer to start, control various peripherals, and offer basic functionality to the hardware. That's all software, often referred to as *firmware*.

The operating system is software, and it's the most important piece of software because it controls the entire computer.

Beyond the firmware and the operating system, software consists of those programs you run to get work done, to be social, to goof off, and so on. This software is referred to by a collection of specific terms:

App: An abbreviation for *application,* although the term technically describes smaller, specific software found on a smartphone or tablet. Apps in Windows 10 are designed to look good on a PC, laptop, tablet, or mobile device.

Application: Traditionally refers to productivity software. An application is a program that does the work or creates something. For example, word processing is a software application.

Driver: A special type of program that controls specific hardware. For example, a *video driver* is required for the operating system to use the PC's graphics hardware.

Game: Software for fun, of course.

Malware: Refers to nasty software — the viruses, Trojans, spyware, and other nasty programs that are designed to cause you angst. No one installs this type of software on purpose.

Program: A general term for all software. Whether it's an app, a game, or a driver, it's a computer program.

Utility or tool: Software designed to help you manage the computer or diagnose or fix problems. For example, you may use a tool to optimize the performance of your computer's storage system.

No matter what the term, it's all software on your PC.

Run That Program

Your computer day involves more than just staring blankly at the monitor. Of course, I'm assuming that your supervisor is watching while you use the computer. When you work by yourself or are at home, please feel free to stare blankly at the monitor. When you want to get something done, you need to rustle up some programs.

Hunting down programs in Windows

Microsoft tries to make things super easy for Windows users. Rather than have one boring, standard way to start a program — which would be easy and simple — you have a multitude of options.

In each case, start a program by locating its icon and clicking or double-clicking that icon. Here's where to hunt:

The desktop: Locate a program icon or shortcut affixed to the desktop. Double-click to open the icon and run the program.

The taskbar: Programs pinned to the taskbar are opened with one click. I keep my most favorite programs on the taskbar.

The Start menu: Programs you open frequently appear atop the Start menu, on the right. Other programs are pinned as tiles on the left. Click once on the program icon or tile to run the program.

The All Apps menu: Click the All Apps item on the Start menu to view a list of all apps installed on your PC. Click an item to run that app. Sometimes, you have to open a folder to find the app you're looking for.

Figure 14-1 illustrates the All Apps menu in Windows 10. The tiles appear on the right side of the Start menu, even when the All Apps menu is displayed.

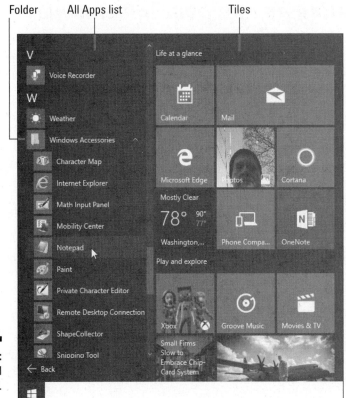

Figure 14-1: The All Apps list.

- ✔ Press the Win key to see the Start menu.

- ✔ The All Apps menu is named All Programs or just Programs in some versions of Windows.

- ✔ Some programs or apps may run automatically. For example, a program may start up when you first sign in to Windows.

- ✔ Programs that run "in the background" may pop up on the screen from time to time. For example, the Steam online gaming system always runs, even though you don't see its window on the desktop.

- ✔ Clicking on a taskbar notification might launch a program.

- ✔ Newly installed programs appear highlighted on the All Apps menu. That way, you can easily find stuff you've just installed.

- ✔ The All Apps menu doesn't show *all* the programs on your PC, but rather all the most useful ones. Though your computer has thousands of programs, you use only a handful regularly.

Starting an app from Tablet mode

If you run your PC with Tablet mode active, you see things the way people who disliked Windows 8 saw things: The Start menu is replaced by a tile-spangled screen. All programs and apps run full-screen in Tablet mode.

To activate Tablet mode in Windows 10, follow these steps:

1. Press Win + A to summon the Action Center.

2. Click the Tablet mode tile.

Tablet mode is illustrated in Figure 14-2. Officially what you see — tiles and other icons — is called the *Start screen.* To start an app, click a tile, as illustrated in the figure.

The All Apps menu is still available: Click the All Apps button, illustrated in Figure 14-2. It works the same way as described in the preceding section.

To exit Tablet mode, repeat the steps in this section.

Show the left side
of the Start menu

Tiles

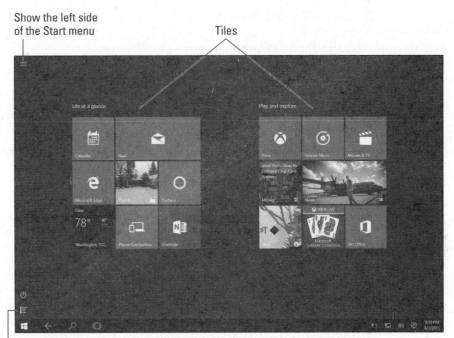

Figure 14-2:
Windows 10
Tablet mode
Start screen.

All Apps menu

Finding a program when you know its name

Sometimes you know the name of the program you want to start. A fast, easy shortcut is to press the Win key to pop up the Start menu and just start typing the name.

For example, to run the Notepad program, press the Win key and, on the keyboard, type **note** — that's all you need to type because Notepad appears at the top of the Start menu. Press the Enter key to launch the program.

Pinning a program

The best way to start a program is to click its icon on the taskbar. Second best is to double-click an icon on the desktop. Third best is to find a program right on the Start menu. How do these programs relocate to such prime Windows real estate? They are pinned.

To pin a program to the taskbar or Start menu, follow these steps:

1. **Click the Start button or press the Win key.**

   Up pops the Start menu.

2. **Click All Apps in Windows 10; otherwise, choose All Programs.**

3. **Right-click the program you want to pin to the taskbar, desktop, or Start menu.**

4. **Choose the location where you want to pin a copy (or shortcut) for the program.**

   Your options are Pin to Start and Pin to Taskbar.

If the item is already pinned, the commands (refer to Step 4) read *Unpin* instead of *Pin.* That's the command you choose to remove an item from that specific location.

Placing a program shortcut on the desktop is a bit trickier, and it would be nifty if Microsoft had placed that shortcut on the menu in Step 4, but they didn't. So in Step 4, choose the Open File Location command. A File Explorer window appears with the program file highlighted. Right-click that icon and choose Send To➪Desktop (Create Shortcut).

- ✔ Programs pinned to the Start menu become tiles, shown on the right side of the menu. These tiles also appear on the Start screen when the PC is using Tablet mode.

- ✔ Not every program's shortcut menu features the Open File Location command.

- ✔ To remove an icon from the desktop, drag it to the Recycle Bin.

- ✔ I pin only my most frequently used programs to the taskbar; maybe only three or four items. Any more and the taskbar becomes too crowded.

Install and Remove Programs

Computer programs don't magically spawn on your computer, growing like mutating fungus in some post-apocalyptic nightmare. Nope, you must invite the programs in. Invitations are extended directly, obtained from the Internet as a download, or installed from media such as a thumb drive or an optical disc.

Just as you let software in, you eventually let software back out of your computer. The process is called *uninstalling,* and it rarely involves the use of high explosives.

Obtaining software from the Internet

The most common way of installing software today is over the Internet. You either browse to a website where you can download the software or you obtain download instructions inside a software box you bought at a brick-and-mortar store.

Generally speaking, the process works like this:

1. **Purchase the software, if required.**

   Sometimes you can download a free trial version. Or you can obtain the real version and use it in a limited capacity until you pay for and register the software.

2. **Visit the web page that contains the download link.**

3. **Click the link or graphical image that initiates the download.**

   Pay very close attention at this point! Ensure that you're obtaining the program you want and no extras, add-ons, toolbars, or other programs. You may have to uncheck items on the page to decline these offers. Don't be too hasty with the installation options, or else you may end up stuck with some software on your PC — software that you don't want and which is trouble to remove.

   If you're presented with a choice of different types of files to download, choose the program file link, which often ends with the EXE filename extension. Avoid choosing a compressed folder, Zip, or archive file, because doing so involves extra steps before you can actually install and run the program.

4. **Mind the security warning.**

   Some web browsers alert you whenever software attempts to flow into your computer. You must grant permission; otherwise, who-knows-what might be downloaded into your PC.

   If you ignore my warning in Step 3, the web browser and PC security programs won't catch the "bonus" software you download. Technically — and legally — you are granting permission for that extra software to be installed.

5. **Sit and watch as the file is copied from the Internet to your computer.**

   Doh-dee-doh-doh.

   By the way, what's downloaded is often an install or setup program, which will configure and install the software you'll eventually use.

6. Choose the option to run the program.

7. If you're greeted with a security warning, click the Allow button.

8. Obey the directions on the screen to finish the installation.

The directions are specific to whatever it is you're installing.

After installing the program, you can run it or do anything you would normally do with any software installed on your computer. The only difference is that the new software was obtained from the Internet instead of installed from an optical disc or other media.

✔ In Windows 10, freshly installed software appears at the top of the All Apps list.

✔ The software downloaded from the Internet can be free, a trial version, a one-time paid version, or a subscription.

✔ If the software requires a product key or purchase code, write down that code! If the information arrived in an email message, print out the message. Keep that information in an easily accessible location.

✔ Get used to obtaining software from the Internet. It's the way most software will be installed on PCs in the future. Well, actually *now*. It's the way software is being installed right now.

✔ If you search for hacker tools or free movies, music, books, or other illegal material, odds are good that you'll end up at an illegitimate website. The result may be a virus or another infection on your PC, not the software you wanted.

Installing a program from external media

In the physical realm, new software is purchased at the store, or it arrives bright and shiny from a friendly, sweaty guy driving a delivery truck. Either way, your job is to get the software out of the box and into your PC in a fully functional state. Here's how to do that:

1. Open the software box and locate the installation media.

If more than one optical disc is present, note in which order they're used; the discs should be numbered, and you start with the first disc.

2. Insert the installation media into an appropriate drive on the PC.

If you're lucky, the installation program runs automatically after the media is inserted. Otherwise:

3. If you see a notification about what to do with the media, choose the option to install the software.

Sometimes this process involves two steps, as illustrated in Figure 14-3. First, you must acknowledge the new media, and second, you direct Windows in what to do.

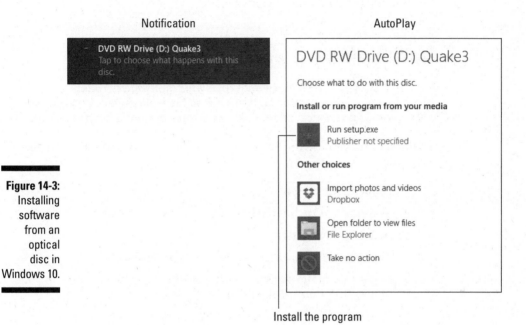

Notification

AutoPlay

DVD RW Drive (D:) Quake3
Tap to choose what happens with this disc.

DVD RW Drive (D:) Quake3

Choose what to do with this disc.

Install or run program from your media

Run setup.exe
Publisher not specified

Other choices

Import photos and videos
Dropbox

Open folder to view files
File Explorer

Take no action

Figure 14-3: Installing software from an optical disc in Windows 10.

Install the program

4. If prompted with a User Account Control (security warning), click the Yes button to confirm installation.

Only when you're not actively installing something would you refuse the request.

5. Follow the instructions on the screen.

Work through the directions on the screen to install, set up, and configure the new software.

It takes time to learn new software — even computer games. It's natural to be frustrated at first. That's okay; you're only human. Just keep trying, and eventually you'll learn the program. Of course, buying a good book about the software is an excellent idea!

- Generally speaking, few — if any — stores let you return computer software after you open the box.

- I recommend keeping the box. Use it to store the installation media as well as the manual or whatever trivial items came in the box.

- If the software requires a registration number or installation code, keep it in the box or another handy location.

Uninstalling a program

Nothing makes Windows more irate than when software is rudely and abruptly removed from your computer. Don't use pliers, and especially don't use a periosteal elevator. Instead, follow the proper uninstall procedure.

In Windows 10, you use the Settings app to uninstall software. Obey these directions:

1. **Open the Settings app.**

   Press the Win+I keyboard shortcut.

2. **Click the System button.**

3. **On the left side of the screen, choose Apps and Features.**

   The right side of the screen fills with a list of all installed apps on your PC. It may take time for the list to populate.

4. **Click to select the program or app you want to evict.**

   Two buttons appear below the item's entry: Move and Uninstall.

5. **Click the Uninstall button.**

   A pop-up featuring a second Uninstall button appears.

6. **Click the second Uninstall button to confirm the program or app's removal.**

7. **If prompted with a security warning, click the Yes button to proceed.**

8. **Continue following directions on the screen.**

   Some software removes itself instantly, while others attempt to quiz you on removal, set options, and perhaps offer another series of buttons to click.

In Windows 7 and earlier versions of Windows, follow these steps to remove software:

1. **Open the Control Panel.**

   Directions to the Control Panel are found in Chapter 13.

2. **Click the Uninstall a Program link, found below the Programs heading.**

   The Programs and Features window appears, listing all software installed on your PC.

3. **Select the program you want to uninstall.**

4. **Click the Uninstall or Uninstall/Change button on the toolbar.**

5. **If prompted by a User Account Control, type the administrator password or click the Continue button to proceed.**

6. **Continue reading instructions on the screen to uninstall the program.**

   The uninstall directions vary from program to program, but eventually the program is removed.

 Use these steps to uninstall software. Deleting a shortcut icon doesn't uninstall a program. Deleting a program file doesn't uninstall the software, either. No, follow the steps in this section to properly, officially, finally remove software.

Chapter 15

Fun with Files and Folders

Here's a tip: Understand what a *file* is and you and your computer will have a far more productive relationship. Understand a *folder*, and you're well on your way to earning a doctorate in computer-human relationships. Both items — file and folder — are containers into which digital stuff is kept. You use files and folders to keep your PC organized and your sanity intact.

Behold the File!

All that digital information stored inside your computer doesn't float around, wild and loose like grains of sand in a dust storm. Instead, that information is kept neat and tidy inside little digital jars. Those jars are called files.

> ✔ A *file* is a chunk of information stored in a computer.

> ✔ Unlike the jars Aunt Trudy uses for her pear preserves, the container that holds a file isn't of a fixed size. It can be as big or as small as needed to hold the information.

> ✔ Computer programs create files. When you save information, such as a document in a word processor, you create a file. The file is separate from the program that created it.

> ✔ Files start out in computer memory and are then saved on the *mass* storage system. See Chapter 7.

Describing a file

Since the Mann Act was passed in 1910, files are required to carry several forms of ID, chief among them a name and an icon.

> **Name:** All files have a name, or *filename*. The name is given to the file when it's created and, ideally, the name describes the file's contents or gives you a clue to the file's purpose.

> **Icon:** Icons are pictures used in the Windows operating system to visually represent a file and maybe even its contents.

Figure 15-1 illustrates several files, showing their icons and names. Some files, such as Word documents, all use the same icon. Other files, such as the Picture and Fax examples in the figure, show a document or image preview. A generic icon appears for files where the file type is unknown or not recognized.

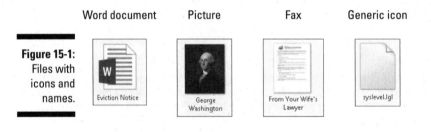

Word document   Picture   Fax   Generic icon

Figure 15-1:
Files with
icons and
names.

Beyond the name and icon, files sport various trivial details, including the file size, date, and type. The size is the amount of storage required for the file's contents, measured in bytes. The date is applied when the file is created, but also whenever it's updated or modified. The file type is set by the file's contents, such as plain text, graphics, or audio.

Files also dwell in a specific folder on the PC's mass storage system. See the later section "Folder Folderol" for details.

✔ The file type is related to the file's icon, which relates to the program that created the file or the program used to view or access the file's contents.

✔ A file can be any size, from zero bytes to billions of bytes. Refer to Chapter 6 for more information on bytes.

✔ To see all file details, right-click the file icon and choose the Properties command. Click the OK button to close that dialog box should you become light-headed.

Creating a new file

Files are born in the programs you use, conceived in the computer's memory, and eventually saved to the PC's mass storage device. The command responsible for that last task is called Save As.

When you use the Save As command, the Save As dialog box appears, similar to what's shown in Figure 15-2. Use that dialog box to create the new file.

Favorite folders and other
locations for saving files

Folder where the
file will be saved

Create new folder   File's location ("Address bar")

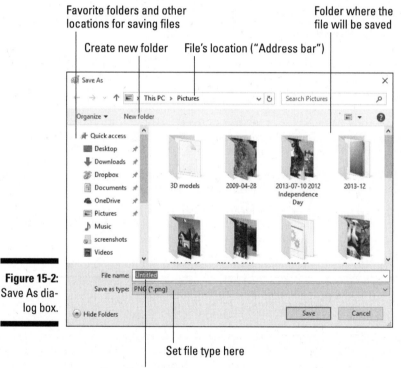

Figure 15-2:
Save As dialog box.

Set file type here

Type filename here

Of all the mischief you can get into when using the Save As dialog box, three tasks are key: Give the file a name, set the file's location or folder, and choose a file type. Here's how these tasks work:

1. Choose the Save As command to summon the Save As dialog box.

The Save As command can be found on the File menu or on the File tab in newer apps. The Ctrl+S keyboard shortcut also activates the Save As command. Some programs feature a Save toolbar button, as shown in the margin.

2. Type a filename into the File Name text box.

See the nearby sidebar, "File naming rules."

3. Confirm that the file is being created in the proper folder.

If not, use the folder portion of the dialog box to select or browse to a new folder. See the later section "Working with folders in the Open and Save As dialog boxes."

4. Ensure that the file type menu shows the proper file type.

Most of the time, it's the proper file type. Only when you must save a file in a specific format (which is rare) do you need to change the type.

5. Click the Save button to create the new file.

After a file has been saved, the file's name appears on the title bar (at the top of the window). That's your clue that a file has been saved. From that point on, use the Save command to update the file.

✔ Some apps use a Save screen as opposed to the traditional Save As dialog box. The Save screen's function is the same as the Save As dialog box, although the appearance is different.

✔ New files can also be created when an existing file is copied. See "Copy a file from hither to thither," later in this chapter.

✔ The Save As command obliterates an existing file. That happens should you attempt to save the new file by using an existing file's name. In that case, choose another name to save the new file.

File naming rules

The best rule for naming files is to be descriptive and brief. Feel free to use letters, numbers, and spaces. You can start the name with a letter or a number, but avoid starting the name with a space, as it's just plain weird.

Windows gets cranky when you use any of these characters to name a file:

   * / : < > ? \ | "

Periods are okay in a filename, but don't begin the name with a period or name a file with all periods. Also, keep in mind that at least one period is used in a filename to identify the filename extension.

The good news: If you screw anything up, Windows flashes a rude warning on the screen when you try to save or rename a file. The warning explains the problem, such as a long filename, duplicate filename, or forbidden character.

Understanding the filename extension

An important part of a filename is the extension, which is like the file's last name. In Windows, the extension identifies which program created the file, determines the file's contents, and sets the icon associated with the file. All that information is collectively known as the file's *type*.

The weird part about the filename extension is that you may or may not see it. Windows hides filename extensions by default. If you'd rather see the extensions, you must direct Windows to show them.

To display filename extensions in Windows 10, follow these steps:

1. **Press Win + E to summon a File Explorer window.**

2. **Click the View tab.**

3. **In the Show/Hide group, click to place a check mark by the option File Name Extensions.**

In earlier versions of Windows, abide by these steps to display the filename extension:

1. **Open the Control Panel.**

2. **Click the Appearance and Personalization heading.**

3. **Below the Folder Options heading, click the Show Hidden Files and Folders link.**

    The Folder Options dialog box appears.

4. **Remove the check mark by the item Hide Extensions for Known File Types.**

5. **Click OK to close the Folder Options dialog box and close the Control Panel window.**

With the extensions visible, you see them appended to all the filenames in Windows.

  ✔ The filename extension is added automatically to files you create. You don't need to type it into the Save As dialog box; the Save As Type menu sets the type and appends the extension automatically.

  ✔ When you elect to show filename extensions, be careful never to change or delete the extension when you rename a file.

✔ The filename extension starts with a period and is followed by one to four characters. For example, the TXT filename extension is used to identify text files. Web page files use the HTM or HTML filename extension. Graphics files have a number of filename extensions, depending on the graphics file type: GIF, JPG, PNG, or TIFF, for example.

✔ Gazillions of filename extensions are out there, too many to list here. If you're curious, you can visit the website `www.filext.com` to review or look up a filename extension.

Folder Folderol

A *folder* is a container for files, designed to keep your files organized. It was chosen over the earlier file container, the rubber band, which was too constricting on larger files.

✔ All files dwell in folders.

✔ Folders keep like files grouped together — the way barbed wire keeps prisoners, vicious animals, and toddlers from wandering off.

✔ Without folders, your PC's mass storage would contain tens of thousands of files, all listed one after the other. It would take you months to find anything.

✔ To open the folder, double-click it. Folders open into a window that displays the folder's contents. The program that displays folder windows is called File Explorer.

✔ Folders may also be referred to as *directories*. This term is merely a throwback to the early days of computing and the Unix operating system, which was used by Julius Caesar.

Understanding subfolders and parent folders

Folders exist in a hierarchy, with folders containing other folders, called *subfolders*. The folder hierarchy is often visualized as a tree structure because once, a long time ago, a programmer actually walked outside and saw a tree.

All storage devices feature a main folder, called the *root* folder. Every other folder on the storage device is a subfolder of the root. As an example, the primary storage device on your PC contains a root folder. The Windows folder is a subfolder of that root folder. The Windows folder contains the Windows operating system files, as well as other subfolders.

For your own files, you can use subfolders to keep your stuff organized. For example, Figure 15-3 illustrates a folder named Vacations. It has a subfolder named Disneyland. Into the Disneyland folder you could put files associated with your Disney vacation.

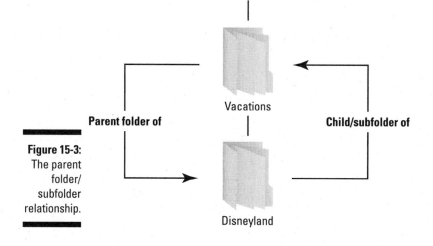

Parent folder of   Vacations   Child/subfolder of

Figure 15-3:
The parent
folder/
subfolder
relationship.

Disneyland

- ✔ Creating subfolders is part of organizing your files. See the later section "Making a new folder," for the details.

- ✔ No limit exists on the number of subfolders you can create. A folder can be inside a folder inside a folder, and so on. If you name the folders well, it all makes sense. Try to smile and imagine it all making sense.

- ✔ A folder's location in the mass storage system is referred to as a *path*. The path lists all parent folders up to the root folder. In Windows, the backslash character, \, separates individual folder names within a path. That character also represents the root folder.

Finding a place for your stuff

All user accounts in Windows feature a specific location for your stuff, your own folder, which I call the *home* folder. It's given the same name as your user account, so if you log in as Lord Huckleberry, your home folder is named Lord Huckleberry.

To view your home folder, press Win+E to summon a File Explorer window, and then choose your account name from the address bar menu, as illustrated in Figure 15-4.

Contents of your home folder

Choose your account name from here

Figure 15-4:
Your home
folder.

To help get you accustomed to the concept of file and folder organization, Windows equips your home folder with a slew of preset folders, such as the Contacts, Documents, and Downloads folders, shown in Figure 15-4. You can use these folders, create more folders, and add subfolders, all depending on how organized you want to keep your files.

✔ Most programs select either your home folder or one of its subfolders when you use the Save As dialog box to save a file. For example, in Figure 15-2 you see the Pictures folder, which is where images and photographs can be saved.

✔ Cloud storage folders also appear in the home folder, including your OneDrive, Dropbox, Google Drive, and other cloud storage folders. See Chapter 16 for information on cloud storage.

✔ Some documentation refers to the home folder by its utterly obnoxious name, the User Account folder. I find that too confusing with the user account, which is the name used to sign in to Windows. Internally, the home folder is known as the User Profile folder, which is equally vapid.

Making a new folder

New folders are born in several ways, none of which involves a stork.

Perhaps the most common way to create a new folder is to use a File Explorer window. Obey these steps:

1. **Press Win + E to open a File Explorer window.**

2. **Navigate to the folder in which you want to create the new folder.**

   For example, open your home folder or perhaps the Documents folder.

3. **In Windows 10, click the Home tab.**

4. **Click the New Folder button.**

   The New Folder icon appears in the window, ready to be given a new name.

5. **Type the new folder's name.**

   Make it short and descriptive; the same rules for naming files also apply to folders. See the sidebar "File naming rules," earlier in this chapter.

6. **Press the Enter key to lock in the name.**

A New Folder button is also found in the Save As dialog box. See the earlier section "Creating a new file."

Avoid reading about silly libraries

Windows 7 introduced the concept of the library, which has since been downplayed in more current versions of Windows. Essentially, a library is a collection of multiple folders whose files and subfolders are referenced from a single spot.

For example, you may see a Documents or Pictures folder in the This PC window. They look like folders, but when you open them, you see files and subfolders from a variety of locations on the computer storage system.

Working with folders in the Open and Save As dialog boxes

Both the Open and Save As dialog boxes feature a mini-File Explorer window. You use that window to find a file to open or to set the location for a file to create.

Figure 15-5 shows a typical Open dialog box. Use the controls in the mini-File Explorer window to find files or folders to open. Click the Up button to move up a level in the folder hierarchy. Double-click a folder icon to open.

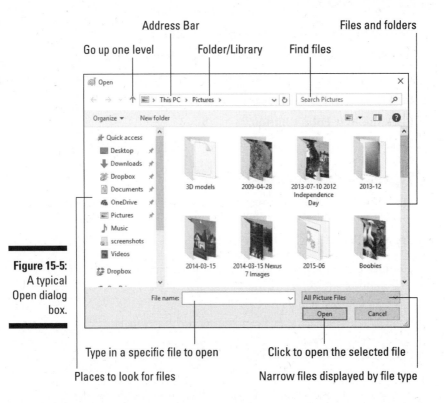

Address Bar

Go up one level   Folder/Library   Find files   Files and folders

Figure 15-5:
A typical
Open dialog
box.

Type in a specific file to open   Click to open the selected file

Places to look for files   Narrow files displayed by file type

✔ Similar to the Open dialog box, the Browse dialog box is used to find a file. The file isn't opened directly, but is merely referenced for whatever nefarious purposes.

✔ Narrow the quantity of files displayed in the Open dialog box by choosing a file type. Only files matching the specified type are displayed.

✔ Some newer programs use an Open screen instead of the traditional Open dialog box. The functionality is the same, but the look is changed to keep you on your toes.

✔ Not every program can open every type of file. Programs work best with the files they create themselves.

Manage Files Because They Can't Manage Themselves

Managing files is nothing like taming lions, so put away that whip and the chair. To work with files and folders, you need to know two things: how to select a file or folder and how to use the various file management tools available in Windows.

✔ *File management* is the process of organizing files and folders on your computer's mass storage system. If it were a class at Hogwarts, Professor Snape would teach it.

✔ The operating system provides the tools necessary to manage files. Specifically, you use a program called File Explorer.

✔ If you did everything properly with files and folders the first time, file management wouldn't be necessary. But, no, you did things wrong. See? This is all your fault.

Selecting files

Files (and folders) must be *selected* before you can mess with them. Similar to a pogrom, you can select files individually or in groups.

Select a single file

To select a single file, click its icon once with the mouse. Click. A selected file appears highlighted in the File Explorer window, similar to the file Reunion shown in Figure 15-6.

Figure 15-6: The icon (file) on the right is selected.

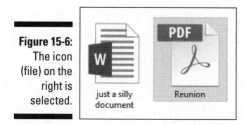

Select a random smattering of files

Suppose that in a folder brimming with files, you need to select the four ugliest icons, similar to the ones shown in Figure 15-7.

Figure 15-7: A random smattering of files is selected.

BIO.DOC DOC File 11.0 KB	chap3.txt Text Document 852 bytes
conspiracy theory.rtf Rich Text Document 205 bytes	Edgar Allan Poe The Raven.txt Text Document 7.10 KB
EDITOR.DOC DOC File 3.56 KB	ENGLISH.DOC DOC File 14.5 KB
FIND ME.pfx Personal Information Exchange 2.49 KB	LOG File 5.07 KB

Here's how:

1. **Click to select the first file.**

2. **Press and hold down the Ctrl key.**

3. **Click to select the next file.**

4. **Repeat Step 3 to select additional files.**

5. **Release the Ctrl key when you're done selecting files.**

Now you're ready to manipulate the selected files as a single, guilty group.

To deselect a file from the group, just Ctrl+click it again.

Select a swath of files in a row

To select a queue of files, such as those shown in Figure 15-8, pursue these steps:

Figure 15-8: A queue of files is selected.

Name	#	Title	Contributing artists	Album
01 A Hard Day's Nigh...	1	A Hard Day's Night	The Beatles	A Hard Day's Night [UK]
02 I Should Have Kno...	2	I Should Have Known Better	The Beatles	A Hard Day's Night [UK]
03 If I Fell.wma	3	If I Fell	The Beatles	A Hard Day's Night [UK]
04 I'm Happy Just to ...	4	I'm Happy Just to Dance Wi...	The Beatles	A Hard Day's Night [UK]
05 And I Love Her.wma	5	And I Love Her	The Beatles	A Hard Day's Night [UK]
06 Tell Me Why.wma	6	Tell Me Why	The Beatles	A Hard Day's Night [UK]
07 Can't Buy Me Love...	7	Can't Buy Me Love	The Beatles	A Hard Day's Night [UK]
08 Any Time at All.wma	8	Any Time at All	The Beatles	A Hard Day's Night [UK]
09 I'll Cry Instead.wma	9	I'll Cry Instead	The Beatles	A Hard Day's Night [UK]
10 Things We Said To...	10	Things We Said Today	The Beatles	A Hard Day's Night [UK]
11 When I Get Home....	11	When I Get Home	The Beatles	A Hard Day's Night [UK]
12 You Can't Do That...	12	You Can't Do That	The Beatles	A Hard Day's Night [UK]
13 I'll Be Back.wma	13	I'll Be Back	The Beatles	A Hard Day's Night [UK]

1. **Line up the files in the window.**

   In Windows 10, click the View tab and choose List or Details from the Layout group. In older versions of Windows, choose List or Details from the View menu button on the toolbar.

2. **Click to select the first file in your group.**

3. **Press and hold down the Shift key.**

4. **Click to select the last file in your group.**

5. **Release the Shift key.**

The files are now ready for abuse. Well, maybe not "ready" for it, but it's coming.

Lasso a group of files

If you want to treat your files like the bovine vermin that they are, use the mouse to lasso them into a group. Figure 15-9 illustrates how it's done.

Figure 15-9:
Lasso a group of files with the mouse.

To lasso the files, start by pointing the mouse above and to the left of the icon herd you want to rope. Holding down the mouse button, drag down and to the right to create a rectangle surrounding ("lassoing") the file icons (refer to Figure 15-9). Release the mouse button, and all the files you have lassoed are selected as a group. A vocal "Yee-ha!" is considered appropriate — and intimidating — in this circumstance.

Select all files in a folder

To select all files inside a folder, press the Ctrl+A keyboard shortcut. This command highlights all files in the window — including any folders (and all their contents). The A in Ctrl+A probably stands for "All the guilty ones."

Deselect files

To deselect a file, simply click anywhere in the File Explorer window (but not on an icon). Or you can close the window, in which case Windows immediately forgets about any selected files.

To answer your question: No, the files don't feel any sense of relief from being deselected. They fully accept that there will always be a next time.

Manipulating files

Once selected, a file or group of files is subject to your merciless whims. Of all the taunts you can tender, the most common methods for manipulating files are copy, move, rename, and delete.

- ✔ The main reason to manipulate files is organization. You copy, move, rename, and delete files in various folders to keep your digital stuff organized.

- ✔ All file manipulation commands also apply to folders, but with a special caveat: When you copy or move a folder, you're copying or moving all files and subfolders within that folder. And when you delete a folder, you're potentially deleting a lot of stuff. Be careful!

- ✔ If you make a mistake when performing any file action, you can immediately undo the procedure by pressing Ctrl+Z, the Undo command shortcut. The key word is *immediately.* Don't wait.

Copy a file from hither to thither

To *copy* a file is to make a duplicate. For example, you copy your big presentation from the PC's primary storage device to a thumb drive. The copy operation works like this:

1. **In a File Explorer window, select the files or folders you want to move or copy.**

2. **Press Ctrl+C.**

   Ctrl+C is the common keyboard shortcut for the Copy command.

3. **Open the folder where you want the files to be copied.**

4. **Press Ctrl+V to paste the files.**

   The duplicate files appear in the window.

Copying files makes duplicates; after you copy the files, you have the original as well as the copy you just made.

Paste a shortcut

When you don't need to junk up your PC's storage system with duplicates, create file shortcuts instead: Copy a file as you normally would (see the preceding section), but instead of pasting it, right-click the folder window and choose the Paste Shortcut command. A file shortcut is created instead.

A file *shortcut* is a copy of the original file, but without all the bulk. It's merely a signpost that says, "The real file is over there somewhere." When you open a shortcut, Windows is smart enough to find the original and open it instead.

 A file shortcut sports a tiny arrow nestled in the lower left corner over its icon, as shown in the margin. That's your clue that the file is a shortcut and not a full-blown copy.

Move a file from thither to yon

To move a file, you cut and paste instead of copy and paste: Select the files or folders, and press Ctrl+X to cut. Open the folder where you want to move the files, and press Ctrl+V to paste them, moving them from the first folder to the second.

Copy or move files graphically

Providing that you have two folder windows open, you can drag one or more icons between the windows to copy or move the files.

When both folders are on the same storage device, dragging moves the files. When one of the folders is on another storage device, dragging copies the files.

You can override the copy or move operations: Press the Ctrl key while dragging to ensure that the files are copied; press the Shift key while dragging to ensure that the files are moved.

Rename a file

When you fail to properly name a file upon its creation, you can go back and bless it with a new, more appropriate name. Gleefully obey these steps:

1. **Select the file.**

2. **Press the F2 key, the keyboard shortcut for the Rename command.**

   Just to let you know, the person who thought that the F2 key would make an excellent keyboard shortcut for the Rename command has been killed in a prolonged and cruel manner.

3. Type a new name or edit the current name.

The goal of renaming a file is to be descriptive and clever.

4. Press the Enter key to lock in the new name.

The only time this operation fails is when you abuse the file naming rules (refer to the sidebar "File naming rules," earlier in this chapter), or you attempt to use the name of an already existing file in the same folder.

If you forget the F2 keyboard shortcut (and I don't blame you), right-click the icon and choose the Rename command from the pop-up menu.

Rename a whole gang of files

Windows lets you rename a group of icons all at once. The process is the same as with renaming a single icon, except that when the operation is complete, all selected icons have the same new name plus a numeric suffix.

For example, you select a group of icons and press the F2 key. When you type Picture as the group filename, each file in the group is given the name Picture (2), Picture (3), and so on, to the last file in the group — Picture (274,369), for instance.

Delete files

When it's time to go on a file-purging binge, approach the task of file deleting with eager relish. Follow these steps:

1. Select the file or group of files.

2. Press the Delete key on your keyboard.

3. If you see a confirmation prompt, click Yes.

The file is gone.

The files you delete aren't killed off. They're banished to a digital limbo called the Recycle Bin. In fact, if you see the Recycle Bin icon on the desktop, you can drag icons to the Recycle bin directly.

Files dwelling in the Recycle Bin can be recovered. See the later section "Finding files lost, missing, or dead."

Never delete any file or folder unless you created it yourself.

Delete a program

Programs aren't deleted in Windows; they're uninstalled. See Chapter 14.

Finding files lost, missing, or dead

Files get lost every day. They slip off and hide in some bizarre, unknown folder, or you banish them to the Recycle Bin. Either way, you can find a file and potentially get it back from the dead.

To locate a lost file, use the Search text box located in the File Explorer window; look in the upper right corner of the window, as shown in Figure 15-5. In the text box, type the file's name or text that might be found in the file. Press the Enter key, and Windows begins a fanatical search for matching files.

If the Search command fortuitously finds a file, you see it in the Search Results window. You can open the file directly or move the file from that window back into a folder where it more properly belongs. See the earlier section "Move a file from thither to yon."

The only place the Search command doesn't look in is the purgatory of the Recycle Bin. To rescue a deleted file, follow these steps:

1. **Open the Recycle Bin on the desktop.**

   If the Recycle Bin icon isn't visible on the desktop, press Win+E to summon a File Explorer window. In the address bar, type **Recycle Bin**.

2. **Select the file you want recovered.**

3. **In Windows 10, click the Recycle Bin Tools Manage tab.**

4. **On the toolbar, click the Restore the Selected Items button.**

   In some versions of Windows, the button is named Restore This Item.

The file is magically restored afresh to the folder from which it was so brutally condemned.

Oh, you can close the Recycle Bin window.

> ✔ When searching for a file, start the search in a parent folder, such as your home folder. The search progresses downward through the folders. See "Finding a place for your stuff," earlier in this chapter, for information on locating your home folder.

> ✔ You can also use the Cortana feature in Windows 10 to locate files on your computer.

✔ If you just deleted a file — and I mean *just* deleted it — you can use the Undo command to get it back: Press Ctrl+Z on the keyboard. There. It's back.

✔ Over time, the Recycle Bin purges its contents, similar to the way top fashion models stay thin, but not as frequently. If a deleted file cannot be located in the Recycle Bin, you might be able to recover a copy from a recent backup. See Chapter 23.

Chapter 16

Life On the Cloud

. . . .

. . . .

*T*hanks to the Internet, your digital life extends well beyond your own PC. In addition to the web and email, you can use the Internet to store your stuff. This storage includes files, music, videos, contacts, and more. That information is available anywhere you can get Internet access. The oddball and nonsensical term for this type of service is *the cloud*.

The Cloud Thing

The idea behind the cloud is simple: You want to keep all your files, contacts, appointments — your digital life — accessible no matter where you are. Ideally, you log in to any computer using your Windows account and you see your desktop on the screen. Then you can use that computer just as you use your own PC.

Most cloud computing services don't actually display your own desktop on the screen. Windows 10 may echo some common settings, but more common is being able to access your files and other personal information from any Internet-connected computer. That's the type of service provided by cloud computing.

You need just two things to make the cloud thing happen: a broadband Internet connection and access to a cloud service.

The Internet connection can be provided by your desktop PC, but also by a laptop on the road or even a mobile device, a phone, or a tablet.

Many cloud services are available. In Windows 10, Microsoft offers OneDrive cloud storage as well as other cloud services coordinated with your Windows or Microsoft account.

- ✔ The advantage to cloud storage is that you don't really have the excuse, "That information is in my computer back at home." Anywhere you can get on the Internet, you can grab your cloud information.

- ✔ You don't have to use cloud storage. You especially don't have to understand why the word *cloud* was even chosen. Obviously, humidity isn't an issue.

Cloud Storage

The most common cloud service is file storage. A branch of folders and files on your PC's mass storage system are duplicated on the Internet, available on the web or from any other Internet-connected gizmo.

Adding a cloud storage service

Whether your PC has a cloud storage subscription or not, you can always get one. Several services are available, which include a modicum of free online storage. They all work in a similar manner:

1. **Install the cloud storage software on your computer.**

   This is the program that synchronizes your files from the PC's mass storage system to the Internet.

2. **Create an account.**

   The account provides the Internet access, not only to coordinate the files but also to a website where you can access your files online.

3. **Start using the service.**

   You copy files to the folders on your PC, which are echoed to the Internet and synchronized across any device that also uses that cloud storage.

Three popular online storage services are Microsoft's OneDrive, Google's Google Drive, and Dropbox. Table 16-1 lists these services and their web addresses. Visit the address to download the software.

Table 16-1	Online Storage Services
Service	*Website*
OneDrive	`onedrive.live.com`
Google Drive	`drive.google.com`
Dropbox	`www.dropbox.com/home`

To add the cloud storage to your PC, follow the general steps in this section. Visit the web page to install the software, create an account, and then start using the service.

- ✔ One drawback to cloud storage is limited storage capacity. That can be addressed if you're willing to pay for more storage.

- ✔ More cloud storage options exist than the three presented in this section. Some are open to anyone, but many are paid subscription only — for example, Adobe's Creative Cloud.

- ✔ Microsoft's cloud storage service was originally called SkyDrive. Then they found out someone else owned the name SkyDrive, so Microsoft changed it. I have older PCs that still sport SkyDrive folders, although they're linked to OneDrive.

Copying a file to cloud storage

To make cloud storage work, save files and create folders within the cloud storage folder tree on your PC's mass storage system. The folders are found in your account's home folder, given the name of the cloud service that you're using. For example:

Dropbox

Google Drive

OneDrive

Open those folders and you often find additional folders, such as Documents, Pictures, Music, and so on. You may find documentation on how to use some of the folders.

As an example, here are the steps to copy a file from your home folder's Documents folder to the OneDrive Documents folder:

1. **Press Win + E to summon a File Explorer window.**

2. **Choose Documents from the left side of the window.**

   What you see is actually a library, not the specific documents folder for your account. That's okay; the same files are available.

3. **Click to select a file, and then press Ctrl + X to move (cut) the file.**

   File manipulation details are concealed in Chapter 15.

4. **From the left side of the window, choose OneDrive.**

   It should appear in the Quick Access list. In fact, you may also see Dropbox and Google Drive in that list as well.

5. **Double-click on the Documents folder to open it.**

   Technically, you're now looking at the contents of the OneDrive\ Documents folder.

6. **Press Ctrl + V to paste the file.**

   The file is moved from the Documents folder to the OneDrive\Documents folder. (If you want to move it back, press Ctrl+Z to undo the operation.)

After the file is copied, it's immediately synchronized with cloud storage on the Internet. After a few information superhighway moments, that file is available via the web or on any other device that has access to cloud storage.

- ✔ This section demonstrates copying a file to cloud storage, but you can also copy a file from cloud storage, move files, rename them, add folders, and so on.

- ✔ When you delete a file from cloud storage, it's removed from *all* cloud storage devices.

- ✔ I move files between my desktop PC and laptop by copying them to cloud storage.

- ✔ Both Google Drive and Dropbox folders are accessible through teensy-weensy icons in the taskbar's notifications area.

- ✔ You can still use your PC's cloud storage folders while the Internet is offline. Any files you add or modify in the cloud storage folders are instantly synchronized after the connection is resumed.

- ✔ Windows uses the backslash character, \, to separate folder names when specifying a path. The term *path* describes the folder hierarchy, listing all parent folders for a specific folder or just the relevant parent folders.

Accessing cloud storage from another device

The most common way to access your cloud storage is from any web browser; navigate to the cloud storage website (refer to Table 16-1) and log in, and there are your files. OneDrive even lets you preview and examine files online; you can edit Microsoft Office documents if you subscribe to the Office 365 service.

On other devices, you must obtain the cloud storage app. For example, on Android phones and tablets, visit the Google Play Store to obtain apps for Dropbox and OneDrive; Google Drive is included on all Android devices (the app is named Drive).

In Figure 16-1, you see the Dropbox folder on my PC right next to how that folder looks when accessed on an Android tablet. To do so, I opened the Dropbox app. Files and folders are identical — and synchronized — between both devices.

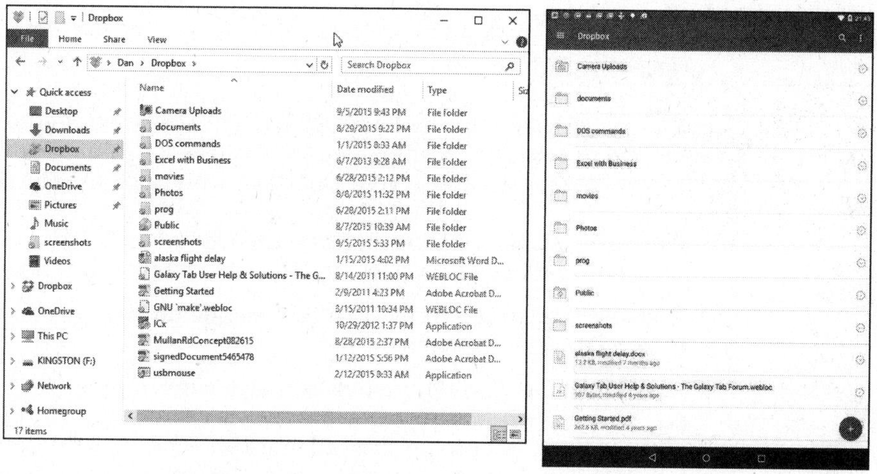

Figure 16-1: Dropbox on a PC and a tablet.

Dropbox files on a PC

Dropbox files on a tablet

For a laptop or another PC, add the cloud storage software as you did for your first PC. On Windows 10, the OneDrive connection is made automatically, so there's nothing more to set up.

Online Media

In addition to storing files, various cloud services provide specific features for sharing media. These services include photo sharing, music, and video. In some cases, you can use the service to listen to your music or watch your home movies from any Internet-connected device.

You have two ways to expose your photos, music, or videos to the online universe: You can use cloud storage, or you can sign up for a media sharing service.

Keeping your pictures on cloud storage

The simplest and most direct way to share your pictures online is simply to use the Photos or Pictures folder in your cloud storage. All major services offer such a folder. In your Home folder, look for the following:

Dropbox\Photos

Google Drive\Google Photos

OneDrive\Pictures

For example, in your home folder, use the folder OneDrive\Pictures. Any image saved or copied to that folder — or to any subfolders inside that folder — is synchronized with your OneDrive storage on the cloud.

✔ Windows creates a Pictures folder within your home folder on the PC. That's the default location where photos and images are saved.

✔ You can copy images from the Pictures folder to a cloud storage folder to place those images online, but:

✔ Keep in mind that you have only so much cloud storage, especially if you're not paying for the service. Pictures can occupy a lot of storage and you don't want to be charged more for exceeding the allotted capacity, nor do you want images to be arbitrarily deleted.

✔ The Dropbox service has a second location for images, which appears when you activate the photo upload service on a mobile device. When it's active, any pictures you snap on a phone or camera are automatically saved to the Dropbox\Camera Uploads folder. See my book *Android Phones For Dummies* (Wiley Publishing) for more information on this service.

Accessing cloud storage pictures

To visit your cloud storage photos on the Internet, navigate to the web page where you can access your files; refer to Table 16-1 for specifics. After you log in, open the Photos or Pictures folder. You see your images displayed, similar to what's shown in Figure 16-2.

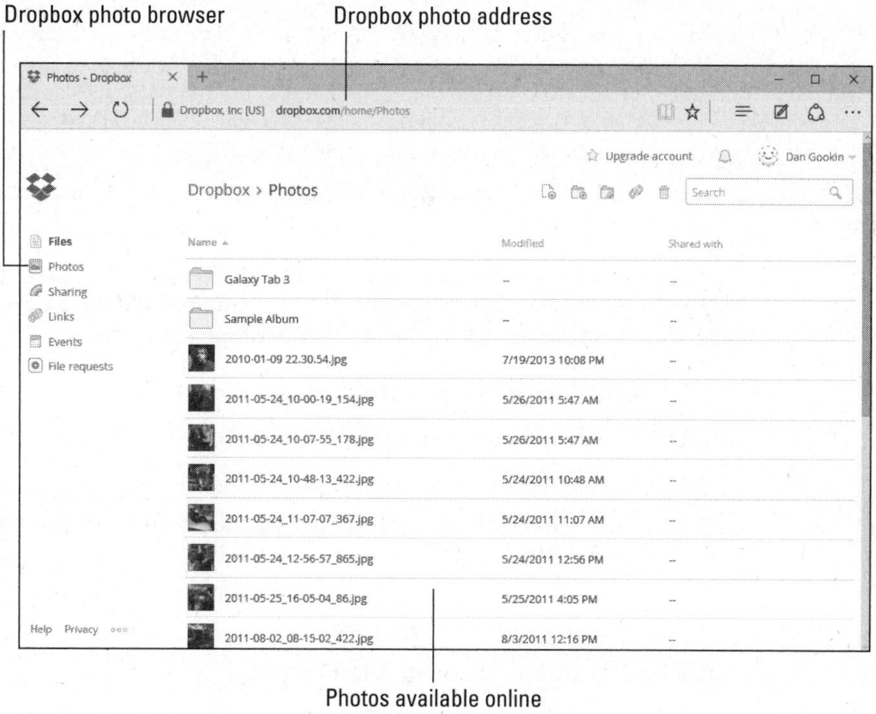

Dropbox photo browser   Dropbox photo address

Figure 16-2: PC images available via cloud storage.

Photos available online

Of course, if the other device you're using (computer, tablet, phone) has access to a cloud storage app, you can use the app instead of a web browser.

What can you do with the online photos? Well, you can look at them. Most cloud storage sites offer a photo viewing tool, such as the Photos link for Dropbox, shown in Figure 16-2.

Sharing a picture from cloud storage

You don't have to tell everyone your cloud password when you want your friends to enjoy the cloud storage pictures. Instead, you share a photo.

Photo sharing services

Cloud storage is really the way to go for sharing files and photos. Back in the old days, and even today, the solution for online photo sharing was to subscribe to a photo sharing service. Many were available free and are still available today.

Photo sharing services weren't as well-coordinated with files on your PC. Instead of synchronizing, you had to choose which files to upload (or send) to the photo sharing service. Once there, you used the web browser to organize images and share them with your friends.

A few of the more popular photo sharing services include Flickr at `www.flickr.com`; Image Shack, `http://imageshack.us`; and Photobucket, `http://photobucket.com`. You might also be able to use an online hosting service with a traditional photo developer. For example, WalMart has an online photo service at `photos.walmart.com`.

The photo-sharing technique applies to most cloud storage files: The file is flagged as shared and you send a link to that shared file via email to someone else. Here's how it works for most cloud storage services:

1. **Click the image you want to share.**

   Or it can be any file, such as a PDF, Word document, and so on.

2. **Click the Share button.**

3. **Type the email address for the person or people you want to receive a link to the file.**

   For Dropbox, you have the option of copying and pasting the file's web page link instead of sending an email.

4. **Click the Share, Done, or Send button.**

   In mere Internet moments, the other person receives the message along with the link.

When the recipient clicks the link, their web browser opens and they can view the photo or access the file.

- ✔ On a mobile device, the recipient may be required to choose whether to open the link in the web browser app or use the cloud sharing app. Using the cloud sharing app is best.

- ✔ Most files shared as described in this section are copies of the actual file. The recipient(s) do not have direct access to your cloud storage files.

Listening to your cloud music

As with photos, cloud storage services also dish up audio files shared on your PC. Each service features its own, special audio or music folder. For example, in your OneDrive folder you find a Music folder. In that folder you see any music you may have added to OneDrive or which you copied from your home folder's Music folder.

When you visit OneDrive on the web, you can open the Music folder and listen to your tunes. Click a music file (or any audio file) to play.

For example, Figure 16-3 shows my OneDrive Music folder on the web, which is an echo of the folder I have on my computer. I click a File icon to listen to a given song or open a folder to begin listening to an album.

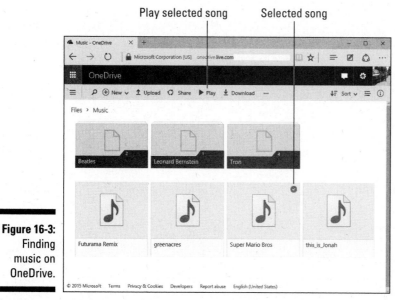

Figure 16-3: Finding music on OneDrive.

 As with storing photos online, mind how much music you keep on cloud storage. Music files consume storage space, and you're allotted only so much cloud storage.

Music on the cloud

Most online music is stored entirely on the cloud, which is apparently the direction the tech industry is going. Music services, such as Apple's iTunes and Google Play Music, keep all your purchased and uploaded music on the Internet. That way, the music doesn't occupy any storage on your PC, but an Internet connection is required if you want to listen to your music. See Chapter 21 for more information on PC music.

Chapter 17

The Weird World of Networking

*E*ven if it's the only computer in the room, if the PC is connected to the Internet, it's part of a network. That makes networking a basic part of owning a computer, like having a printer or a sore neck. Because networking can be vast, uncharted, dangerous ground on which to tread, you better bone up on some basics before you do something foolish.

Why Network?

Networking is about sharing. Specifically, a network allows multiple computers to share their resources. These resources include mass storage devices, printers, media players, and modems. The modems (and it should be only one modem, but my editor believes in parallel lists) are what provide Internet access.

Like everything computerish, networking involves hardware and software. The hardware part is included with your computer as well as specific network components described elsewhere in this chapter. The software part is supplied by Windows.

Avoidable network jargon

The realm of networking hosts its own jargon festival. Strange terms and funky words dot the landscape like piles of straw in a field, with some of the piles on fire.

802.11: This number describes the wireless networking standard. It's followed by one or more lowercase letters of the alphabet, which is potentially significant in some way to someone, but not to most people. You pronounce 802.11 as "eight oh two eleven." You can also say, "Eight oh two *dot* eleven" if you're feeling cheeky.

CAT5: Networking cable is described as CAT5 or sometimes CAT6. You say "cat" and then the number. It doesn't really matter what CAT stands for.

Ethernet: This term refers to the standards and protocols used for networking. Say "*Eeth*-r-net."

Gateway: Often incorrectly called a router, the gateway is the interface between your computer network (or LAN) and the Internet. The gateway manages network traffic, receiving information and sending it to the proper location.

Hub: It's a central location into which network hardware connects.

LAN: This is the acronym for *local area network,* which is what you create when you configure one or more computers to share resources. You pronounce LAN like *land* without the *d* at the end, like how Aunt Minnie pronounced "Land sakes!"

Modem: This device connects the big bad Internet to your home or office network. Modems come in dialup and broadband varieties, although pretty much all modems today are broadband modems, which means they're so fast that they don't need vowels: They're sprfst! The modem sits between the gateway and the Internet, and in some cases the modem and the gateway are the same gizmo.

Router: It's a more common term, though technically incorrect, for a gateway.

Wi-Fi: This term describes a wireless network. Supposedly, it stands for *wireless fidelity,* but the nerds debate whether or not that story is true.

✔ Networks come in wired and wireless varieties. The difference is in how you connect to the network.

✔ A non-network way to access the Internet is to use the old phone system and a dialup modem. This type of connection is very rare these days. Odds are good that if your PC uses a dialup connection, it's already configured and ready to go. If so, don't mess with it!

Network Hardware

The nifty thing about network hardware is that once you set it up, you're done. Add the modem and the gateway and connect whatever cables you bother to use, and the network itself is complete. It may not work all the time, but you seldom if ever need to reconnect or reconfigure network hardware.

- ✔ Most networks today are wireless, meaning that connecting to the existing network hardware is a software operation. See the later section "Connecting to a wireless network."

- ✔ The best way to fix a network is to turn off the modem and gateway, wait, and then turn each one on again: Turn on the modem. Turn on the gateway. This procedure fixes most network woes.

Reviewing the network configuration

A typical computer network setup includes several items, some of which have oddball names. Here's the list:

- ✔ Computers, printers, phones, tablets

- ✔ The networking adapter, or NIC

- ✔ The cables (or not)

- ✔ The gateway or router

- ✔ A broadband modem

These items are illustrated in Figure 17-1, which lovingly maps out the parts of a typical computer network. As you can see, it's possible and pretty much standard to mix wired and wireless devices on the same network.

The network devices — computers, printers, and mobile devices — each sport a NIC, or network interface card. That's the hardware that connects the device to the network, either wired or wirelessly.

For a wired network, cables connect all network devices to a central location. One end of the cable connects to the PC's Ethernet jack. The other end plugs into the gateway. If the gateway runs out of jacks, a switch or hub can be added to accommodate more connections.

At the center of the computer network is the *gateway*. It's the location where all the network devices connect. Wires connect the wired network devices; magical leprechauns connect the wireless devices.

The gateway's job is to coordinate local network activity and to communicate with a larger network, the Internet. It may also provide firewall support, which helps prevent bad guys on the Internet from accessing the computers on your local network.

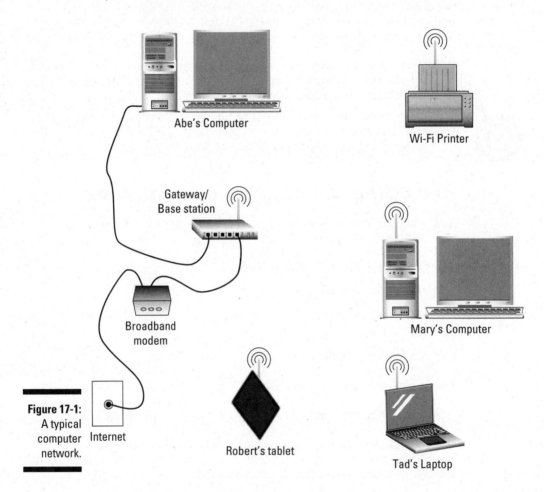

Abe's Computer

Wi-Fi Printer

Gateway/
Base station

Broadband
modem

Mary's Computer

Figure 17-1:
A typical
computer
network.

Internet

Robert's tablet

Tad's Laptop

The final piece of the network puzzle is the broadband modem. It bridges the connection between the gateway and the Internet.

- ✔ NIC is pronounced "nick," as in "nick-nack paddywhack."

- ✔ All PCs sold today come with a wired NIC. Laptops come with both wired and wireless NICs.

- ✔ You can add a wireless NIC to a desktop PC by connecting in a USB Wi-Fi adapter or installing a Wi-Fi expansion card. See Chapter 10.

- ✔ For a wired NIC, you plug the network cable into the Ethernet adapter on the PC's rump.

- ✔ Wireless NICs show no visual parts, although some desktop PC wireless NIC's feature one or more antennae.

- ✔ Computer network cable comes in a variety of lengths and in several bright and cheerful colors.

- ✔ There is no incorrect way to plug in a network cable; you can plug either end into the computer's NIC. Plug the other end into the gateway. Snap, snap.

- ✔ Network cables are often cleverly disguised, hidden behind furniture or drapery, or run through walls and ducts. The presence of such ugly cables has motivated most people to use Wi-Fi instead of wired networking.

- ✔ Several types of broadband modems are common: cable, DSL, satellite, and WiMAX. Your ISP supplies the modem, either for lease or sale.

- ✔ You should leave the broadband modem on all the time. Oh, what the heck: Leave the gateway on all the time as well. These devices are designed to operate 'round the clock.

Setting up a gateway

If you're setting up your own network, one task is more important than all the others. That's the proper configuration of the gateway, or "router." (You can call it a router all you want, but it's a gateway.)

The two items you must set are the administrator's password and the Wi-Fi password. If you neglect to set either one, you run the risk that your friendly neighbors might initiate a hostile takeover of your network. That's a bad thing.

Directions for configuring the gateway are found on a flimsy sheet of paper that you probably lost when opening the box. The steps work like this:

1. **Plug in the gateway so that it has power.**

2. **Connect the gateway to the modem.**

   The modem plugs into a special jack, often labeled *WAN,* which stands for *wide area network.*

3. **Connect any wired devices to the gateway.**

4. Use a connected computer to access the gateway's web page.

You type the gateway's IP address into your PC's web browser window. The address might be supplied on that flimsy sheet of paper you lost. It looks similar to 192.168.0.1 — a series of numbers.

5. Log in to the gateway.

Use the default account name, usually *admin*, and the default password, either *admin* or *password* or whatever's printed on the flimsy sheet of paper.

6. Change the gateway's administrator password.

This is an important step. The bad guys know the default password for every router. It's the first thing they try.

7. Assign a network name for the Wi-Fi network, set up security, and set a Wi-Fi network password.

How you perform this step varies, but all three tasks are important, especially the Wi-Fi password.

8. Write down the admin and Wi-Fi network passwords.

Write them down on a sheet of paper. Tuck that paper beneath the gateway so that you'll always know where it is. And don't put anything else on the paper that may confuse you in the future; just write down and label the passwords you set and put nothing else on the paper!

9. Continue obeying directions to configure the gateway.

Often the final step is to restart the gateway, which is done via software. Only unplug the gateway if you're required to do so for maintenance or troubleshooting.

The good news: Once you've configured the gateway, you're done. The only other time you need to access it is for an update or when troubleshooting your network.

✔ Don't get cute or fun with the Wi-Fi network password. Use something complex and tough to guess.

✔ Bookmark the gateway's website; save it in your PC's web browser.

✔ Setting Wi-Fi network security can be a tough decision. Trust me, few people know what those acronyms mean. Definitely use security, and most likely the suggested security setting is best.

✔ When you need more wired connections for the gateway, obtain a *switch*. It's basically just a gang of Ethernet ports, which let you add more computers, printers, and other gizmos to the network. The switch helps you expand a wired computer network.

> ✔ If the wireless signal can't reach everywhere in your home or office, get a Wi-Fi extender. Any gateway works, actually. Use the main gateway's configuration web page and direct it to extend its network to the second Wi-Fi gateway. This type of setup is called a *wireless distribution system,* or WDS.

The Network Connection

With the hardware in place, you might ask the question, "How do I connect to the network?" Good question, although you don't connect to the network — your computer does. This ain't *The Matrix*.

Connecting to a wired network

Windows automatically finds any network into which the PC is plugged. So, by turning on your computer and having that network hose connected, you're more or less done with network configuration for a wired connection.

Upon the initial connection, you may see a prompt asking you about the network type. Choose the option Private or Home for a home or office network, or any location you know is secure. Otherwise, or when in doubt, choose Public. See the later section "Checking the network type" for more details.

Connecting to a wireless network

Accessing a wireless, or Wi-Fi, network involves more steps than connecting a wired network. Primarily, you must choose the Wi-Fi network and enter the password. The good news is that Windows remembers Wi-Fi connections, so once the initial connection is made, the PC reconnects automatically to the Wi-Fi network whenever it's in range.

In Windows 10, follow these steps to access a Wi-Fi network:

1. **Open the Settings app.**

   The keyboard shortcut is Win+I.

2. **Click the Network & Internet button.**

3. **Ensure that Wi-Fi is chosen from the left side of the window.**

4. **Choose a wireless network from the list.**

   Networks are shown by their name and signal strength. Those at the top of the list have a better connection.

5. **Place a check mark by the option Connect Automatically.**

This option ensures that the laptop automatically reconnects to the network whenever it's in range.

6. **Click the Connect button.**

7. **Type the network password and click the Next button.**

8. **If you're on a home or work network, click the Yes button; otherwise, click No.**

Click Yes to set the Private or Home network type. Click No for a public Wi-Fi network, such as in a café or at the airport. See the later section "Checking the network type."

In Windows 7, follow these steps to connect to a Wi-Fi network:

 1. **Click the Wireless Networking icon, found in the notifications area.**

When you click the Wireless Networking icon, a list of available wireless networks appears, as shown in Figure 17-2.

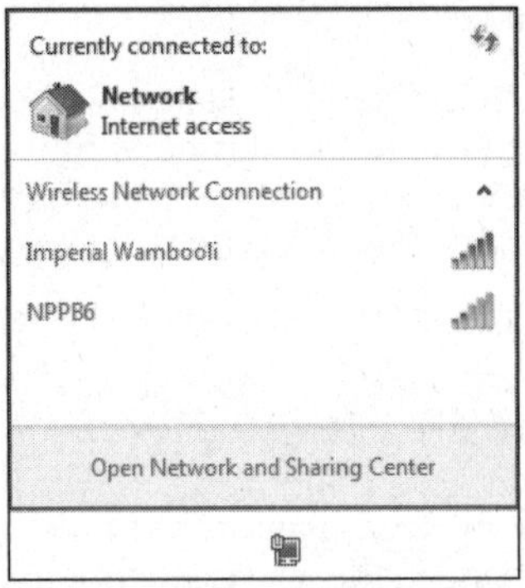

Currently connected to:

Network
Internet access

Wireless Network Connection ^

Imperial Wambooli

NPPB6

Open Network and Sharing Center

Figure 17-2:
Available
wireless
networks.

2. **Choose a network from the list.**

The list shows the network name and its signal strength.

3. **Place a check mark by the Automatically Connect option if you plan to use the same wireless network in the future.**

4. **Click the Connect button.**

Windows attempts to "make friendly" with the wireless network.

5. **If you see a warning that the network is unsecured, click the Connect Anyway option.**

   This message is common for certain free wireless networks that don't require a password for connection. Click the Connect Anyway option to proceed.

6. **Enter the network's password, if you're prompted to do so.**

Some public Wi-Fi networks require that you log in or pay to complete the connection process. If you're unsure, open a web browser window and navigate to any web page. If you're successful, the connection is good. Otherwise, heed the directions on the web page that appears to sign in and complete the connection.

Connecting to a hidden Wi-Fi network

Some Wi-Fi networks don't broadcast their name. It's hidden for security reasons; obviously, you can't access the network unless you know the name. Assuming that such a Wi-Fi network is in range, and you have the name, follow these steps to access it:

1. **Open the Control Panel.**

   In Windows 10, press the Win+X key combination and choose Control Panel from the super-secret menu that pops up.

2. **Below the Network and Internet heading, click the View Network Status and Tasks link.**

   The Network and Sharing Center window appears.

3. **Click the link Set Up a New Connection or Network.**

4. **Choose the Manually Connect to a Wireless Network option, and click the Next button.**

5. **Type the network name in the Network Name box.**

   You obtain the name from whoever is in charge of the network. The name is also known as an SSID.

6. **Fill in the rest of the information as provided by the same source as the network name.**

   Set network security and encryption and whatever other options appear.

7. **Ensure that the option Start This Connection Automatically is enabled.**

   This step saves you some time by preventing you from having to repeat these steps later.

8. Click the Next button.

Windows goes out and finds the unnamed wireless network.

9. Choose the Connect To option.

At this point the network has been added to the list of visible Wi-Fi networks. You must still connect to the network and enter a password. Refer to the preceding section.

The network name is referred to as the SSID, where *SSID* stands for Service Set IDentifier.

Checking the network type

One of the most important things you do when first connecting to a network is to set the network type. This step is about security. Obviously, you want more network security when connecting to the car mechanic's Wi-Fi than you do when connecting to your home network.

In Windows 10, the two network types are: Public and Private. The Public setting offers more security, which you need when accessing a public network. The Private setting is best for home or the office.

To review the current network type, follow these steps:

1. Open the Control Panel.

In Windows 10, right-click the Start button and choose Control Panel from the super-secret pop-up menu. In Windows 7, choose Control Panel from the Start menu.

2. Below the Network and Internet heading, click the link View Network Status and Tasks.

The currently connected network is shown in the Network and Sharing Center window, shown in Figure 17-3. The current network type is displayed beneath the network name, such as Private Network, shown in the figure.

3. Close the Control Panel window when you're done.

Or, if you need to reset the network type in Windows 7, keep reading in the next section.

In Windows 7, the network types are Home, Work, and Public. The Windows 7 Home type is the same as the Windows 10 Private type. The Windows 7 Work and Public types are the same as Public in Windows 10.

Network type

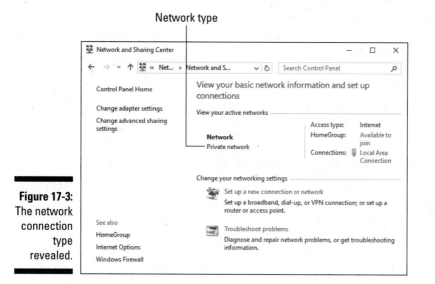

Figure 17-3:
The network
connection
type
revealed.

Resetting the network type

Say you goof and accidentally choose Public for your home network or Private (or Home) for Starbucks. If so, you need to change the network type.

In Windows 10, to change the network type for a wireless connection, you must disconnect from the network and forget that connection. Only when you reconnect to the network can you choose another type. See the later sections "Disconnecting from a network" and "Forgetting a Wi-Fi connection."

To change a wired connection's network type in Windows 10, follow these steps:

1. **Press Win + I to summon the Settings app.**

2. **Click the Network & Internet button.**

3. **On the left side of the window, choose Ethernet.**

4. **On the right side of the window, click the tile that reads Local Area Connection.**

   The tile may have a different name, but it's the one at the top of the right side of the window.

5. **To make the network private, set the toggle switch to the On position; for a public network, ensure that the setting is Off.**

   The setting controls network access to your PC, so for a private or home network, turning on the setting is fine; for a public network, you want to turn off that setting.

In Windows 7, follow the steps from the preceding section to display the Network and Sharing Center window. Click the network type link, such as Home Network or Private Network. Choose a new network type from the Set Network Location window.

Always choose the Public network type when you're using your PC or a laptop in a public location. This choice is the most secure.

Disconnecting from a network

There's no need to disconnect from a wired network. Just leave the cable plugged in all the time and Mr. PC will be fine.

You can manually disconnect from a wireless network by turning off the PC or simply moving out of range. Otherwise, follow these steps to disconnect from a network in Windows 10:

1. **Open the Settings app and click the Network & Internet button.**

2. **Click the currently connected wireless network.**

   The word *Connected* appears below the network name.

3. **Click the Disconnect button.**

   The Wi-Fi network connection is broken.

To manually disconnect from a wireless network in Windows 7, click the Network icon in the notification area and choose the wireless network from the pop-up window. Click the Disconnect button.

The wireless network will automatically reconnect if you've configured it to do so, as recommended in this chapter. That happens if you move out of range and then back into range, or if you restart the computer.

Forgetting a Wi-Fi connection

Windows remembers which Wi-Fi networks your computer has accessed. That way, you can reconnect to an established network instantly — unless you direct Windows to forget about a network.

To forget a Wi-Fi network connection or simply review the list of saved networks, follow these steps in Windows 10:

1. **Open the Settings app.**

   The keyboard shortcut is Win+I.

2. **Click the big button labeled Network & Internet.**

3. **On the right side of the window, click the Manage Wi-Fi Settings link.**

4. **Scroll down the list to locate the heading Manage Known Networks.**

   At this point, you could be done and simply behold the list of former Wi-Fi sweethearts. If you need to purge a network, such as that motel in Bakersfield you know you'll never return to, continue with:

5. **Click the name of network to forget.**

6. **Click the Forget button.**

   Windows discards the network information, which includes the saved network password.

Of course, you can always reconnect to any network. You need to supply the password again, as well as set the network type, as described elsewhere in this chapter.

On the Network

Networking is about sharing resources. To view those resources shared on the network, open the Network window:

1. **Press Win + E to summon a File Explorer window.**

2. **From the items on the left side of the window, click Network.**

   You see shared network resources, similar to what's shown in Figure 17-4.

The Network window organizes available network resources by category. In Figure 17-4, you'll find icons for computers, media-sharing devices, storage devices, network printers, and even a scanner.

✔ Access to network resources, such as those shown in Figure 17-4, happens primarily over Private (or Home) networks. See the earlier section "Checking the network type" for details.

✔ Available network printers are accessed automatically. See Chapter 11 for details on printing.

✔ When your computer is connected to a public network, you won't see as many resources in the Network window. That's because Windows automatically cranks up the network security and restricts network access on such networks.

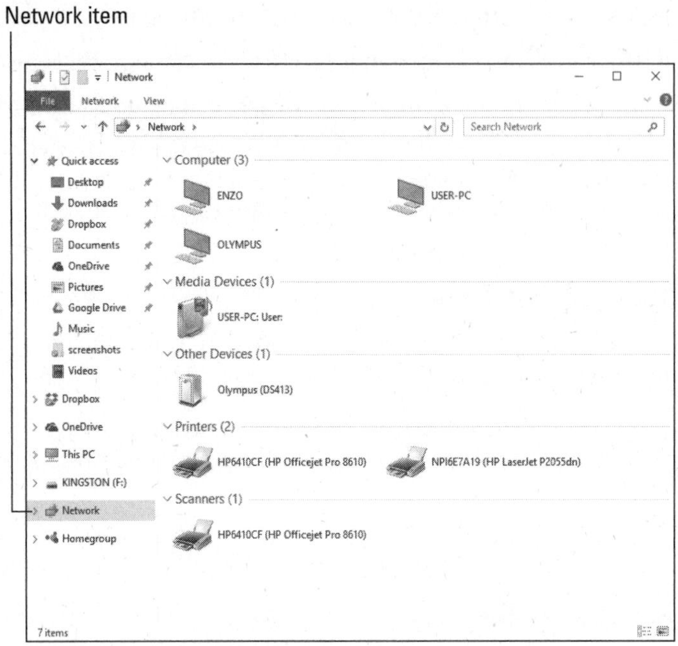

Network item

Figure 17-4:
The
Network
window.

Accessing a network folder

You access a folder elsewhere on the network just as you would access any folder on your PC's mass storage system. The difference is that you need to browse to the folder from the Network window and sign in to the other system to use the folder. Follow these steps:

1. **Open the Network window.**

   Refer to the steps in the preceding section.

2. **Open a computer icon to see which folders it's sharing.**

   If the computer shows no shared folders, try another or contact the computer user and order them to buy a copy of my book and learn how to share a folder, as covered in the later section "Sharing a folder."

3. **Double-click a folder to access its contents.**

   Folders with security — which should be all of them — require a user account and password for full access.

4. **Log in to the shared folder; type your username and password.**

5. **Browse the files in the shared folder.**

   At this point, using the folder works like using any other folder on your PC.

A better way to share files is to use cloud storage, as described in Chapter 16. It's possible to share a whole folder with someone else, in which case you both have access to the folder's files. Cloud storage services work across a local network as well as the Internet.

Mapping a network drive

If you find yourself accessing a shared network folder all the time, consider mapping that folder to a drive letter in your PC's mass storage system. Follow these steps:

1. **Press Win + E to open a File Explorer window.**

2. **In Windows 10, choose This PC from the left side of the window.**

   This step isn't necessary in Windows 7, because you already see the My Computer window. Like the This PC window, it lists local storage and network locations.

3. **In Windows 10, click the Computer tab.**

4. **Click the Map Network Drive button.**

   The Map Network Drive dialog box appears.

5. **Choose a drive letter.**

   Pick something from the list of available letters. I recommend using something high-up so that the mapped network drive won't interfere with any removable storage you add to your PC. For example, I map drive letter V to my network file server.

6. **Click the Browse button.**

   A mini network window appears, listing available storage devices on the network. These are locations flagged for shared folders, as described in the preceding section.

7. **Select a network computer or server and then a shared folder.**

8. **Type the username and password to access the network resource.**

   You must have an account on the other computer, or know the username and password, to map a shared folder.

9. **Ensure that the Reconnect at Sign-in (or Logon) option is checked.**

10. **Click the Finish button.**

You see a new "drive" appear in the window, one with the letter you assigned in Step 5. Opening this drive icon displays the contents of the shared folder on the network.

Sharing a folder

If you want other people on the network to have access to your PC's mass storage system, well, they can't. But they can have access to a folder on your computer. To do so, you must *share* the folder. Sharing makes the folder — and its contents (all files and subfolders) — available to all other computers on the network. Here's how to share a folder:

1. **Right-click the folder you want to share.**

   You must be in the parent folder to share one of its subfolders. See Chapter 15 for details on how parent and subfolders work.

2. **Choose Properties from the folder's pop-up menu.**

   The folder's Properties dialog box appears.

3. **Click the Sharing tab.**

4. **Click the Advanced Sharing button.**

5. **Put a check mark by the option labeled Share This Folder.**

   You can set a share name, which helps to better identify the folder on the network.

   If you want others to have full access — to add as well as delete files — click the Permissions button and place a check mark in the Allow column by the Full Control item.

6. **Click OK.**

   The folder is now shared.

7. **Click the Close button to dismiss the folder's Properties dialog box.**

Other PCs can now access the folder on the network, as described in the preceding section.

✔ To unshare a folder, repeat the steps in this section, but in Step 5 remove the check mark.

✔ Others can access the shared folder only if they know your username and password on your computer. You can add an account for them on your PC, which can be used to access the shared folder.

✔ Don't share an entire storage device, such as Drive C. Don't share your entire Home folder. Doing so is a security risk. Share only specific folders, such as a project folder.

Accessing shared media

Some PCs, as well as specific network devices, cough up their media for network sharing. For example, you can access photos, videos, or music on another computer on the network. The topic is called *media sharing*.

If any PCs or other gizmos on the network have activated media sharing, you can use a media player to access that media. The most obvious way to do so is to open an item listed in the Network window under Media Devices. Follow the directions on the screen to determine what to do next, such as choose an app to access the pictures, music, or video.

Activating media sharing on your PC

No computer willingly coughs up its media for sharing. You must command Windows to provide your PC's media as a resource, open and shared on the network. Heed these directions:

1. **Open the Control Panel.**

   In Windows 10, press Win+X. In Windows 7, press the Win key. Choose Control Panel from the menu.

2. **Below the Network and Internet heading, click the link View Network Status and Tasks.**

   The Network and Sharing Center window appears.

3. **From the left side of the Networking and Sharing Center window, click the link Change Advanced Sharing Settings.**

4. **Scroll down the list to locate the Media Streaming entry.**

   You may need to click one of the down-arrow buttons to expand part of the sharing settings to find Media Streaming.

5. **Click the Choose Media Streaming Options link.**

   The Media Streaming Options window appears.

6. **Click the Turn On Media Streaming button.**

   If you don't see that button, media sharing is already configured. You're done. Otherwise:

   The screen that appears lists network computers and various sharing options. You can fiddle around here, but everything is pretty much set to share pictures, videos, and music from your PC to those network devices.

7. **Click the OK button, and close the various other windows you've opened.**

   You're all done.

Your PC is now sharing its media to other network devices. It's the digital equivalent of a Craigslist ad saying, "Come into my house and take my pictures, albums, and videos," but far less chaotic.

Part IV
Your Digital Life

In this part . . .

- ✔ Discover useful web and email tricks
- ✔ Add images, music, and video to your PC
- ✔ Work with digital photos
- ✔ Entertain yourself with music, TV, and video

Chapter 18

An Internet Refresher

*T*he Internet is ubiquitous. Even if you haven't memorized all the bit fields in a packet header, you probably know about the web, have sent and received email, and perhaps even stuck a digital big toe in the enticing waters of social networking. That's great! I assume you need only a minor refresher on the big topic that is the Internet.

What Is the Internet?

The Internet consists of all the computers connected to the Internet. That definition seems weird, mostly because people think of the Internet as a single computer or a program. It's not. Whenever your computer is *on* the Internet, it's part of the Internet.

✔ The computers on the Internet send information, they receive information, and — most important — they store information. That's the Internet in a nutshell.

✔ No one owns the Internet, just as no one owns the oceans. The company you pay for Internet access is merely providing you with the access, not with the Internet's content.

Internet Access

The Internet comes pouring in from a hole in the wall. Or you may pull in its wireless signal from the ether. Either way, some other outfit provides the connection. That outfit is known as an *Internet service provider,* or ISP.

In exchange for the Internet service, you cough up some money — or not: Free Internet access can be found at various public locations and many businesses. Your office or another large, imposing organization might also provide Internet access. Most of the time, however, you subscribe to an Internet service.

- ✔ Your ISP can be your telephone company, cable company, wireless provider, or satellite outfit, all of which compete to provide you with broadband Internet access.

- ✔ Most Internet access these days is broadband. That means the signal is on all the time and you don't need to log in to the Internet. It's always available!

- ✔ Before broadband access, people used dialup modems to access the Internet. Those days are long gone. Today, about 98 percent of the Internet users have broadband connections.

- ✔ To test the Internet connection, run the web browser. If a web page appears, you're on the Internet. If not, contact the ISP for assistance.

- ✔ The *S* in *ISP* stands for *service.* You pay a fee, and the ISP provides you with Internet access *and* service. Service means technical support: someone you can phone for help, classes, software — you name it.

It's a World Wide Web We Weave

Yeah, you probably know how to use a web browser fairly well. Most people do. But I'll bet lots of people could still use some of the information held in this section.

Finding another web browser

Most definitely you're not stuck with the web browser that comes with Windows. You can use any web browser you want. You can even use your current web browser to obtain a new one. Here are just three options:

Chrome: www.google.com/chrome

Firefox: www.mozilla.org/firefox

Opera: www.opera.com

Even more web browsers are available. My point is that you're not stuck with using any web browser.

To obtain and install another browser, follow these general steps:

1. **Visit one of the web browser websites listed in this section.**

2. **Click the link to download the browser.**

   The link is titled Download or Download Now.

3. **After it's downloaded, open your home folder's Downloads folder.**

   Downloaded files are automatically saved in the Downloads folder.

4. **Double-click to open the downloaded file.**

5. **Click the Yes or OK button to confirm that you want to run the program.**

6. **Continue obeying the directions in the installation or setup program.**

   When installation is completed, the new web browser is installed on your PC.

When you install the new web browser, it asks whether you want to make it the default browser. Click Yes. That way, all web page links and web requests will start that browser, not the old browser.

In Windows 10, the browser is called Edge, but everyone refers to it as Internet Explorer, which is the traditional Windows web browser.

Locating the web browser commands

As software developers fulfill their desire to completely befuddle the user (that's you), they design programs — or "apps" — that hide what were once easily accessible features. Gone are menus. Present are buttons and graphics and whacky things.

In Figure 18-1, you see the assortment of popular web browsers — specifically, Chrome, Edge, and Firefox. The figure illustrates where to find the hidden commands in each web browser. Generally, it's located near the upper right corner of the window, as illustrated in the figure.

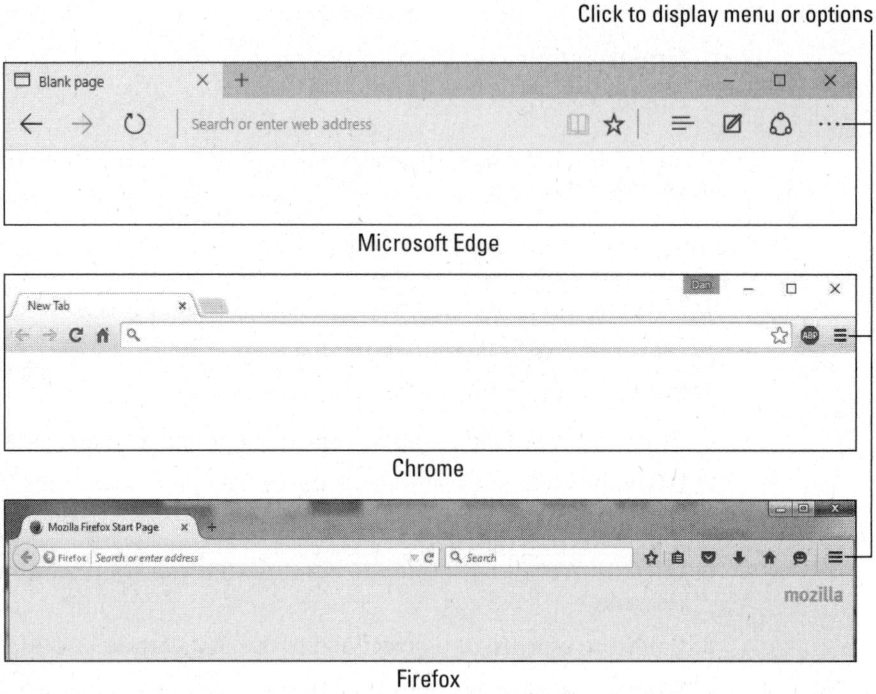
Click to display menu or options
Blank page
Search or enter web address
Microsoft Edge
New Tab
Chrome
Mozilla Firefox Start Page
Firefox
Search or enter address
Search
mozilla
Firefox

Figure 18-1: Locating the web browser commands.

Another trick is to press the F10 key. If you're lucky, you see a traditional menu bar pop up, in which case you can have at it with the mouse and various commands as you were originally trained.

Going undercover on the web

As you meander through the World Wide Web, efforts are made to track your path. These efforts include things like cookies and other information that web pages keep to monitor what you look at, track which ads you click, or simply remember account information on what you've saved in a shopping cart. All that tracking is normal and benevolent.

When you don't want to be tracked, you open an undercover tab in the web browser. Different browsers refer to the undercover tab by different names, but the end result is the same: As you browse undercover, your history isn't tracked and cookies are not saved.

- In Edge and Internet Explorer, going undercover is referred to as InPrivate browsing. Press Ctrl+Shift+P to create a new InPrivate browsing window.

✔ In Chrome, it's referred to as Incognito. The keyboard shortcut is Ctrl+Shift+N.

✔ Firefox uses the term Private window. To bring up a Private window, press Ctrl+Shift+P.

With these browsers, the first undercover window displays a summary of how the browser behaves in this mode as well as offers some tips and suggestions on how to use it.

To exit your undercover adventures, close the undercover window or tab.

Using an undercover tab isn't just for porn. I do my pre-shopping in an undercover window. That way, I'm not bombarded with advertising for the items I've browsed.

Browsing tips

Here are my collected web-browsing tips, honed and polished over the past two centuries:

✔ Use the Zoom control to make web pages with small text more visible. A graphic control may be found at the bottom of the window. The common Zoom command keyboard shortcut is Ctrl++ and Ctrl+- (the plus and minus keys on the keyboard).

✔ If a web page doesn't load, try again! The web can be busy, and often when it is, you see an error message. Reload a web page by pressing Ctrl+R on the keyboard.

✔ Refreshing a page is one quick way to fix the "missing picture" problem.

✔ When a web page isn't found, you probably didn't type its address properly. Try again.

✔ Most web links are text, but quite a few are graphical. The only way to know for certain is to point the mouse pointer at what you believe may be a link. If the pointer changes to a pointing hand, shown in the margin, you know that it's a link you can click.

✔ When you accidentally click a link and change your mind, click the Stop button, which appears on the address bar with an X symbol. The Internet then stops sending you information.

✔ Press Ctrl+D to add any web page you're viewing as a bookmark or to add it your favorites. Don't be shy about it! It's better to add it now and delete it later than to regret not adding it in the first place.

Printing web pages

It may not be a big deal in other programs, but printing a web page can be an ordeal. The problem is that a web page is formatted for a computer screen, not a piece of paper. So unless the page is designed like a document, generating a printed copy can be an ordeal.

Here are my suggestions for getting a web page to print properly:

- The print command is Ctrl+P for all web browsers. You might also find a Print button on the toolbar or hidden on a menu. Press Ctrl+P to summon the Print dialog box or screen. It contains settings for controlling the printer.

- Change the page orientation from portrait (tall) to landscape (wide). This setting can be found in the Print dialog box.

- Use the Shrink to Fit or Shrink to Page command in the Print dialog box to reset the web page's size to match the paper size.

- Consider saving the web page to disk; press the Ctrl+S keyboard shortcut. After the page is saved, you can open the web page file in Microsoft Word or Excel or any web page editing program and edit or print it from there.

Searching-the-web tips

The web is full of information, and some of it accurate. The issue is locating the information you want. Here are my web-page-searching tips:

- My main search engine these days is Google, at `www.google.com`, but I can also recommend the Microsoft search engine Bing, at `www.bing.com`.

- Web search engines ignore the smaller words in the English language. Words such as *is, to, the, for, are,* and others aren't included in the search. Therefore:

- Use only key words when searching. For example, to look for *The Declaration of Independence,* typing *declaration independence* is good enough.

- Word order matters. If you want to find out the name of that red bug with six legs, try all combinations: *bug red six legs, red bug six legs*, or even *six legs red bug*. Each variation yields different results.

- When words *must* be found together, enclose them in double quotes, such as *"electric chair" setup*. A quoted search finds only web pages that list the words *electric chair* together and in that order.

Get Stuff from a Web Page

The text and pictures you see on a web page can easily be copied and saved to your PC. Well, actually, the information you see on the display *is* already on your computer: The text, images, and other stuff you see are sent from the Internet and stored temporarily while you're viewing that web page. Your desire may be to retain that information.

Saving an image from a web page

To save an image from a web page to your PC, right-click the image and choose Save Picture As from the pop-up menu. That command may be worded differently, depending on which web browser you use. Regardless, use the dialog box that appears to find a happy home for the picture on your hard drive.

- ✔ Nearly all images on the web are copyrighted. Although you can save a copy to your hard drive, you're not free to duplicate, sell, or distribute the image on 20,000 T-shirts at a rock concert without the consent of the copyright holder.

- ✔ To set the image as the Windows desktop wallpaper, choose Set As Background from the pop-up menu after right-clicking the image, if that command is available.

Copying text from a web page

You can copy text from a web page and save it for later or paste that text into another document or email message. Here's how:

1. **Drag to select the text you want to copy.**

2. **Press Ctrl + C to copy the text.**

3. **Start your word processor, email program, or what-have-you.**

4. **Paste the text into a document or an email message.**

   Press Ctrl+V on the keyboard or choose Edit ⇨ Paste from the menu.

5. **Print. Save. Whatever.**

   Use the proper commands to save or print or edit the text.

If you can't paste the text, you need to choose a program into which text can be pasted.

Sharing a web page

When you love a web page so much that you must share it with everyone you know, follow my friendly-yet-threatening words of advice: Share only the web page address.

There is no need to copy and paste the entire web page into an email message or on Facebook. Instead, just copy the web page's address from the address text box. Follow these steps:

1. **Click the mouse in the web browser's address bar.**
2. **Select the entire text — all of it.**

   With some web browsers, the keyboard shortcut to instantly select the current web page address is Ctrl+L. The F4 key might also work.
3. **Press Ctrl+C to copy the text.**
4. **Switch to whichever program you're using to share that address.**

   For example, switch to your email program or perhaps Facebook in another web browser tab or window.
5. **Press Ctrl+V to paste the web page address.**

Some web browsers may feature a Share button. Click that button to bring up a list of places to share the web page address. This trick may not work in all browsers, because the command called "Share" might do something else.

Email Messages

Few of the kids who first sent email never sent a real letter. Today, few kids who send text messages have ever bothered with email. Where once email was listed as the number-one reason to use the Internet, today it's considered passé. It's something your parents use. Based on that, I figure you have kids or grandkids, so email is still a concern.

Understanding email acronyms

Not all email is the same. To drive home that point, the nerds use different acronyms to describe a few popular forms of email:

POP or POP3: This is the traditional type of email, the kind supplied by an ISP. POP stands for Post Office Protocol. It has nothing to do with the government mail service.

IMAP: This is the most common type of email, usually found on the web. Also known as webmail, IMAP stands for Internet Message Access Protocol.

SMTP: This service is used in combination with POP and provided by a traditional ISP. POP picks up the email, but SMTP sends it. It stands for Simple Mail Transfer Protocol.

I'm glad you didn't read all those items. That's because all you need to know is that POP (or POP3) is an option to choose for traditional, ISP email. And IMAP is the option to choose for webmail.

- ✔ IMAP is easier for email software to configure because all you need is an email account name and password. The POP setup involves more variables and can be burdensomely painful to configure.

- ✔ The current trend is for even ISPs to offer a form of webmail.

Finding an email program

An email program was once the cornerstone of your PC's Internet software suite. If you used AOL back in the dark times, before the empire, your email program and web browser were one and the same. Today, using a specific email program isn't necessary; most users simply use the web browser to visit the host's webmail page and read their email that way.

If you're sorely stuck in the past, you can still use an email program. In fact, by doing so, you can collect all your email messages in one central location. That's why I use such a program.

- ✔ In Windows 10, the email app is named Mail. It comes with Windows 10.

- ✔ Windows 7 didn't really come with an email program.

- ✔ Older versions of Windows used a program called Windows Mail or Outlook Express.

- ✔ Microsoft Office comes with the Outlook program, which can be used for email. Be aware that Outlook works best on networks with an Exchange Server.

Other email programs are available on the Internet, such as Mozilla Thunderbird. Due to the popularity of webmail, these email programs aren't as common as they once were.

Upon starting an email program, you're asked to add your email accounts. Fill in the information to add all of your various email incarnations.

Once configured, the email program pulls all your messages into a central mailbox. I keep the program open all the time for that reason; I can check messages as they arrive — but don't tell anyone that, because sometimes I take a few days to write and send my reply.

Chapter 19

Hello, Other Gizmo

*E*ventually something will be attached to your PC. You can plug in, snap on, shove in, insert, or toss at your PC a variety of fun and fabulous things, from video cameras to tablets to music CDs. The PC is more than happy to say, "Hello!" And, of course, you pay a role in that conversation as well, even if you're unwilling to do so.

AutoPlay

Your PC doesn't just sit there when other gizmos bump into it. The PC reacts instantly, installing software to access the gizmo. If the gizmo contains media, Windows asks you what to do next. That prompt is called AutoPlay.

Dealing with another device

Connecting another gizmo to your PC is met by a flurry of activity. If the device, or its type, is familiar to your computer, predicted actions occur. For example, inserting a musical CD might result in that music playing automatically.

For devices unknown to your computer, Windows attempts to make nice. First, Windows installs special software to control the device. This software falls under the category of device driver or just *driver*. Once that software is installed, you can begin using the device, such as a digital camera or perhaps a cell phone.

For storage devices and other media, you see a notice appear, similar to what's shown in Figure 19-1. Click or tap the notice to view an AutoPlay list, also shown in the figure.

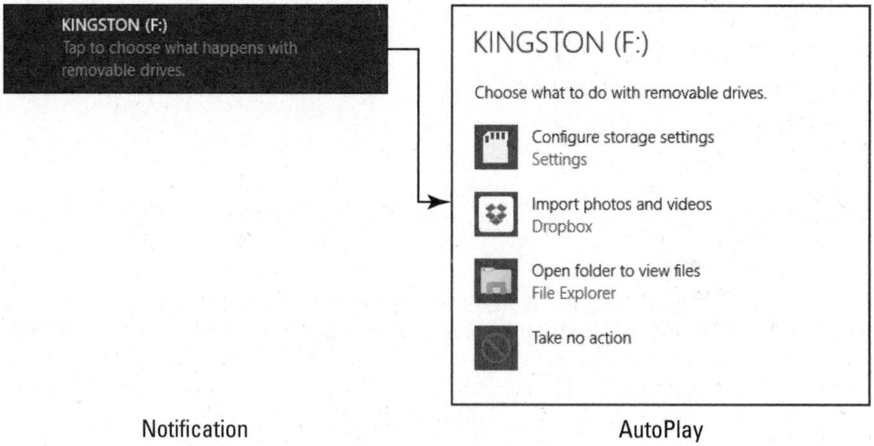

KINGSTON (F:)
Tap to choose what happens with removable drives.

KINGSTON (F:)

Choose what to do with removable drives.

Configure storage settings
Settings

Import photos and videos
Dropbox

Open folder to view files
File Explorer

Take no action

Figure 19-1:
Dealing with an external gizmo.

Notification   AutoPlay

In some versions of Windows, the AutoPlay list appears automatically, without the need to click a notification.

You use the AutoPlay list to instruct the PC how to handle the new device. Your choices are presented in a list, or you can choose to do nothing by dismissing the AutoPlay list or choosing the option Take No Action.

Here an example of how you can deal with another device:

1. **Attach the device to your PC.**

   Connect a digital camera, phone, tablet, thumb drive, or other item to one of the computer's USB ports. Or you can insert an optical disc.

2. **Click the notification to display the AutoPlay list.**

3. **Choose a command, such as Open Folder to View Files.**

   For most external storage, you could open a File Explorer window to manage its files. For a media card from a digital camera, you might choose the option to import the photos.

4. **Complete whatever action you chose in Step 3.**

   Some options, such as importing pictures or videos, require additional steps.

More specific examples of dealing with other devices are covered elsewhere in this chapter.

   ✔ The AutoPlay choice appears as a list in Windows 10 (and in Windows 8). In earlier versions of Windows, AutoPlay shows up as a dialog box.

   ✔ Windows may need to venture out to the Internet to hunt down drivers. If you see a prompt asking whether the PC can locate drivers on the Internet, click the Yes or OK button to proceed.

Manually summoning AutoPlay

If the AutoPlay list or dialog box doesn't appear, or if it vanishes before you made a choice, you can display it again. Follow these steps:

1. **Press Win+E to summon a File Explorer window.**

2. **In Windows 10, choose This PC from the list of locations on the left side of the window.**

   In older versions of Windows, the Computer window appears when you press the Win+E keyboard shortcut, which is where you need to be.

3. **Right-click the drive icon representing the media you inserted.**

4. **Choose Open AutoPlay from the pop-up menu.**

   The AutoPlay list or dialog box appears, from which you can select an option.

Other items on the pop-up menu may actually be shortcuts to some of the items shown in the AutoPlay list. For example: Open to view a File Explorer window and examine files; Install or Run program; Import Pictures and Videos; and so on. Choose that item in Step 4.

Setting AutoPlay options

AutoPlay may prompt you or it may not. Or maybe you get sick of the prompts and just want to plug in a gizmo and deal with it later. To make such adjustments, you need to visit the AutoPlay settings.

In Windows 10, follow these steps to adjust the AutoPlay settings:

1. Open the Settings app.

Press the Win+I keyboard shortcut.

2. Click the Devices button.

3. From the left side of the window, choose AutoPlay.

You see the three categories for removable devices on the right side of the window, illustrated in Figure 19-2.

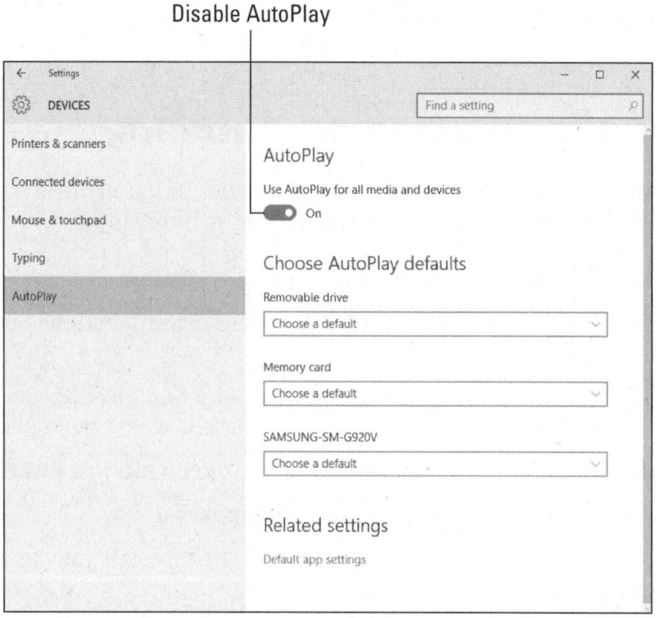

Disable AutoPlay

Figure 19-2:
AutoPlay
settings in
Windows 10.

In Windows 10, you can disable AutoPlay by clicking the toggle and setting it to the Off position (refer to Figure 19-2.) Otherwise, set your choices for the three categories; choose an item from the menu based on what you want the PC to do automatically when that type of media is inserted.

In Windows 7, obey these directions to configure AutoPlay options:

1. Open the Control Panel.

Choose Control Panel from the Start menu.

2. Click the heading Hardware and Sound.

3. **Click the AutoPlay heading.**

> You see a list of several — way too many — options for various items that can be inserted into your PC.

Three AutoPlay options are worth noting, and they apply to all AutoPlay conditions:

> **Choose a default.** This setting appears when no option is chosen. Windows prompts you every time you insert the media.
>
> **Take no action.** This option directs Windows not to do squat when you insert the media.
>
> **Ask me every time.** This setting confirms that Windows always displays an AutoPlay list or dialog box.

Choose one of these options to control how Windows reacts when inserting specific media.

Another thing you can do in the AutoPlay settings window is reset a previous "do this all the time" type of setting. For example, if music always plays when you insert a CD, change that setting to Take No Action or Ask Me Every Time.

Connect Something to Your PC

Generally, when you insert media into your PC, Windows splashes up an AutoPlay. Specifically, you need to know what to do with that media. That means more than moving files around. In fact, for some specific types of media, Windows is eager to do more than let you stare at a folder window.

Importing images

The pictures you take with a digital camera or phone are stored on a mass storage device in exactly the same confusing manner as information is stored on your computer. To move those images from the camera into the computer, follow these steps:

1. **Connect the digital camera or phone to the computer.**

> You can use the USB cable to connect the device, which is the most popular method. If the digital camera features removable storage, you can insert that media card into the computer's media drive.

2. **From the AutoPlay list, choose the option Import Photos and Video, which might also be titled Import Pictures and Video.**

    The images stored on the digital camera or phone are imported.

3. **Type a name for the album or some text that will help you later identify the images.**

    The name becomes the album name in the Photos app or the name of a folder in the Pictures folder, located in your account's home folder.

The app or program you use to view the pictures varies with the different versions of Windows. In Windows 10, the Photos app is in charge. Some versions of Windows may use the Windows Photo Gallery program.

✔ Other image-importing options might also appear on the AutoPlay list. These may be custom to an image management program installed on your PC. If you use such a program, choose it in Step 2.

✔ The name you assign the imported photos is important! That is how you will be able to locate the images later.

✔ Some versions of Windows prompt you to type tags for the imported images. These *tags* are single words or short phrases that help you locate the images. For example: *birthday*, *Disneyland*, *summer*, *chipped tooth*, and so on.

✔ Refer to the "AutoPlay" section, earlier in this chapter, for information on working the AutoPlay list or dialog box. See the earlier section "Manually summoning AutoPlay" for what to do when the AutoPlay list doesn't automatically appear.

✔ After you import the images, feel free to remove the originals from the digital camera's media. Erase or reformat the media card using the digital camera's control panel. That way, you have plenty of room to store a new batch of pictures.

Getting video into your PC

Video slithers into your PC from a digital video camera. It can come in live, such as from a *webcam,* or you can import images directly from a digital video camera's storage media.

The webcam: The simplest digital camera you can get for your PC is the desktop video camera, also referred to as a *webcam.* Many monitors come with a webcam built-in, found dead-center above the screen. Otherwise, you can obtain a USB webcam that clips to the top of the monitor.

Video camera: For more traditional moviemaking, you'll probably use some type of digital video camera. That device stores video on internal or removable storage, usually in the form of a media card. To transfer the video from the camera into the PC, you either connect the camera directly or plug its media card into a slot on the computer console.

Generally speaking, the process of importing video works similarly to the steps for importing photos, described in the preceding section. After the videos are imported, you see them displayed in a folder window. You can then mess with them as you please: Create a movie, send them as email attachments, or upload them to the Internet, for example.

- ✔ No, you cannot save or import video from a movie DVD. Those films are copyrighted, and copying them from the DVD is restricted.

- ✔ Webcams are normally used for video chat, though the software that comes with the camera lets you save snippets of video to the PC's mass storage system. It's not Hollywood, but it works.

- ✔ Video files are *huge!* They not only are the most complex type of files but also gobble up lotsa disk space.

Ripping music from a CD

The current trend is for music to be stored digitally on the Internet. You don't really buy a CD and then rip it into your PC, although you still can. If you have a CD handy, you can quickly copy its tracks from the PC's optical drive to long-term storage inside the computer. Follow these steps:

1. **Insert a musical CD into the PC's optical drive.**

   Windows Media Player automatically begins playing the CD. If not, open the Windows Media Player program.

2. **Click the Pause button if you don't want to listen to the CD now.**

   The Pause button is found at the bottom center of the window.

 3. **If necessary, click the Switch to Library button to display the Windows Media Player Library view.**

   Library view is shown in Figure 19-3.

4. **Click the Rip CD button on the toolbar.**

   Windows Media Player begins copying every track from the CD, storing it on the computer. You see the progress updated in the window.

Rip CD button

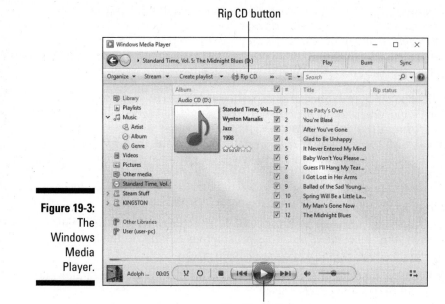

Figure 19-3:
The
Windows
Media
Player.

Play/Pause button

5. Press the Ctrl+J keyboard shortcut to eject the disc.

Repeat Steps 1 through 5 to rip another CD.

After the songs from the CD are ripped, they're available for your listening enjoyment at any time in the Windows Media Player library.

Chapter 20

Images Digital

*G*rabbing a digital image is about more than knowing that hexadecimal bytes 63 68 65 65 73 65 spell out *cheese*. You need a digital camera to snap new images, or you can use a scanner to convert your old paper images (or slides) into digital images. The end goal is to get those images into the computer. Then you can enjoy them, send them to friends, or print them out on paper.

✔ Refer to Chapter 16 for information on sharing digital photos.

✔ Chapter 19 covers extracting images from a digital camera, phone, or tablet.

Image Resolution

When you deal with digital images, the topic of resolution rears its hideous head. It has nothing to do with New Year's. You don't have to know Robert's Rules of Order to properly make an image resolution. And it has nothing to do with chemistry. Even so, resolution is an important part of taking and working with digital images.

Understanding resolution

Image resolution deals with two separate and equally confusing things.

At the most basic level, *resolution* measures the number of dots in an image, vertically and horizontally — although it might be horizontally and then vertically. See? Confusing.

Those dots are called pixels, which is a word created when the words *picture* and *element* get into a traffic accident: picture element = pictelem = pixel.

The number of pixels in the image determines the image's detail. An image with a low resolution — say, 320 by 255 pixels — may look good on a computer screen but lousy when enlarged to an 8-by-10 inch picture.

Obviously, more pixels in an image is better, but they tend to add up quickly. A huge, finely detailed image is great, but it occupies megabytes of storage. That's okay for images you plan to edit or print, but for sharing with Facebook or an online photo album, the high resolution is too much.

The second factor that plays into resolution is *dots per inch,* or *dpi.* This measurement goes in one direction only, so you see value such as 600 dpi, which might be what the PC's printer can produce. A monitor typically shows an image at 100 dpi.

The dpi is related to image resolution in that, depending on the dpi density, an image of a given resolution may look huge or tiny. For example, a 2400-by-1800-pixel image would appear 4 inches wide on a 600 dpi printer, but 24 inches wide on a 100 dpi computer monitor.

- Resolution determines the amount of detail in an image.

- The higher the resolution, the more information is available in the image, but the larger the image file.

- Higher resolutions are best for photo-editing or printing an image at a large size, say 8-by-10 inches.

- Lower resolutions are ideal for sharing on the Internet, where the computer screen has a lower resolution anyway.

 - Another aspect of a digital image is the number of colors available. When digital cameras first appeared, they could capture only a handful of colors. Today's cameras capture millions of colors, so the color density is no longer an issue — especially for amateur digital photographers.

Setting resolution

An image's resolution is set when that image is created. When using a digital camera, set the resolution first, then shoot. The same rule applies for using a phone or tablet: Set the resolution and then shoot the picture.

✔ Though you can reduce an image's resolution, you cannot effectively increase it. Pixels cannot be added where none existed before. Even good photo editing software manages to increase resolution only by making the image blurrier.

✔ Set the resolution based on the output device. If the output device is the Internet, low resolution (or lower) is fine. Set high resolution only when you plan to print the image or edit it later.

✔ When I go on vacation, I set a medium resolution for images. That way, I have detail if I need it later for printing, but the images aren't occupying too much storage space.

Digital Camera Tips

Here are some digital camera shooting tips, many of which were invented back in the 19th century. I'm not kidding! Using a film camera is the same as using a digital camera, only without the developer.

✔ Set the resolution before you shoot. See the preceding section.

✔ Hold the camera in a horizontal or landscape orientation — wide as opposed to vertical or portrait orientation. Use portrait orientation for taking pictures of tall things, like skyscrapers or dinosaurs up close, but for just about every other image, orient the camera horizontally.

✔ Keep the camera steady. The image will snap quickly, but if you're using one hand, the image might end up blurry. Use a tripod if you have one available.

✔ A digital camera's flash has three settings: On, Off, and Auto. On means the flash always works; Off sets the flash to never work; and Auto sets the flash for only low-light situations.

✔ Set the flash to On when taking a picture of a dark object in front of a light object, such as little Petunia holding a brown kitten while she's standing in front of an exploding munitions factory.

✔ Most digital cameras feature autofocus, so the camera automatically sets the focus to whatever it's pointed at. Manual focus can override this setting.

✔ If autofocus is set and you're taking a picture through a window, the focus is set on the window, not what's outside.

The Scanner

Your prehistoric paper photographs, slides, and daguerreotypes aren't barred from entering the digital realm. You can use a gizmo called a *scanner* to take those flat pictures and transform them into digital images, stored right inside your PC.

Introducing the scanner

A scanner works like a combination photocopier and digital camera. You place something flat, like a photograph, in the scanner — just like it's a photocopier. Press a button or run a program and the image is scanned and then beamed into the computer, ready for you to save, edit, or print.

Figure 20-1 illustrates a typical, standalone computer scanner. Your printer may also function as a scanner, if it's an all-in-one model. In that case, it looks more like a printer or copy machine than the lovely illustration shown in Figure 20-1.

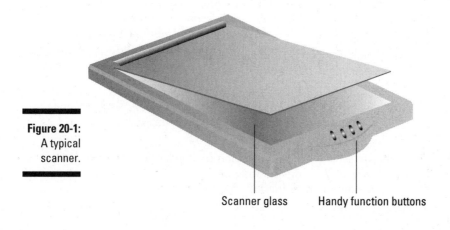

Figure 20-1: A typical scanner.

Scanner glass   Handy function buttons

Most scanners are thin (like the model in the picture), use the USB interface, and have handy function buttons that let you immediately scan, copy, fax, email, or read text from whatever item is placed on the scanner glass.

✔ The scanner must have something called a *transparency adapter* to be able to scan slides and film negatives.

✔ Those buttons on the scanner can be handy. For instance, I use the Copy button all the time to make quick copies. The only reservation I have about the buttons is that the tiny icons by the buttons are confusing; if need be, use a Sharpie and write down the button's function in English.

Scanning an image

Scanners come with special software that helps you scan an image and transfer it into the PC. The scanner might also come with some primitive form of image editing software. My advice is to use the software that came with the scanner, which is often your best choice.

If you don't have any scanner software, you can use Windows to scan an image. Follow these steps:

1. **Turn the scanner on, if necessary.**

   Some USB scanners are on all the time, so there's no power switch.

2. **Open the Control Panel.**

   In Windows 10, press Win+X and choose Control Panel from the menu. Otherwise, choose Control Panel from the Start menu.

3. **Beneath the heading Hardware and Sound, click the View Devices and Printers link.**

   You see a list of hardware attached to your computer. One of those items listed should be the scanner. If not, ensure that the scanner is plugged in and turned on.

4. **Open the scanner's icon in the Devices and Printers window.**

   Double-click the scanner's icon to open it.

   If you see the new New Scan window, similar to Figure 20-2, skip to Step 6. Otherwise:

5. **Click the Scan Photos or Documents link.**

   A New Scan window appears, looking similar to the one shown in Figure 20-2.

Set file type

Portion of image to scan

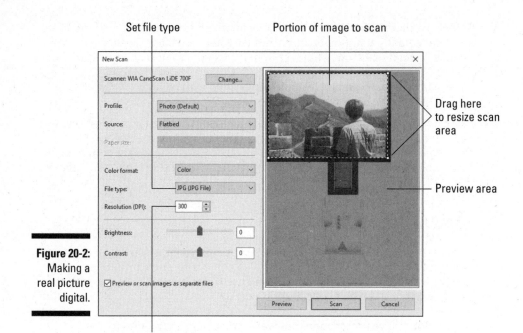

Drag here
to resize scan
area

Preview area

Figure 20-2:
Making a
real picture
digital.

Set resolution

6. **Place the material to be scanned into the scanner, just as though you were using a photocopier.**

7. **Click the Preview button.**

   The scanner warms up and shows you a preview of the pictures in the scanner, as shown in Figure 20-2.

8. **Adjust the scanning rectangle so that it encloses only the part of the image you want scanned.**

   Drag the corners of the rectangle by using the mouse to resize it. Only the portion of the preview inside the rectangle is scanned as an image and stored on the computer.

9. **Click the Scan button.**

   The scanner reads the image, turning it into digital information to be stored in your PC.

10. **Type a tag for the images.**

    The *tag* is a general description of all the images. Use short, descriptive text, such as *Summer 2015 Vacation, Meteorite Hit.*

Scanners that read documents

One of the scanner's software features is optical character recognition (OCR) software. This feature directs the scanner software to process text from an image, transforming it from graphical bits into editable text.

The OCR scan procedure works just like scanning an image: You place the document in the scanner and then run the OCR software to start a new scan. The OCR software "reads" the document being scanned and saves the information as a text file. You can then edit the text file, print it, and so on. It's not perfect, but using OCR software is better than having to sit and type text.

11. **Click the Import button.**

    The image is saved to the PC's storage system and displayed in a folder window.

12. **Close the folder window.**

13. **Repeat Steps 6 through 12 to scan additional images.**

After you become comfortable with scanning, you can add some extra steps. For example, you can set the image resolution, brightness, and contrast options, and even choose another source for scanning, such as the scanner's transparency adapter.

✔ When you have lots of images to scan, such as a lifetime of vacation slides, consider sending the slides to a scanning service. No, this option isn't cheap, but consider what your time is worth and how badly you yearn to digitize your pictures.

✔ Information about graphics file types and image resolution is found elsewhere in this chapter. Bone up on that stuff to help you make the best scans possible.

Picture Files

After an image makes the journey from a digital camera scanner into the computer, it becomes a *file* on your PC's mass storage system. Specifically, it becomes a *picture* file. Windows allows you to do quite a few things with picture files, and you should be familiar with a few picture-file concepts if you plan to get the most from your PC as the center of your digital photography universe.

- ✔ To best work with picture files, you need an image editing program. Your version of Windows may have come with such a program, such as Windows Photo Gallery. In Windows 10, you can obtain the Photo Editor from the Store app.

- ✔ Photoshop is the king of all image editing programs. It has a lite cousin named Photoshop Elements. For serious digital photographers, consider Adobe Lightroom, which works like a digital darkroom to do all sorts of fancy photo manipulation.

- ✔ See Chapter 15 for more information on the fun topic of computer files.

Storing pictures in Windows

Windows organizes your pictures into the Pictures folder. Any images you import or scan into the PC using Windows eventually end up in that location.

To view the Pictures folder, press the Win+E keyboard shortcut to summon the File Explore window. From the list of categories on the left side of the window, choose Pictures.

The Pictures folder window looks similar to what's shown in Figure 20-3, although that image shows a specific album. The folders represent albums. Icons represent images. In Windows 10, the Picture Tools Manage tab appears, which offers commands to rotate images, start a slide show, and use other handy tools — but no editing.

See the next section for what you can do with pictures in the Pictures folder or any other folder containing pictures both clean and dirty.

Viewing pictures in Windows

Images are viewed automatically in Windows simply by setting the proper icon size. The icon size is set using the folder's window.

In Windows 10, click the View tab. Use options in the Layout group to choose how icons are displayed. The Large Icons and Extra Large Icons settings are ideal for previewing pictures.

In Windows 7, use the View menu to choose Large Icons or Extra Large Icons.

Picture Tools Manage tab

Pictures folder   Pictures in the album/folder

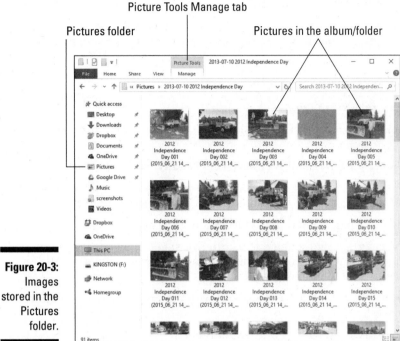

Figure 20-3:
Images
stored in the
Pictures
folder.

 You can also preview images simply by opening their icons. Unless you've installed specific image editing software, Windows displays the image in a preview app or program. You can press the left or right arrow keys on the keyboard to page through the images.

Printing your digital photos

You don't need a fancy photo management program to print out your PC's digital images. The File Explorer program deftly handles the job.

To print a swath of images, follow these steps:

1. **Press Win + E to open a File Explorer window.**

2. **Click the Pictures item on the left side of the window.**

3. **Navigate to the folder containing the images you want to print.**

4. **Select one or more images.**

   All the images print one after the other, so you don't have to repeat these steps unless you're printing images from different folders.

   Refer to Chapter 15 for image-selection rules.

5. **In Windows 10, click the Share tab.**

6. **Click the Print button.**

   You see the Print Pictures dialog box, similar to what's shown in Figure 20-4.

7. **Choose a printer and set paper size, quality, and paper type.**

   These items may already be set for you, but if you're printing on special photo paper, choose it from the Paper Type menu button.

8. **Choose a page layout option from the scrolling list.**

   You can print more than one picture per sheet, such as the four images shown in Figure 20-4. Each time you choose a different option, the preview area of the screen updates.

9. **Ensure that the printer is stocked with the proper paper and ready to print.**

   Refer to Chapter 11 for printer information.

10. **Click the Print button.**

    The images are squirted out on paper as fast as the printer can manage.

Printer settings   Choose page layout

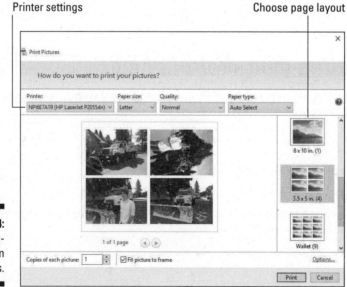

Figure 20-4:
Printing pictures in Windows.

Picture file formats

Just as different flavors of ice cream are available to delight your tongue, different flavors of picture files are available to frustrate your brain. Not that you should care: Your computer can open, display, and even edit just about any odd picture file format. The problem comes when you deal with someone who isn't as graphically flexible. In that case, knowing a modicum of information about the PC picture file formats is unavoidable.

A file format is known by its filename extension, which is the very last part of a filename. The filename extension doesn't show up in Windows unless you recajigger Windows to make it show up. See Chapter 15.

Here are the popular picture file formats:

JPG: Pronounced "jay peg," this image format is used in digital cameras, phones, tablets, and all over the Internet. JPG is also written as JPEG.

PNG: Pronounced "ping," this picture format is also quite common, also used in digital cameras, phones, and tablets.

TIFF: This picture file format is good for keeping detailed images, such as photos you want to edit or enlarge, or images you want to put in documents. It isn't a good format for email or the Internet because, unlike JPG and PNG, TIFF picture files are very large. TIFF can also be written TIF.

BMP: The Windows Bitmap file format is used primarily in Windows — specifically, in the Paint program. BMP files are too large for email or the Internet and, honestly, aren't good for storing digital photographs.

CRW: Camera Raw, or CRW, format is used in an uncompressed, unmodified image taken at high resolutions in certain high-end digital cameras. It's preferred by professional photographers and people who need the purest, rawest images possible. Unless you're doing professional work, you can avoid this format.

GIF: Pronounced "jif," this older, simple format is for storing simple color images. It was (and still is) popular on the Internet because the file size is small, but the files don't contain enough information to make them worthy of modern digital imaging.

Many, many other graphics file formats are out there, including those specific to various photo editing programs. My bottom line bit of advice is to keep and save all your digital images in either the JPG or PNG file format.

I highly recommend obtaining special photo paper upon which to print your memories. This paper absorbs ink far better than standard printer paper. It may also sport a fancy finish, glossy or satin.

Don't fret over buying paper at a specific size. Windows prints out multiple images on a standard sheet of paper. Use scissors or a paper cutter to trim the images to whatever size you need.

Changing picture file formats

Occasionally, you need to convert an image from one picture file type to another. For example, you may have been silly and saved scanned images as TIFF files. Although that file format has its purposes, and TIFF images are by no means shoddy, they're just *too freakin' huge* to send as email attachments. Instead, you're better off converting the TIFF image to PNG. Here's how I do it:

1. **Open the folder window containing the icon of the image file that you want to convert.**

2. **Right-click the image icon.**

3. **Choose Open With ⇨ Paint from the shortcut menu.**

   The picture opens in the Paint program. If it won't open, you need to use another image editing program to accomplish the same process outlined in Steps 4 through 7.

4. **Click the File tab.**

5. **Choose Save As, and then choose the new file format from the Save As submenu.**

   For example, choose Save As ⇨ PNG Picture to save the image in the PNG file format.

   Choosing the Other Formats option merely skips ahead, displaying the Save As dialog box. You can choose a format from the Save As Type drop-down list.

6. **If necessary, work the Save As dialog box to locate a folder in which to save the image, and optionally give the image a new filename.**

7. **Click the Save button to save the image in the new format.**

8. **Close the Paint program's window.**

You can always use a more sophisticated graphics program instead of Paint, such as Photoshop, to make the conversion. Specific image conversion programs and apps are also available.

Chapter 21

Electronic Entertainment

. . . .

In This Chapter

▶ Working with digital video

▶ Sharing a video on YouTube

▶ Viewing TV on the Internet

▶ Getting the Internet on your TV

▶ Enjoying music on the computer

▶ Using Windows Media Player

. . . .

*O*PC, entertain me! You don't really need to bark that order, because the PC — despite its disdain for all humans — is fully capable of providing you with electronic entertainment. It can sing. It can dance. It can put you in a trance. Well, maybe not a trance, but you can watch video, TV, and movies and listen to music by coercing the computer in many ways.

PC Movies

Are you old enough to remember watching home movies? The family would gather in a large room. The projector went clackity-clack as a silent, fuzzy, three-minute color film danced upon a sheet hung on the wall. Then you'd watch it run backward, and everyone would laugh. Many Hollywood producers owe their professional careers to that simple concept.

Today, home movies are shot using digital video cameras, cell phones, or tablets. Sound is recorded. The images are clear. And the movies last as long as you can tolerate sitting in the dark, watching your family's vacation antics, forward or backward.

Video file formats

Video is stored on your computer as a file, just like all the other stuff stored on your computer. Similar to other media files (pictures and sound), the computer universe hosts a whole slate of video file formats, all depending on what gizmo recorded the video, which program edited it, which type of compression is being used, and other tedious details. Generally speaking, the following types of video files are popular in the computer world:

MOV: The MOV file, used by Apple's QuickTime player, can store not only videos but also audio information. MOV is quite popular on the Internet, although you need to obtain a free copy of QuickTime to view or hear MOV files on your PC: `www.apple.com/quicktime`.

MPEG: The Motion Pictures Experts Group is a general compression format for both video and audio.

WMV: The Windows Media Video format is the most popular video format used in Windows and is pretty common on the Internet as well.

Other formats exist, but these are the most common. Also see Chapter 15 for information on the filename extension, which is how you identify file types in Windows.

Storing video in Windows

A folder exists in the PC's mass storage system for video. In your account's home folder, you'll find the Videos folder, also called My Videos in some versions of Windows. That's the location where any videos you add to the computer are saved automatically. Here's how to display the contents of that folder:

1. **Press Win+E to summon a File Explorer window.**

2. **In the list of folders on the left side of the window, choose Videos.**

   The folder lists video files available on your computer's storage system. The files are shown as icons, and even more video files may be available in folders within the main Video folder.

Windows may come with sample videos. If not, don't fret if the folder is empty; you can easily create your own videos. The most common way is by importing a video from a digital camera. See Chapter 19.

Viewing a video

To view a video, double-click its icon. A capable program starts and displays the video, complete with onscreen controls.

In Windows 10, the Movies & TV app opens and plays the video.

In Windows 8, you're hosed. Windows 8 lacks a video viewer. This is but one of hundreds of reasons why so many people detested Windows 8.

In older versions of Windows, the Windows Media Player opens and plays the video.

✔ You can also view a video by inserting a movie DVD into your PC's optical drive. A program starts that plays the DVD on the computer screen, just as though you were watching it on TV.

✔ Other video viewing programs are available, including Apple's popular QuickTime. Go to http://quicktime.apple.com.

About that codec thing

When you deal with media on a computer, such as audio or video stored in a file, you often encounter the word *codec*. It's a combination of two words — *compressor* and *decompressor*. A codec works with compressed information stored in a media file so that you can be entertained or enlightened.

A variety of codecs are used to encode and decode media information. The problem with the variety is that your PC doesn't come with all the codecs needed for every type of media file. So, when you go to view a video, you may see a message saying that a codec is unavailable or prompting you to visit a certain web page to download a codec. And that's where you can get into trouble.

My best advice is to be cautious about installing codecs. Often, the bad guys disguise a malevolent program as a codec required to view a media file — typically, pornography. Installing that false codec is detrimental to your PC.

I'm not saying that all codecs are evil. Many are good and are required in order to view certain media files. But ensure that you obtain codecs only from reliable sources, such as brand-name websites or from Microsoft directly.

Uploading a video to YouTube

You can invite the world into your den and have everyone sit there, smelly feet and everything, and watch your movies on your computer screen. Or — and this is a better choice — share that video on YouTube. That way, the world can stink up the web with their smelly feet, and you can continue to use the computer unmolested.

To upload a video to YouTube, follow these steps:

1. **Visit www.youtube.com.**

2. **Sign in to your Google account.**

   Click the Sign In button or link. If the link isn't there, check the web page to see whether you're already signed in. And if you don't have a Google account, you can create one: Click Sign In, and then click Create Account.

3. **Click the Upload button.**

   The Upload screen appears.

4. **Choose to set whether the video is public or private.**

   I recommend choosing Private for now. You can change the setting to Public later.

5. **Click the screen to use a Browse dialog box to locate the videos.**

   Or you can open a folder window and drag a Video icon into the upload portion of the web page.

6. **Edit video settings.**

   As the video uploads and processes, you can edit more information — video name, description, tags — and change your mind about public and private settings.

7. **Click the Done button.**

   Some videos may continue to process, but short videos are done right away.

Videos are available in your channel. To view your channel, go to YouTube's main page and choose My Channel from the navigation panel on the left side of the window.

- ✔ Only you can view private videos. Their links can't be shared with anyone.

- ✔ A public video is available for anyone to view on YouTube.

✔ An unlisted video is available for anyone to view, but only when you send them an invitation.

✔ To reset a video from Private to Public, view the video: Locate it in your YouTube channel. Click the Pencil (edit) icon and change the setting from Private to Public.

✔ Google eventually sends you an email when your video has been processed and is finally ready for viewing and sharing.

Sharing your videos

It's easy to share your videos with others using YouTube. Basically, you simply send your pals a web page link to your video. Because the link consists only of text, the email message doesn't take an eternity to send and receive, nor is there any worry about malware-infected file attachments. The process works like this:

1. **Visit your account on YouTube, at `www.youtube.com/my_videos`.**

   You may have to log in first, but eventually you see a list of all your uploaded videos displayed on the web page.

2. **Right-click the title (link) of the video you want to share.**

3. **Choose the Copy Shortcut command from the pop-up menu.**

   The command might be titled Copy Link Address or Copy Link Location.

4. **Start a new email message to your pal.**

5. **Press Ctrl+V to paste the YouTube video link into your email message.**

YouTube videos all have a similar-looking link or URL. For example: `www.youtube.com/watch?v=-QIQhoahbQ8`

That's it! Clicking that link is how others can view your video on the Internet.

When you view a video on YouTube, you see sharing options listed on the web page. For example, click the Facebook button to quickly share a video on Facebook. The Embed option is used to stick the video into a blog or another web page.

Your PC Is a TV

Thanks to high-speed Internet, watching TV on your computer is no longer considered unholy. It used to be that to accomplish such a thing, you needed a hardware TV tuner jammed inside your computer. That's still possible, though it's more common these days to use the Internet to keep track of your favorite programs.

Getting a TV tuner

If it's been on your bucket list to use your PC as a DVR, or digital video recorder, you can gleefully cross off that item. Computers have been able to host television for quite some time. The procedure involves buying TV tuner hardware and then using DVR software to watch and even record your favorite TV shows.

Two types of TV tuners are available: internal and external. The internal cards are more sophisticated but require that you endure the prospect of opening the computer's case to install them. A saner alternative is the USB TV tuner, which hangs out the back of your PC like a limp noodle. In both cases, you connect the tuner to a TV cable, just as you would connect the TV cable to a TV set.

For DVR software, you can use the Windows Media Player Center program to watch and record TV. In Windows 10, the Movies and TV app can also be used to view TV over a USB tuner.

✔ Using the TV tuner with your PC doesn't add to the cost of your cable or satellite subscription any more than adding a second TV in the house would.

✔ The DVR software that comes with the TV tuner may also allow you to burn DVDs of your favorite shows. The DVD storage option is better than keeping video long-term on your computer. That's because:

✔ Recording television consumes a *ton* of storage space. The more you record, the more you should review the video library (by using the DVR software) and purge older programs. Otherwise, your PC runs out of mass storage space faster than a politician runs out of excuses.

Watching Internet TV

Broadcast TV is entering its final decade. In fact, my kids use their cable TV subscriptions only for Internet access. I will too, someday. That's because more and more people are relying on the Internet to deliver their video entertainment.

Here are three sources I offer as consideration for your PC TV entertainment:

- ✔ YouTube
- ✔ Netflix
- ✔ Hulu

More options exist, but these — the big three — are excellent places to get started.

YouTube is perhaps the largest video repository on the planet. The idea is to "broadcast yourself," so you'll find lots of homemade and amateur content on YouTube. Some of it is very good and quite entertaining. But true to Sturgeon's law, 90 percent of it is crap. Visit YouTube at `www.youtube.com`.

Netflix is the premiere online video content-delivery system. It's stocked full of TV shows, movies, documentaries, foreign films, and other professionally produced content. You need a subscription, which is presently under $10 a month, and then you can watch that content as much or as little as you like. Sign up for Netflix at `http://signup.netflix.com`.

Hulu is a fine example of a useful website where the name is completely unrelated to the content. In this case, the content consists of TV shows and older movies, all of which are free to watch. Well, yes, they do have commercials, but so does regular TV, and the point of this section is to watch TV on your PC. You can visit Hulu at `www.hulu.com`.

Your TV Is a PC

This section has nothing to do with computers. That is, unless you consider the plethora of modern digital devices to be computers. Common items such as your car, game consoles, portable music players, and Optimus Prime all feature full-blown computers in their gizzards. One of the newest kids on the block is the high-definition television, or HDTV — specifically, an *Internet-ready* HDTV.

The Internet-ready HDTV is essentially a PC unimpaired by the burden of Microsoft Windows. In addition to receiving high-definition TV signals, an Internet-ready HDTV often comes with Internet access and a complete software suite. That list often includes Netflix, Hulu Plus, YouTube, a web browser, Skype (for online chat), Facebook, Twitter, and other popular Internet programs and digital content providers.

Like other network gizmos, Internet-ready HDTV connects to the computer network, either by wire or wirelessly. The purpose of the connection is to access the Internet and give you all that nifty downloaded content. As a bonus, the Internet-ready HDTV may also act as a media station, letting you view pictures and videos, as well as listen to music, stored on other network computers and devices.

Will the PC be jealous? No. Computers are still far more flexible than devices designed for a specific purpose, such as HDTVs. In fact, there's little you can do with an HDTV that you can't already do on your PC, as described elsewhere in this chapter.

- ✔ Unless you have a wired network connection everywhere that there's an Internet-ready TV, you need to use wireless networking to connect them. See Chapter 17.

- ✔ If your HDTV doesn't offer an Internet connection or a software suite, you can purchase an Internet TV set-top box that provides the same features. Apple manufactures Apple TV for that purpose. Google provides a set-top Internet box called the Nexus Player. And Amazon offers the Fire TV Stick.

- ✔ The biggest problem with Internet-ready HDTV is in the human interface. A TV remote — even one with upward of 60 buttons — is no substitute for a mouse or computer keyboard.

Your PC Is Your Stereo

Who calls it a stereo any more? Back in the olden days, your home would have a radio. Then the radio was combined with the record player to form a stereo system. On the fancier models, you'd find an 8-track player. It was furniture! Today, your PC provides you with a source for musical entertainment. I do confess, however, that mobile devices — the phone and tablet — are rapidly eclipsing the computer in that category.

Enjoying music from the stream

The strategy for digital music today is not to bother with ripping CDs and storing music on your computer. Instead, you buy music online, and that music stays online. To listen, you visit a website and play the music.

Sources for online music include

> **Amazon Prime Music:** `www.amazon.com/PrimeMusic`
>
> **Apple Music:** `www.apple.com/music`
>
> **Google Play Music:** `play.google.com/music`

Other sources are available as well, although I can guess you may already have an account at one of the services in this list.

Beyond buying music, Internet radio stations are available. You don't own the music, but you can listen — and for a fee you can listen without commercial interruption.

Although you can't get specific software to listen to Internet radio music, you can pop open your favorite web browser and tune into web pages abundant with songs and sounds from around the world. Here is a sampling of websites you can browse for your listening enjoyment:

> **iHeart Radio:** `www.iheart.com`
>
> **Pandora Internet Radio:** `www.pandora.com`
>
> **Slacker Personal Radio:** `www.slacker.com`
>
> **Tune-In radio:** `tunein.com`

Other services are available as well, including websites that deliver up specific music genres, such as a jazz or classical.

- ✔ Windows 10 comes with the Groove music app, which can also be used to buy and listen to streaming music.

- ✔ One major advantage of storing music online is that the audio files don't occupy storage space on your computer. Another advantage is that your music is available anywhere and on any device that has Internet access.

- ✔ Some online music sources also provide subscription services. For a flat fee, you can listen to any music in the online library. So you never have to purchase an individual song or album.

- ✔ The topic of *ripping* a CD, which refers to copying music from that media to your PC's mass storage system, is covered in Chapter 19.

Running Windows Media Player

The musical capital of Europe is Vienna. The musical capital of a Windows computer is a program called Windows Media Player. The program still lingers in Windows 10, even though Microsoft would appreciate your subscription to its online music service. For ripping CDs and listening to that music, however, Windows Media Player is still the king.

To start Windows Media Player, follow these steps:

1. **Click the Start button.**

2. **Click the All Apps button or All Programs button.**

3. **Click Windows Media Player in the list.**

   You have to scroll through the list to find it.

If you rip CDs, as covered in Chapter 19, you see your CD collection in the Windows Media Player window. Choose the Music category from the left side of the window to explore your digital jukebox. Click a song to select it. Click the big Play button at the bottom of the screen to start listening.

- Windows Media Player may start automatically when you insert a music CD into your PC.

- Other musical jukebox programs are available, including Apple's iTunes. These programs aren't as popular as they once were, mostly because the value for computer companies today lies in online subscriptions, not in playing music you already own.

Part V
Security and Maintenance

In this part . . .

- ✔ Beef up your PC with security measures
- ✔ Create a backup of your digital life
- ✔ Maintain and troubleshoot your computer

Chapter 22

System Security

I wish it weren't so, but to be a good PC user today, you must accept responsibility for system security. Nasty programs prowl the ether, looking for humble, innocent electronics to infect. Worse, naive users welcome vile software into the computer, despite the system's digital protestations. What follows is unbound woe, gnashing of teeth, and eternal despair. You can avoid that hellish state by following a few simple rules for keeping your PC safe.

Tools to Fight the Bad Guys

Computer bad guys have a host of names as rich and colorful as any comic book supervillain. Knowing those names is important only when you also know the names of the superheroes who help you thwart the plans of the evil ones. Windows has many such superheroes:

Windows Firewall: A firewall helps to close the holes into which Internet nasties can ooze, gaining access to your PC. Plug them or perish!

Windows Defender: The Windows Defender program scans for and removes a clutch of bad guys, especially insidious start-up programs and spyware.

UAC warnings: Whenever Windows suspects something could go awry, you see a blistering onscreen message. Pay attention! Something foul may be afoot.

Privacy settings: Windows 10 offers options that control access to sensitive PC hardware, such as the microphone and webcam.

Windows Update: Keeping your PC's software up-to-date is important because the bad guys like a target that stands still.

Backup: To keep your stuff safe, I recommend that you back it up. The backup procedure creates a safety copy of all files on your PC so that if disaster strikes — naturally created or motivated by evil — you can recover your stuff.

PC supervillain roundup

As with most computer jargon, malicious software — or *malware* — is named in either a highly technical or extremely silly manner. Neither name helps: The technical name is confusing, and the silly name is clever for only people who would otherwise understand the technical names. Here's your handy guide:

✔ **Phishing:** Pronounced "fishing," this term applies to a web page or an email designed to fool you into thinking that it's something else, such as your bank's web page. The idea is to *fish* for information, such as account numbers and passwords. The web page or email tricks you into providing that information because it looks legitimate. It isn't.

✔ **Hijacking:** You want to visit one web page, but you're taken to another. Or you discover that the home page you see when you start the web browser is something unexpected. Perhaps the Google search page is now something else, covered with advertising. This redirection is known as *hijacking*.

✔ **Spyware:** A rather broad category, *spyware* refers to a program that monitors, or spies on, what you do on the Internet. The reasoning is advertising: By knowing where you go and what you do on the Internet, information obtained about you can be sold to advertisers who then target ads your way.

✔ **Trojan:** A program is labeled a *Trojan* (horse) whenever it claims to do one thing but does another. For example, a common Trojan is a special screen saver that saves the screen but also uses your PC on the Internet to relay pornographic images.

✔ **Virus:** A *virus* is a nasty program that resides in your PC without your knowledge. The program may be triggered at any time, taking over the computer, redirecting Internet traffic, sending a flood of spam messages, or doing any of a number of nasty and inconvenient things.

✔ **Worm:** A *worm* is simply a virus that replicates itself, by sending out copies to other folks on your email list, for example.

Most of these tools are covered in this chapter. Backup is a big deal, so it's covered as the sole topic of Chapter 23.

You can avoid many nasty programs by using common sense. In fact, the most successful computer malware has propagated simply because of human nature. It's that *human engineering* the bad guys count on, or your ability to be tricked into doing something you wouldn't do otherwise, such as opening a questionable email attachment or clicking a web page link because you're fooled into thinking it's okay.

Take Action Against the Barbarian Hoard

In ancient times, when the bad guys would attack, they'd just ride into the village and take what they wanted. Then the villagers came upon the idea of building a wall. For centuries, walls were a common feature of any city. On your PC, the wall is known by many names.

Finding the Action Center

The headquarters for security issues in Windows is a location called the Action Center. Alas, Windows 10 calls its notification list the "Action Center," so the name is confusing. Still, Windows 10 also retains the traditional and security-specific Action Center, which is illustrated in Figure 22-1.

The Action Center window provides a quick summary of your PC's current security state. High-priority items are flagged in red in the window, and lower-priority items are flagged in orange. Some areas may be hidden, which means no issues are pending; click the chevron to display those areas, as illustrated in Figure 22-1.

To open the Action Center, follow these steps:

1. **Open the Control Panel.**

   In Windows 10, right-click in the lower left corner of the screen and choose Control Panel from the super-secret pop-up menu. In Windows 7, choose Control Panel from the Start menu.

2. **Below the System and Security heading, click the link Review Your Computer's Status.**

   Behold the Action Center window.

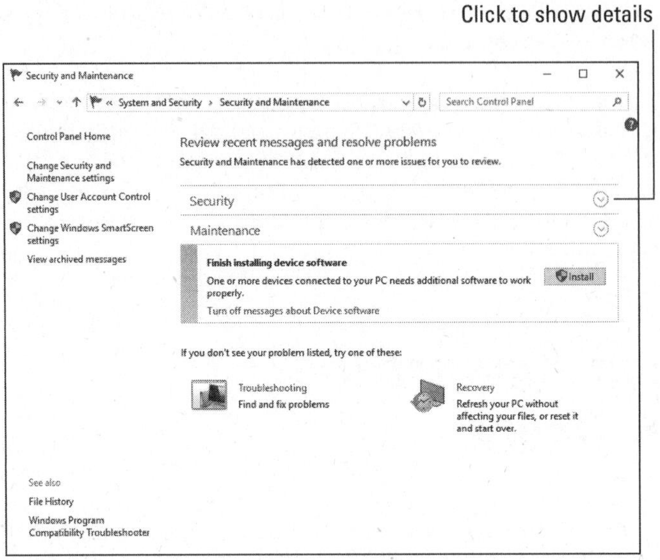

Click to show details

Figure 22-1:
The Action
Center.

Generally speaking, follow the advice in the window. Click a button to activate a feature or run necessary protection.

- ✔ In Windows 7, you can quickly review your PC's security status by clicking the Action Center notification icon on the taskbar, shown in the margin.

- ✔ In Windows 10, press the Win+A keyboard shortcut to display the notification-laden Action Center. This slide-in window is not the same as the Action Center shown in Figure 22-1.

Setting up the Windows Firewall

In construction, a *firewall* slows the advance of a fire. It's created from special slow-burning material and rated in *hours*. For example, a three-hour firewall takes, theoretically, three hours to burn through — and that helps protect a building from burning down before the fire department shows up.

On a computer with an Internet connection, a *firewall* is designed to restrict Internet access, primarily to keep uninvited guests from getting into — or out of — the computer. The firewall effectively plugs holes left open from when the Internet was originally designed.

Windows comes with a firewall named, coincidentally, Windows Firewall. It's accessed from the Control Panel. Follow these steps:

1. **Open the Control Panel.**

   Refer to Step 1 in the preceding section for details on finding the Control Panel.

2. **Click the System and Security heading.**

3. **Click the Windows Firewall heading.**

   The Windows Firewall window appears, as shown in Figure 22-2.

Firewall control

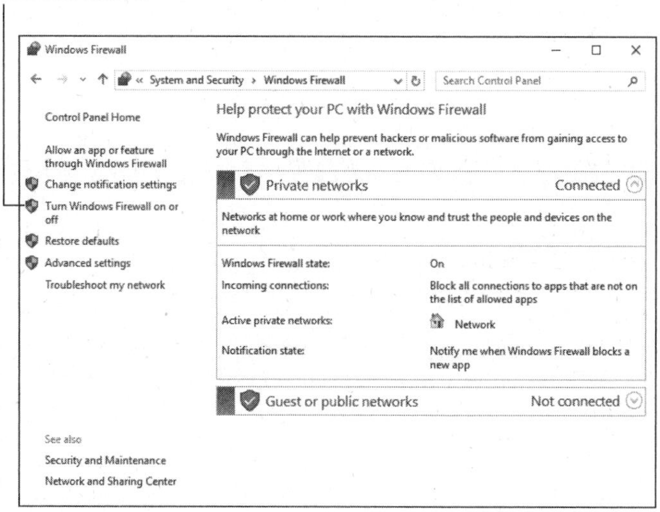

Figure 22-2:
The
Windows
Firewall
window.

As far as you're concerned, Windows Firewall has only two settings: on and off. To change the setting, click the Turn Windows Firewall On or Off link on the left side of the Windows Firewall window (refer to Figure 22-2).

Once activated — and it should be activated — the Windows Firewall goes to work. When unwanted access is detected, either to or from the Internet, you see a pop-up window alerting you to the intrusion, such as the one shown in Figure 22-3. At that point, you can choose to allow access by the named program by clicking the Allow Access button. If you want to continue blocking the program, just click Cancel.

In Figure 22-3, the Skype program desires Internet access. Because I started that program, the request is legitimate and I click the Allow Access button. If, on the other hand, I didn't recognize the program name or the warning showed up while I wasn't running a specific program, I click the Cancel button, and the firewall thwarts the program's attempted access.

Program attempting access

Figure 22-3:
Windows
Firewall in
action.

Protecting the PC with Windows Defender

Windows Defender is a single name given to a slate of tools used to guard your PC against snooping spyware, irritating start-up programs, and even viruses. Therefore, the *defender* name is apt.

Windows Defender program runs automatically. You're alerted to any problems in the Action Center window or via a taskbar notification.

To specifically visit the Windows Defender program window, follow these steps:

1. **Press the Windows key to pop up the Start menu.**

2. **Type** Defender**.**

   As you type, matching programs appear in a list. Before you reach the second *D* in Defender, the top item in the list should be the Windows Defender program.

3. **Click the Windows Defender item on the Start menu.**

Like most antivirus and antispyware programs, Windows Defender features two modes of protection.

The first mode is a passive scan: As you open files or download items from the Internet, Windows Defender checks for signs of mischief. If a vile file is found, you're alerted and the file can be squished like a bug.

Windows Defender's second mode of operation is an active scan. In the Windows Defender program, choose a scan option: Quick, Full, or Custom. Click the Scan Now button to direct the program to rifle through all your PC's files and look for anything stinky.

When a suspicious file is located, you're given the opportunity to eliminate it or quarantine it. I recommend the quarantine. Files sent to quarantine are safely removed from your PC's file system, stored in a location where they can do no harm. Continue to use your PC for a while to ensure that everything works. If so, you can return to Windows Defender and kill off the quarantined files. If not, you can restore the quarantined files, because sometimes — as with all antivirus software — false positives occur.

✔ Windows Defender must be updated frequently to keep pace with the rapidly expanding world of PC malware. See the later section "The Latest Version."

✔ It's okay to run other, more aggressive PC security software in addition to Windows Defender.

✔ Windows Defender may not be successful in removing all infections. In fact, if you accidentally allowed malware into your PC, it cannot be removed. This happens frequently when you download a program and forget to deselect the "bonus programs" box. Such software may require professional assistance for removal. Turn to a local computer dealer or computer consultant for help.

Paying attention to the UAC warnings

In its efforts to make Windows a more secure operating system, Microsoft has presented you (the human) with something called the UAC, or User Account Control. It displays various warning dialog boxes and pop-up windows whenever you attempt to change something in Windows, such as a computer setting or option, or when you try to download software from the Internet. A typical UAC is shown in Figure 22-4.

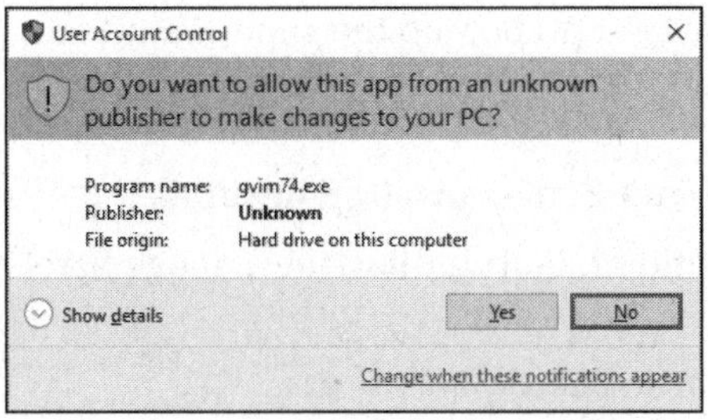

Figure 22-4:
A typical
UAC.

User Account Control	×

Do you want to allow this app from an unknown publisher to make changes to your PC?

Program name: gvim74.exe
Publisher: **Unknown**
File origin: Hard drive on this computer

⌄ Show details   Yes   No

Change when these notifications appear

The UACs are to be expected whenever you see a link or button flagged with the UAC Shield icon, shown in the margin. It's your clue that a UAC warning will appear. If the action is expected, click the Continue button or, if prompted, type the administrator's password and then click the OK button.

If you see a UAC warning when you're not expecting one, cancel it: Click the No or Cancel button. For example, when you're on the Internet and you see a UAC warning about installing software or changing your home page, click Cancel.

System Privacy Settings

Perhaps the most common PC privacy question I'm asked is how to assign individual passwords to a file. The eagerly awaited yet completely disappointing answer is that you can't. You can, however, apply a password to your user account in Windows, which is what I strongly recommend.

Beyond your account password, it's good to keep a lock on things while you use your computer. It's also good to ensure that your computer, no matter its degree of beneficence, understands your desire for privacy.

Setting the screen saver lock

A *screen saver* is an image or animation that appears on the monitor after a given period of inactivity. After your computer sits there, lonely and feeling ignored, for 30 minutes or whatever, a pleasant image or animation appears on the monitor. It's jocular, but it can play a role in PC privacy when you direct Windows to lock the PC when the screen saver starts.

To set up a screen saver, or to confirm that a lock is in place, obey these steps:

1. **Open the Control Panel.**

   In Windows 10, press Win+X to pop up the super-secret menu, and then choose Control Panel. In Windows 7, choose Control Panel from the Start menu.

2. **Click the Appearance and Personalization heading.**

3. **Under the Personalization heading, click the Change Screen Saver link.**

   The Screen Saver Settings dialog box appears.

4. **Choose a screen saver from the Screen Saver button menu.**

5. **Set the Wait timeout value.**

   The screen saver you choose (refer to Step 4) takes over the display when you don't touch the keyboard or move the mouse for the given interval.

6. **Place a check mark by the option On Resume, Display Logon Screen.**

   That's the security setting you want.

7. **Click the OK button.**

When the screen saver kicks in — which means that you may be away from your computer or sneaking in a nap — you need to know your account password to regain access: Wiggle the mouse or tap a key on the keyboard to dismiss the screen saver. Type your account password, and the PC is unlocked.

- ✔ Beware of downloading screen savers from the Internet. Although some are legitimate, most are invasive ads or programs that are impossible to uninstall or remove. If you download this type of screen saver, you're pretty much stuck with it. Be careful!

- ✔ You may never see the screen saver, especially if you're using the PC's power management system to put the monitor to sleep. See Chapter 24 for more information.

- ✔ Screen savers actually have a serious history. When the old CRT (glass) monitors were popular, images could *burn* into the screen's phosphor, rendering the monitor less than desirable. The screen saver would kick in to literally save the screen from the perils of phosphor burn-in. Today, it remains as an amusement, but also a form of security.

Reviewing Windows 10 privacy options

The Windows 10 Settings app features a long list of privacy settings. These allow you to control which programs or apps have access to specific PC features as well as how your personal information is shared between apps.

To view the slate of privacy settings, heed these directions:

1. **Press Win+I to open the Settings app.**

2. **Click the big and obvious Privacy button.**

In the Settings app, categories appear on the left side of the window, and individual settings appear on the right. For Privacy, the top category is General, and it lists several settings on the right, each of which is an on-off toggle.

If privacy is a concern to you, my advice is to deactivate every setting in all the privacy categories: Choose each category in turn, and then reset any On toggles to the Off position.

For some settings, you may see a prompt when a program or an app attempts to access a feature you've flagged as private. For example, in Chapter 12 I discuss some Windows apps that use the microphone. Only by enabling the microphone hardware privacy setting can those apps actually use the PC's microphone.

The Latest Version

It's a common saying in the computer industry that software is never done. In fact, if it weren't for management, programmers wouldn't stop coding. Even when they do finish, things called bugs need to be fixed, and people demand new features, which are added. The result is the *software update,* or the more drastic *software upgrade.*

Updating and upgrading

It's easy to confuse the terms *update* and *upgrade,* which leads me to suspect that Microsoft invented them. These terms are not, however, interchangeable.

An *update* is a gradual change or tiny improvement to software. It might also be called a *patch.* An update may fix a bug or problem, or it can fine-tune some features. Updates are usually free.

Upgrades are complete revisions of programs. An upgrade presents a new release of the software, along with a new version number. For example, the latest version of Microsoft Office is an upgrade, not an update. Upgrades cost money, although the Windows 10 upgrade was offered for free to existing Windows 7 and Windows 8 users.

My advice: Update frequently. If the manufacturer offers a patch or a fix, install it as recommended. On the other hand, upgrades are necessary only when you desperately need the new features or modifications or when the upgrade addresses security issues.

> ✔ Updates are distributed by the manufacturer. Sometimes you're alerted in the program itself, although you may receive an email notice if you've registered the program.

✔ Software updates and upgrades are downloaded over the Internet, installed just like software you download from the Internet.

✔ If you're prompted with a UAC to accept the upgrade, click the Yes button or OK button. Even so, you must initiate the upgrade process in some way. For example, don't expect an update to arrive as an email attachment.

✔ Here's something else to keep in mind: If you're still using DoodleWriter 4.2 and everybody else is using DoodleWriter 6.1, you may have difficulty exchanging documents. After a while, newer versions of programs become incompatible with their older models. If so, you need to upgrade.

✔ You might discover that your software upgrade is incompatible with older versions of Windows. If so, you must upgrade Windows to use the new program.

✔ In an office setting, everybody should be using the same software version. Everybody doesn't have to be using the *latest* version, just the *same* version.

Updating Windows

I highly recommend that you keep your PC's operating system updated. This task requires regular communications between your PC and the Microsoft mother ship. No need to fret: The scheduling happens automatically. If any new updates, or patches, are needed, they're automatically installed on your computer. You need to do nothing — except confirm that the Windows Update service is active and running.

To confirm the status of Windows Update in Windows 10, follow these steps:

1. **Open the Settings app.**

   Press Win+I.

2. **Click the Update and Security button.**

3. **Ensure that Windows Update is chosen from the items listed on the left side of the window.**

   If any updates are pending, you see them listed on the right side of the screen. Click the Install Now button to apply the updates. Or continue with these steps to check the Windows Update status:

4. **Click the Advanced Options link.**

   The Advanced Options screen is where you choose how updates are installed.

5. **If you don't mind Windows restarting your PC to install an update, choose Automatic from the button menu; otherwise, choose Notify to Schedule Restarts.**

   I prefer the second option, Notify to Schedule Restarts, which lets me control when an update is installed.

In Windows 7, follow these steps to configure or check the status of Windows Update:

1. **Open the Control Panel.**

2. **Click the System and Security heading.**

3. **Below the Windows Update heading, click the link Turn Automatic Updating On or Off.**

   The Change Settings window appears.

4. **Below the Important Updates heading, choose Download Updates But Let Me Choose Whether to Install Them from the menu button.**

   The other acceptable setting is titled Install Updates Automatically. If you choose that setting, however, Windows may restart your PC after downloading an update.

Depending on how you've directed Windows to keep itself updated, you may be prompted to install an update or the updates may happen automatically. If you're prompted, simply restart your PC and the updates are installed. Or you may discover that your computer restarts automatically, especially if you leave it on all night. Either way, keeping Windows up-to-date is important.

Chapter 23

That All-Important Safety Copy

* *

In This Chapter

▶ Restoring modified files

▶ Creating a backup copy

▶ Understanding compressed folders

▶ Extracting files from a compressed folder

▶ Installing software from a Zip file

* *

It's sad, but I hear occasionally about someone who regrets losing all their vacation photos because the computer crashed. They seem to accept this fate as an inevitable part of owning a computer. It's frustrating to me, because digital material can stay active for a long time, providing you make a safety copy. The only reason you'll ever lose anything — a document, a photo, a video, music, or any file — is because you failed to create a backup.

The File You Had Yesterday

If a file is lost, you can find it. When a file has been deleted, you can recover it from the Recycle Bin. But when a file has been changed or overwritten with new information, getting it back requires some sorcery. That sorcery is provided by a backup program.

✔ Refer to Chapter 15 for information on finding lost files or lifting them from the electronic purgatory that is the Windows Recycle Bin.

✔ You're warned when a file is about to be overwritten. But if you're working on the file and you save a new version, you cannot get the old version back unless you use a tool called Previous Versions. This tool is part of the Windows backup program.

✔ In Windows 10, the backup program is called File History. In Windows 7, the backup program is called Backup.

Obtaining an external backup device

Before you even think about implementing the vital tool of file backup, some type of external storage must be available to your PC. It can't be a thumb drive, because the capacity is too low. And forget about optical discs. Windows prefers an external hard drive, SSD, or access to network storage.

If your PC lacks an external storage device, rush out and buy one. External hard drives are relatively inexpensive, and you get a lot of storage. In fact, ensure that the backup drive offers at least as much storage as the PC's primary mass storage device. If you can afford a drive with even more storage, buy it!

Hook up the external storage to your PC, as described in Chapter 10. Then you can proceed with configuring the PC's backup program, which is covered elsewhere in this chapter.

It's also possible to use network storage for PC backup, such as a network hard drive. First ensure that you can access the network drive from your PC. In fact, you can map the drive to a letter in your PC's storage system, as described in Chapter 17. That makes the rest of the backup program configuration run smoothly.

Configuring Windows 10 File History

The File History feature in Windows 10 serves two purposes. First, it works as the PC's backup program, which saves archive copies of all your favorite files and folders. Second, it allows you to recover a previous version of a file you may have overwritten or otherwise clobbered.

Follow these steps to ensure that File History is enabled in Windows 10:

1. **Press Win+I to open the Settings app.**

2. **Click the Update & Security button.**

3. **From the left side of the window, choose Backup.**

4. **Ensure that the Automatically Backup My Files toggle is set to the On position.**

   If this item is already enabled, you're done. Otherwise continue with Step 5:

5. **Click the Add a Drive button.**

Windows scans for an external hard drive or even an available network drive. A list of potential backup locations eventually appears. If not, your PC either lacks an external storage device or the device isn't of the capacity required for the File History feature.

6. **Select a drive from the list.**

For example, the external 3 TB hard drive you just bought at Costco for $30 off.

After a location is chosen, the File History feature is activated and is ready for use.

Setting up Windows 7 Backup

The Windows 7 backup program is called Windows Backup, which is so logical that it makes you wonder why Microsoft didn't instead choose the name Shiggity Wiggly Boop-da-lop. Regardless of the name, ensure that this program is set up and configured to back up your vital files. Follow these steps:

1. **Summon the Control Panel.**

Press the Win key to pop up the Start menu and choose Control Panel from that menu.

2. **Below the System and Security heading, click the Back Up Your Computer link.**

If Backup has been configured, in the Backup and Restore window you see the backup media, a schedule, and the results of the last backup. Otherwise, you need to configure the backup. Continue with Step 3.

3. **Click the Set Up Backup link.**

4. **Choose a storage device from the list displayed.**

If you're using a network drive, click the Save On a Network button and choose the network location.

5. **Click the Next button.**

Windows asks you which files to select for the backup.

6. **Keep the default item Let Windows Choose selected, and click the Next button.**

7. **Click the Save Settings and Run Backup button.**

Windows instantly attempts to back up your files to the backup media.

Yes, you need to wait for that initial backup to complete, but you're free to do other things on the PC while the first backup progresses.

Recovering a previous version of a file

You can clobber a file by copying a new file to an existing file's location or by using an existing file's name when saving a new file. In both cases, you're warned of the impending loss. When you update a file, such as editing a list of people who owe you money, the older version is overwritten. To recover the original file in any of these instances, you use a feature called Previous Versions.

The Previous Versions tool works only when you've set up and configured a Windows backup program — either File History in Windows 10 or Windows Backup for Windows 7. When that's the case, follow these steps to recover an earlier version of a clobbered file:

1. **Open the folder window containing the clobbered file.**

   You need to locate the file's icon.

2. **Right-click on the file you want to recover.**

   If the file was deleted, you can recover it from the Recycle Bin, as discussed in Chapter 15. If it can't be found there, you need to run the backup program to restore an archived copy. See the later section "Restoring files from a backup."

3. **Choose Restore Previous Versions.**

   The file's Properties dialog box appears, but, alas, Windows didn't really hear that you wanted the Previous Versions command. So:

4. **Click the Previous Versions tab in the file's Properties dialog box.**

   It may take a few moments for Windows to locate the various previous versions. Eventually, you see a list of previous versions, similar to what's shown in Figure 23-1.

5. **Click to highlight the version of the file you desire to recover.**

   It could be the most recent version or an antique.

6. **Click the Restore button.**

   A special warning dialog box may appear, telling you that the restored, previous version replaces the existing version you have. If you're okay with that peril, click the item to replace the original file.

When you'd rather keep both the historical and current versions of the file, click the down-arrow by the Restore button and choose the Restore To command from the menu. Select a folder for the restored previous version.

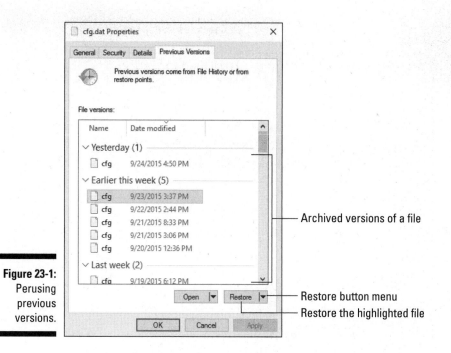

Figure 23-1:
Perusing
previous
versions.

Archived versions of a file

Restore button menu
Restore the highlighted file

Restoring files from a backup

Unlike fetching the previous version of a file, the backup program's restore operation is a broader operation. For example, you can restore all your files to a new hard drive after the old hard drive gets fried after a freak microwave oven experiment. Or you can restore a swath of files obliterated by your brilliant, computer genius nephew, Victor. Or you can restore a file that the Previous Versions feature is unable to fetch.

To initiate the restore operation, heed these steps:

1. **Press the Win+R keyboard shortcut.**

   The Run dialog box appears.

2. **Type** filehistory **in the text box and click OK.**

   That's one word: **filehistory**. Don't type a space between *file* and *history*.

   Yes, other ways exist to get to the File History window, but these steps are the fastest.

   Upon success, the File History window appears, similar to what's shown in Figure 23-2.

Date file(s) backed up   Choose an icon to restore

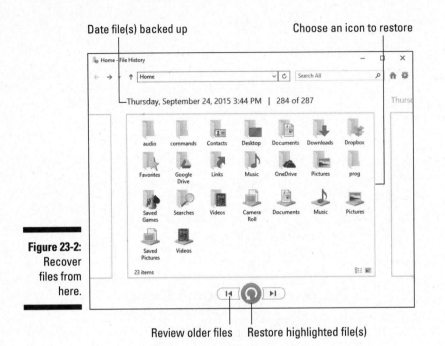

Figure 23-2:
Recover
files from
here.

Review older files   Restore highlighted file(s)

3. Browse the folders to locate the file you want to recover.

You can click the button (illustrated in Figure 23-2) to browse for older versions of the same file.

4. Click to select the file, and then click the Restore button.

The historic version of the file is about to be copied to the same folder as the original, but before the file is restored:

5. Choose the option Replace the File in the Destination.

The historic file replaces the current version.

You can select multiple files or even folders to restore. As long as the File History feature is turned on, you should — in theory — never lose a file.

The File History feature works only when it's enabled. Refer to the sections earlier in this chapter on setting up your PC's backup program.

Exploring Internet backup utilities

Another way to back up your files is to use an Internet backup service. The service regularly copies files from your PC to storage somewhere on the Internet. Beyond being automatic, the advantage of the Internet copy is that if your home or office is crushed by a flaming meteor, your files survive.

Well, I suppose a meteor could smash into the Internet backup company's headquarters, but I think they probably have more than one location for storing your data.

Here is a smattering of Internet backup services to peruse:

- ✔ **Backblaze:** www.backblaze.com
- ✔ **Carbonite:** www.carbonite.com
- ✔ **MozyHome:** www.mozy.com

Most of these services charge a nominal monthly fee, though you might also find a discounted annual rate. Additional fees apply when you back up more than one computer or when you go over a certain amount of storage. Well, you need Internet access too, which is kind of another fee. Fees, fees, fees.

Compressed Folder Archives

Let me be frank: Everyone has a favorite medieval torture device. Am I right? There's the rack, and the iron maiden, and who can count the things you can do with hot, molten lead?

For a computer file, the preferred form of torment is *compression.* It's possible to take multiple files and squeeze out the juice, compacting them into a single unit. That unit, or *archive,* can then be sent quickly over the Internet or stored long-term without occupying the bulk of all those regular-size files.

Compression is a possibility for files because of their digital nature. Thanks to mathematics and other chalkboard writing, a file can be compressed from its original size into a compact unit. It can then — almost magically — be decompressed to its original form with no loss of data, integrity, or self-esteem. Such is the beauty of the file archive.

Whether files enjoy compression or not, archiving is yet another way you can store files for later retrieval. Or you can be traditional and send the archive as an email attachment or somehow fling it out on the Internet.

The archives are officially known as *compressed folders* in Windows. They're also called *Zip* files.

- ✔ Zip files, or compressed file archives, feature their own, unique icon, shown in the margin. See the zipper? Cute.

- ✔ Like a traditional folder, a compressed folder contains files and folders. It's not really a folder, however; it's merely a special type of file. It's an archive!

> ✔ Compressed folders are called *Zip files* because Windows uses the Zip file compression algorithm, and also because the filename extension is *zip*. Zip doesn't stand for anything; the developer chose the name because zippy means *speedy*.

Compressing files

Say you have this group of rowdy files. You want to pack them all up on a media card and send them to a military academy. So you select the files and, lo, they don't fit on the media card. What to do?

The consumer-driven culture would demand that you purchase a higher-capacity media card. This book recommends that you compress and archive the files into a Zip folder. Here's how that process works:

1. **Select the files you want to compress.**

   You can compress files in a group, or you can compress a single, large, bloated file.

2. **Right-click the group of files.**

3. **Choose the command Send To ⇨ Compressed (Zipped) Folder.**

   A new, compressed folder is created. Its name, which is preset and stupid, is selected.

4. **Type a new name for the compressed folder.**

   Make it short, sweet, and descriptive.

The new, compressed folder contains an *archive,* or duplicate copy, of the files you selected in Step 1. You can now copy that compressed folder, email it, or store it on external media. The files remain compressed into that single unit until you extract them. Extracting files is covered in the next section.

> ✔ You can also create an empty compressed folder: Right-click a blank part of a folder window or the desktop, and then choose New ⇨ Compressed (Zipped) Folder. Rename the icon and you're in business.

> ✔ After a compressed folder has been created, you can add new files to it by simply dragging and dropping the file icons to the compressed folder's icon. This action copies the file into the compressed folder; it does not move the file.

> ✔ Files stored in a compressed folder occupy less storage space than the original files. That was the idea behind compressed folders, back in the early days of computer telecommunications: It takes less time to transmit a smaller file, which is important over slow, dial-up modem connections.

✔ Some types of files compress well, such as text files. Other file types don't compress at all. Certain audio and movie file types don't compress, because they're already compressed. You can still archive those files into a compressed folder, but you're not saving any storage space.

Working with a compressed folder

To see which files are lurking inside a compressed folder, open the folder. On the screen, it appears as though you've merely opened any old, boring folder — but you haven't. What you're looking at is a compressed file archive, similar to the one shown in Figure 23-3.

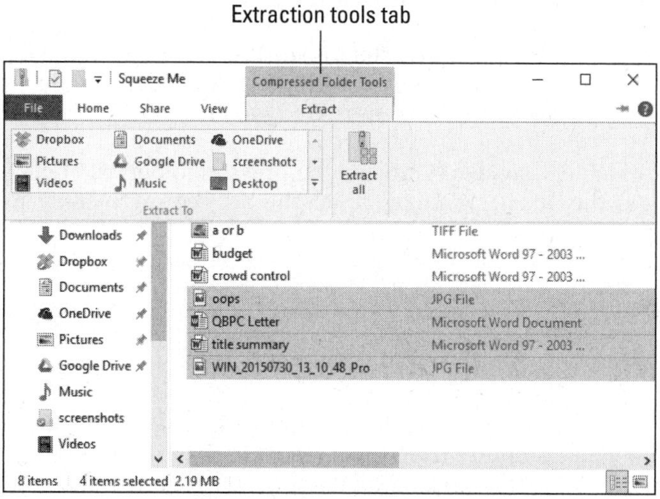

Extraction tools tab

Figure 23-3: Browsing inside a compressed folder.

Despite a potential for aggression, you can really do only three things when looking at files imprisoned in a compressed folder:

Snoop around. You can see what files and folders are inside the archive. Open folders inside the compressed folder to check their contents. You can even open compressed folders inside of compressed folders. If that concept blows your mind, watch the 2010 film *Inception*.

Preview files. Double-click an icon inside the compressed folder window to have a peek. Some files open in programs that let you preview their contents — but you cannot change the file unless you first extract it.

Extract one or more files. To extract one or more files, drag them out of the archive.

Most commonly, you'll want to extract all files from the compressed folder archive. To do that, follow these steps:

1. **Open the compressed folder.**

2. **In Windows 10, click the Compressed Folder Tools Extract tab.**

3. **Click the Extract All or Extract All Files button.**

   The Extract Compressed (Zipped) Folders window appears.

4. **Click the Extract button.**

   Windows creates a folder with the same name as the compressed folder and *extracts* (copies) all files from the compressed folder into the new folder. That new folder then opens on the screen.

5. **Close the compressed folder window.**

Extracting files from a compressed folder does not remove the files from the archive. The files remain in the compressed folder until you delete them individually or simply delete the compressed folder.

To remove a file individually from a compressed folder, right-click its icon and choose the Delete command. Click the Yes button to confirm.

Installing software from a compressed folder

Although I recommend against it in Chapter 14, occasionally new software arrives on your computer from the Internet in the form of a compressed (Zip) folder. Committing this sin isn't damning, but it requires that you perform a few extra steps to install the software.

Specifically, after you extract all files from the compressed folder, as described in the preceding section, you need to locate the Install program or Setup program in the newly created folder. Run that program. Follow the steps on the screen to continue installing the software.

When the Install or Setup program doesn't appear in the window, open the only folder in the window, or open the bin folder. (*Bin* means *binaries,* or programs.)

Chapter 24

Maintenance Chores

. . . .

. . . .

They don't really talk about it in the brochures, and it's not a topic that pops up at cocktail parties, but PC's do require some maintenance. It's a computer, after all. Though you could hire a charming young person who wears a white lab coat, it's probably a better idea that you attempt to undertake the maintenance chore yourself. It's not that difficult to do and, surprisingly, most of the time the PC does its own maintenance for you.

Storage Utilities

Utilities and tools is a definite category of computer software. It's a broad category, including items such as backup, Windows update, networking, and other items strewn through this tome.

Perhaps the most interesting and popular types of computer utility are those that deal with mass-storage devices — the "disk utilities" from days gone by. These programs are still around, although Windows does a lot of self-maintenance, which for the most part renders regular use of these programs optional.

Freeing storage space

I hope you bought a nice, roomy primary storage device for your PC. It's one area that comes back to haunt you when you get skimpy. That's because the primary storage device can fill up with files faster than the exhibition hall for the She-Hulk cosplay contest at Comic-Con.

To check storage stats and potentially free up space, follow these steps:

1. **Press Win + E, the keyboard shortcut to summon a File Explorer window.**

2. **In Windows 10, choose This PC from the list of items on the left side of the window.**

3. **Right-click on a storage device, such as the primary hard drive, C.**

4. **Choose Properties.**

   The storage device's Properties dialog box appears, which lists a chart graphically illustrating hard drive usage, similar to what's shown in Figure 24-1.

Handy graph

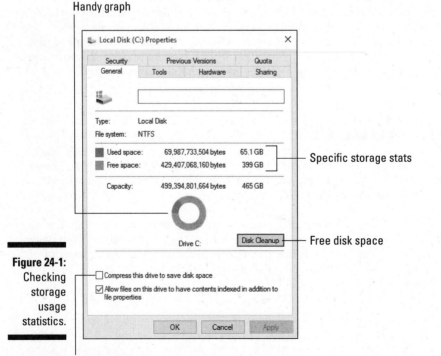

Specific storage stats

Free disk space

Figure 24-1: Checking storage usage statistics.

Don't do this

When storage gets low, it's shown graphically in the storage device's Properties dialog box. The graphic may even turn red in the main This PC or Computer window. That's when you've waited too long and you must take action.

5. Click the Disk Cleanup button.

The Disk Cleanup window appears, showing items you can remove from the device's storage and approximately how much storage will be gained.

6. Peruse the list of files to delete, placing check marks by various categories.

Pretty much everything in the list can go.

7. Click the OK button to free up some space.

The operation may take some time. Be patient.

You can click the Clean Up System Files button before Step 7 to scour non-personal locations on the storage device. This step may add a few extra megabytes of free storage, but don't get your hopes up.

Other ways of increasing storage include:

- ✔ **Remove any programs you don't use.** Refer to Chapter 14 for information on uninstalling programs. Especially if you haven't used a program in a while, get rid of it.

- ✔ **Purge the Downloads folder.** I keep everything I download, but that information could also be archived to external storage to free up space on the primary storage device.

- ✔ **Perform a file search for excessively large files.** Details on this type of search are found in the online bonus material available for this book. Quickly: Use the Windows Search command to locate files larger than 200 MB. Peruse the list and purge those biggies you no longer need.

- ✔ **Copy your music, videos, and photos to the cloud.** These media are still accessed from the Internet, but the files don't occupy storage on your PC.

If you can't free enough space, you need to obtain a larger, primary storage device. Have a PC consultant or another professional clone your PC's current primary mass-storage device onto a higher-capacity device. The key word is *clone*, which creates an exact copy so that you don't lose anything or need to reinstall software.

One solution you may see recommended is to compress the drive. The option is shown earlier, in Figure 24-1. Though that may work as a temporary solution, it involves long-term complications that don't really address the basic issue.

Checking for errors

Windows does its own error-checking on your PC's storage, especially the primary mass-storage device or Drive C. This checking happens automatically. In fact, you may notice Windows performing a media check when you start Windows. That's normal: Windows may have detected a problem and it's working to fix it.

To manually run a media check, follow these steps:

1. **Open the This PC or Computer window.**

   Press Win+E to start the File Explorer program; in Windows 10, choose This PC from the items listed on the left side of the window.

2. **Right-click the storage device you want to check.**

   It can be any storage device, from a thumb drive to the primary storage device.

3. **Choose Properties.**

4. **In the device's Properties dialog box, click the Tools tab.**

   You see two tools available: the traditional file checking tool, once known as check disk, and the defrag tool, both illustrated in Figure 24-2.

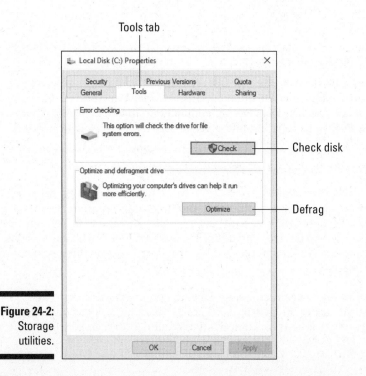

Figure 24-2:
Storage
utilities.

5. **Click the Check or Check Now button.**

   The storage device may not need checking. A prompt appears in that instance, which also reminds you that Windows automatically checks storage devices.

6. **Click the Scan Drive button.**

   Wait while Windows checks out the device.

7. **Peruse the results.**

8. **Close the window when you're done.**

If any errors are found, you may be prompted to correct them, though Windows fixes most errors automatically.

In the old days, PC users would run the check disk, or chkdsk, utility any time they suspected something was wrong with the computer's hard drive. It was almost a type of witchcraft, with the user believing that running the utility would somehow magically cure all hard drive — or even general PC — woes. That's no longer the case.

Running defrag

The defrag utility is sheer genius. Developed in the late 1980s, it corrects a storage problem that drastically slowed down file access. I remember running an early defrag utility on my PC and being utterly blown away by how much faster the system ran afterward.

Today, not only does a defrag or storage optimization utility come with Windows, but your PC also regularly runs that utility to ensure that the storage devices are all running at maximum efficiency. You don't need to defragment anything! But if you're curious, or you just want to run the utility for old-time's sake, follow these steps:

1. **Press Win + E to summon a File Explorer window.**

2. **In Windows 10, choose This PC from the left side of the window.**

   You see a list of storage devices for your computer.

3. **Right-click on the storage device you want to optimize.**

   Do not click on an SSD, a thumb drive, or a media card. Only hard drives can be optimized by using the defrag utility.

4. **Choose Properties.**

5. **In the device's Properties dialog box, click the Tools tab.**

   Refer to Figure 24-2.

6. **In Windows 10, click the Optimize button; in Windows 7, click the Defragment Now button.**

The Optimize Drives window appears, as shown in Figure 24-3. The window is titled Disk Defragmenter in Windows 7.

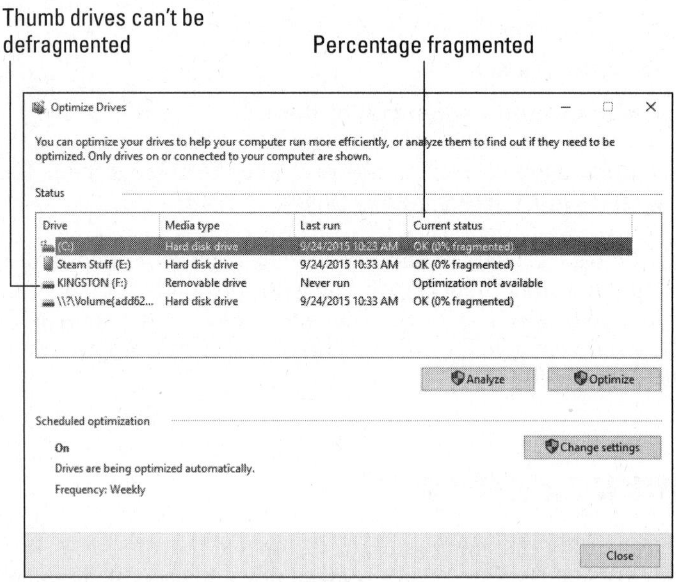

Thumb drives can't be
defragmented   Percentage fragmented

Figure 24-3:
The Optimize Drives window.

7. **Review the current fragmentation status of available storage devices.**

For the most part, you should see a zero-percentage-fragmented statistic on all drives. Some drives, such as SSDs, thumb drives, and media cards, show that optimization isn't available.

8. **If you insist upon moving forward, select a drive from the list.**

9. **Click the Analyze button in Windows 10; in Windows 7, click Analyze Disk.**

Windows may show an updated statistic for the media's current fragmentation status. Or it may not. In the old days, if a drive was less than 5 percent fragmented, you didn't optimize.

10. **Click the Optimize button or Defragment Disk button to defrag the media.**

The process takes awhile. A report is generated when it's complete.

11. **Close the Optimize Drives window or Defragment Now window when you're done.**

Again, this process is done automatically by Windows. Only if you see a truly messed-up value (a value higher than 5 percent after Step 9) should you proceed with optimizing the media. Otherwise, you're just wasting time.

✔ Never, ever, run a defrag utility on an SSD, thumb drive, or media card. These storage media are damaged by the action of the defragmentation process, which isn't a healthy thing. The Windows Optimize utility is smart enough to recognize such a storage device, and it refuses to work on it. Don't force it to!

✔ *Defrag* is short for *defrag*mentation. The operation takes files that have been split into smaller pieces and glues them back together, which optimizes file access. The files are split to take advantage of the storage media in a way that maximizes the number of files that can be stored.

Network Troubleshooting

The Internet is such a vital part of using a PC that you actually do lose some functionality when the network goes down. As with most PC troubleshooting, an easy fix-it cure isn't available. Instead, work through the problem in a logical way. Ask yourself these questions, in order:

1. **Is the modem working?**

   Look at the modem. Are its lights flashing? All its lights on? If not, phone your ISP and ensure that there isn't an outage in your area. They may even be able to test the modem to determine whether the problem is theirs or somewhere on the local network.

2. **Is the Internet down?**

   Try to visit a web page, especially a popular site like Google or Amazon. Sometimes individual websites go offline. Mail service can go down. And Internet outages do occur. If that's true, all you can do is wait.

3. **Can you see other PCs in the Network window?**

   Pop up a network window as described in Chapter 17. Can you see other devices on the network? If not, check the network connection, wired or wireless. Restarting your PC may help reestablish the connection.

4. **Have you restarted the gateway (router)?**

   Unplug the gateway. Wait a few moments. Plug it back in. Restarting the gateway may "clear its head" and get the network back up.

5. Have you restarted the entire network?

The final step is to restart the entire network. Turn off everything: modem, gateway, any hubs or switches, and every network device. The devices include computers, tablets, phones, and printers.

Start with the modem. Turn it on first. Wait. Turn on the gateway. Wait. Turn on any switches or hubs. Wait. Turn on network devices. This process is tedious, but sometimes it resolves network distress.

Change is the number-one reason things go awry in any system. If you've added new devices to the network, updated software, or replaced hardware, that might explain why the network went hinkey.

Manage the PC's Power

Your computer lusts for power. It's not the same power that some megalomaniac or fast-food store manager would want. No, the PC wants power from the wall. Electricity. Juice. As lord of your computer, you can control how much power the PC consumes, managing its thirst so that the system works but your electric bill doesn't go through the roof.

- ✔ *Power management* is a general term used to describe the capability of computers and other appliances, such as television sets and disintegration chambers, to become energy-smart.

- ✔ The power management hardware is what enables a computer to sleep, hibernate, and turn itself off.

Setting power options in Windows 10

One of the many things Windows 10 improved over its ancestors is how to handle power management. Follow these steps:

1. Press Win+I to summon the Settings app.

2. Click the System button.

3. From the list on the left side of the screen, choose Power & Sleep.

Power management settings appear on the right side of the screen.

4. Choose a timeout for the screen.

This timeout determines when the PC cuts power to the monitor. At that point, the monitor enters low-power mode.

If you have a laptop or your PC uses a UPS battery-powered backup, one menu item appears for battery power. The second or only item is the plugged-in power timeout.

I set a sleep timeout of 1 minute on battery power and 30 minutes for wall power.

5. Choose a timeout for the PC's system.

This timeout sets when the computer itself goes into low-power mode.

If the PC is backed up by a UPS power supply, or you have a laptop, the On Battery Power menu appears; otherwise, you see only the When Plugged In option.

As with the screen (or monitor) timeout, I set values of 1 minute on battery power and 30 minutes for standard power.

The timeout values start ticking when you ignore the PC. If you don't touch the mouse or tap a key on the keyboard for the given timeout, the screen or computer itself enters low-power mode.

While in low-power mode, the PC saves energy. To rouse the system from that mode, tap a key on the keyboard or wiggle the mouse.

See Chapter 4 for information on using a UPS. If a desktop PC is connected to a UPS, both with a power and USB connection, the battery-power options appear in the Settings app.

Configuring a power management plan

For Windows 7, as well as Windows 10, you can create a customized power management plan. Follow these steps:

1. Open the Control Panel.

2. Click the Hardware and Sound heading.

3. Click the Power Options heading.

The Power Options window appears, as shown in Figure 24-4.

The Power Options window features various plans for managing the power in your PC, as listed in Figure 24-4. You can see more plans by clicking the downward-pointing arrow button thing, as illustrated in the figure.

Each plan tames two power-mad items in the computer's hardware inventory: the monitor and the console. Specifically, the plans control when to dim or turn off the display and when to sleep the rest of the computer.

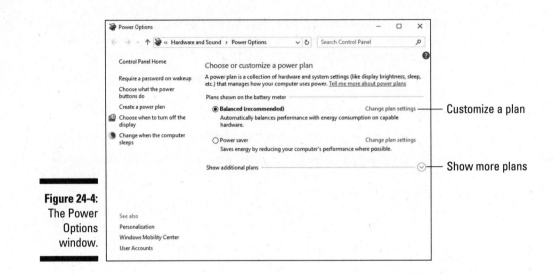

Customize a plan

Show more plans

Figure 24-4:
The Power
Options
window.

The key to invoking the power control is the timeout. The computer observes your activity; when there hasn't been any input for a given amount of time, Windows turns off the display or puts the computer to sleep. That action saves energy.

To choose a plan, select the radio button next to the plan name. Close the Power Options window and you're done.

You can also customize any plan, or create your own plan, by clicking the Create a Power Plan link on the left side of the Power Options window (refer to Figure 24-4). Follow the directions on the screen. Be sure to give your power plan a clever name, such as *Dan's Plan,* which is ideal when your name happens to be Dan.

Adding the Hibernate option

Windows has never put the option to hibernate your PC in an obvious place. Because of that, my advice for putting the computer into Hibernation mode is to assign the Hibernate command to a position on the Power menu. Here's what to do in Windows 10:

1. **Press Win+X and choose the Control Panel command from the super-secret shortcut menu.**

   The Control Panel appears.

2. **Choose Hardware and Sound.**

3. **Below the Power Options heading, choose the link Change What the Power Buttons Do.**

4. **Click the link Change Settings That Are Currently Unavailable.**

5. **Place a check mark in the box by Hibernate.**

   This option is found at the bottom of the window; scroll down to locate it.

6. **Click the Save Changes button.**

7. **Close the Control Panel window.**

After following these steps, the Hibernate command appears on the Start menu's Power menu.

The Windows 10 Do-Over

Life may not have a reset button, but Windows does. Specifically, Windows 10.

If you suffer dire mishap to your PC, or if you intend to sell or give away the computer, you can reset Windows so that all your personal information is removed, programs uninstalled, and settings reverted to the time when Windows 10 was first installed or upgraded.

Obviously, resetting Windows is a drastic step. You don't perform this procedure to fix minor ills. If you're ready and willing, obey these steps in Windows 10:

1. **Press the Win + I keyboard shortcut to bring up the Settings app.**

2. **Click the Update & Security button.**

3. **From the list of items on the left side of the screen, choose Recovery.**

4. **On the right side of the screen, click the Get Started button.**

5. **Choose whether to keep your files or remove everything.**

   If you choose Keep My Files, only Windows is unwound back to its original state. Otherwise, if you choose Remove Everything, the entire PC is reset.

   After you make the choice, Windows examines a few things and provides a summary of the operation and a confirmation message.

6. Confirm that you want to proceed.

You cannot undo or cancel the operation after it begins.

7. Proceed.

Sit back and wait.

After the process is complete, your PC starts and Windows 10 pops up its bright, cheery head. It asks you the same questions it did when you first started your new PC or upgraded your old PC with Windows 10. Yes, you are a complete stranger.

You can either proceed with setting up Windows again or turn off the PC, because it's ready to be sold, traded, bartered, or simply left to die alone in a field somewhere.

Part VI

The Part of Tens

Find a bonus Part of Tens chapter online at www.dummies.com/extras/
pcs-something.

In this part . . .

- ✔ Obey the ten PC commandments
- ✔ Get ten handy things for your PC
- ✔ Contemplate tips from a computer guru

Chapter 25

Ten PC Commandments

Take it from me: I've been there, I've done that. I've survived the worst of using a computer and lived to write about it. Let me share my experiences with you by passing along a chunk of digital wisdom. I may not have descended from Mt. Sinai, and I certainly look nothing like Charlton Heston, but here are my Ten PC Commandments.

I. Thou Shalt Not Fear Thy PC

The computer isn't out to get you. It won't explode suddenly. It harbors no sinister intelligence. Honestly, it's really rather dumb.

Knowledge is the key to overcoming fear.

II. Thou Shalt Save Thy Work

Whenever you're creating something blazingly original, use the Save command at once! In fact, use the Save command even when you make something stupid that you don't even want to save. Trust me — the PC's primary storage device has plenty of room for you to save your stuff.

You never know when your computer will meander off to watch NASCAR or chat with the wireless router across the street while you're hoping to finish the last few paragraphs of that report. Save your work as often as possible. Save when you get up from your computer. Save when you answer the phone. Save! Save! Save!

III. Thou Shalt Back Up Thy Files

Nothing beats having that just-in-case copy of your stuff. The computer itself can run a backup program to make that safety copy, or you can duplicate your files yourself. Either way, that secondary backup copy can save your skin someday.

See Chapter 23 for information on backing up.

IV. That Shalt Not Open or Delete Things Unknownst

Here's the rule, written in modern English: Delete only those files or folders you created yourself.

Unlike computer hardware, where sticky labels with red letters read *Do Not Open*, unknown computer files have no warning labels. They should! Windows is brimming with unusual and unknown files. Don't mess with 'em. Don't delete them. Don't move them. Don't rename them. And especially don't open them to see what they are. Sometimes, opening an unknown icon can lead to trouble.

V. Thou Shalt Not Be a Sucker

The Bad Guys are successful in spreading their evil, malicious software on the Internet because people let down their guard. Don't be a sucker for human engineering. Basically, here's a list of don'ts to adhere to:

✔ Don't reply to any spam email. Doing so brings you even more spam. A popular trick is for spammers to include some text that says "Reply to this message if you do not want to receive any further messages." Don't! Replying to spam signals the spammers that they have a "live one" and you then receive even more spam. Never, ever, reply to spam!

✔ Don't open unknown or unexpected email attachments. Seriously, you're not missing anything if you don't open them. Yet that's how human engineering works: The email fools you into believing that opening the attachment is important. It's not.

✔ Never open any program file attachment. These attachments end with the .exe, .com, or .vbs filename extension. See Chapter 15 for more information on filename extensions and how to display them in Windows.

VI. Thou Shalt Use Antivirus Software, Yea Verily, and Keepeth It Up-to-Date

I highly recommend that you use antivirus software on your PC. Keep that software up-to-date. Windows comes with Windows Defender, which is good. Getting a third-party antivirus program such as Norton, McAfee, or Kaspersky is even better.

See Chapter 22 for more computer security advice.

VII. Thou Shalt Upgrade Wisely

New hardware and software come out all the time. The new stuff is generally better and faster, and it's important to some people to be the First On the Block to have a new hardware gizmo or software upgrade. You don't have to be that person.

✔ Buying a new version, or *upgrade,* of computer software is necessary only when you truly need the new features it offers, when you need that new version to be compatible with your coworkers, or when the new version fixes problems and bugs that you're experiencing.

✔ Buy hardware that's compatible with your PC. Especially when you have an older computer, confirm that the new hardware will work with your system.

VIII. Thou Shalt Compute at a Proper Posture

Using a computer can be a pain. Literally. You must observe the proper posture and sitting position while you operate a PC. By doing so, you can avoid back strain and the risk of repetitive stress injury (RSI).

- ✔ Even if your wrists are as limber as a politician's spine, you might consider an ergonomic keyboard. This type of keyboard is specially designed at an angle to relieve the stress of typing for long — or short — periods.

- ✔ Wrist pads elevate your wrists so that you type in a proper position, with your palms above the keyboard, not resting below the spacebar.

- ✔ Sit at the computer with your elbows level with your wrists.

- ✔ Your head should not tilt down or up when you view the computer screen. It should be straight ahead, which doesn't help your wrists as much as it helps your neck.

- ✔ If you want to be truly trendy, don't sit at all while you use a computer. I don't! That's because I use a standing desk, where I stand up while I work. If you're game, this type of working environment is great for the back and core. And if you're timid, get a standing desk that adjusts its height so that you can sit down once in a while.

IX. Thou Shalt Keepeth Windows Up-to-Date

Microsoft keeps Windows continually fresh and updated. The updates fix problems, but they also address vulnerabilities that the Bad Guys exploit. In my book (the one that you're reading now), that's a good thing, but it's effective only when you use the Windows Update service regularly. See Chapter 22.

X. Thou Shalt Properly Shut Down Windows

When you're done with Windows, shut it down. Choose the Shut Down command from the Start menu. The PC automatically turns itself off.

Refer to Chapter 4 for detailed PC shutdown instructions.

Chapter 26

Ten Things Worth Buying for Your PC

I'm pretty sure that you're not ready to burst out and spend, spend, spend on something else after buying a new computer. Still, who doesn't enjoy getting more toys — or I should write *vital peripherals* — for their home or office? No computer system comes complete out of the box, so consider some or all of these ten items as bonus goodies you can now or in the future obtain for your electronic pal, the PC.

Mouse Pad and Wrist Pad

The old mechanical computer mouse required a mouse pad upon which to operate. It needed that textured surface or moving the mouse was an exercise in frustration. Mouse pads still exist, but with today's optical mice they're not considered necessary. That is — until you run out of room on your desktop or your computer desk surface is too shiny and the optical mouse doesn't register. In that case, get a mouse pad. If anything, the mouse pad sets aside some desktop real estate so that your mouse doesn't compete with that raft of papers and other desktop detritus.

While you're at it, obtain a wrist pad for the keyboard. It enables you to comfortably rest your wrists while you type. This product may help alleviate some repetitive-motion injuries that are common to keyboard users. Wrist pads come in many exciting colors, some of which may match your drapery.

External Mass Storage

If you love your digital data — documents, photos, music, video, and so on — then you need to run a backup program to keep a safety copy. Those instructions are offered in Chapter 23. To make that process work, you need to obtain an external mass storage device, a hard drive or SSD.

External hard drives run about $100 each. Oddly enough, they've maintained that price for years. What changes is the drive's capacity. A few years back, $100 got you a 500GB external hard drive. Today, the capacity is in the multiple gigabyte range — which is awesome.

To accommodate a backup, obtain an external storage device with at least the same capacity as your PC's primary storage device: For a 1 TB primary hard drive, get a 1 TB external hard drive. If you can afford a higher capacity external drive, get one!

Cleaning Materials

I have a high tolerance for a dirty house. It's not as high as my kids' tolerance, and my mother's is much higher, but at least I know the level of crud at which I must clean things. The PC is no exception to the cleaning routine. Here are some items to consider:

Keyboard vacuum: This tiny gizmo is ideal for sucking the crud from between the keyboard's keys. And, oh yes, there's crud in there. Especially if you eat while you compute, you'll find food bits, dust, chunks of fingernail, hair, and all sorts of things that will make you *not* want to eat while you compute. A tiny keyboard vacuum is ideal for removing that crud.

Keyboard cover: Did I gross you out with the reasons for getting a keyboard vacuum? If so, consider purchasing a keyboard cover, something that fits snugly over the keyboard to prevent the crud from getting between the keys. Especially if you have young ones using the PC, get a keyboard cover.

Microfiber cloth: The best way to clean a computer screen is to use a microfiber cloth. One might have come with the monitor. If not, you can obtain a microfiber cloth at any office supply store.

Screen cleaner: When the sneeze globs dry, use a screen cleaner to remove them. Ensure that the cleaner is made for your PC's computer monitor; special formulas are required for LCD monitors and especially touchscreens. You don't want to use abrasive solutions or chemicals like alcohol or ammonia, which can damage a touchscreen monitor.

Internal Expansion

You don't want to hear about it, especially when you've just purchased a new PC, but did you get enough storage? Specifically for memory and mass storage, is the capacity adequate?

Upgraded memory and a new hard drive aren't things you'll buy right away for your PC. Consider them anniversary gifts.

Any PC works better with more memory installed. The upper limit on some computers is something like 32GB of RAM, which seems ridiculous now, but who knows about two years from now? Still, upgrading your system from 4GB to 8GB of RAM might improve performance.

The PC's primary storage device may fill up more quickly than you anticipated. The first time, it's because you have kept lots of junk on your hard drive: games, things people give you, old files, and old programs you don't use any more. You can free up some space, as described in Chapter 24, but eventually a larger, roomier storage device may be in order.

✔ Upgrading memory and replacing a hard drive are operations best carried out by computer professionals.

✔ Sometimes, upgrading memory requires that you purchase all new memory chips to replace those currently in the PC. That may seem illogical, but it's how memory works.

✔ If possible, get the professional to clone your old hard drive on to the newer, larger hard drive. That process doesn't require that you reinstall anything.

✔ Before taking your PC into the shop, always ensure that you have an up-to-date backup handy.

USB Hub and Cables

Most PCs seem to come with plenty of USB ports, both on the front of the console and the back. Difficult as it is to imagine, at some point in the future, those ports may not be enough. The solution is to obtain a USB hub.

Plug the hub into a USB port on the PC. I recommend getting a powered-USB hub because it can connect to powered-USB devices, which is a requirement for some external gizmos. If so, plug the powered-USB hub into a wall socket as well as the PC.

With the hub, you may need some USB cables. These are items you'll more likely collect than purchase. I keep my phone's USB cable plugged into a USB hub that lingers just below the PC monitor. That way, I can quickly connect the phone for a charge or to send over files.

Better Keyboard and Mouse

When you buy a PC, the manufacturer doesn't burden you with a top-o'-the-line keyboard or mouse. Usually you get something cheap — unless you specify a better input device when you first configure the computer. Otherwise, you're free to obtain a better keyboard and mouse.

Keyboard varieties abound, giving you options for wireless connections, ergonomic designs, multimedia functions (play/pause, volume controls, and so on), and special keys for computer gaming. Because I'm a writer, I pay top dollar for a mechanical keyboard that's far more enjoyable for touch-typing.

Computer mice come in plenty of varieties, including wireless. Some mice sport an abundance of buttons. My son uses a gaming mouse that features an accelerator button as well as options for increasing or decreasing the weight of the mouse. Trackball mice are available for graphic artists. And if you're a laptop fan, you can get a touch pad for your PC and use it instead of a mouse.

An Uninterruptible Power Supply (UPS)

The *uninterruptible power supply (UPS)* is a boon to computing anywhere in the world where the power is less than reliable. Plug your console into the UPS. Plug your monitor into the UPS. If the UPS has extra battery-backed-up sockets, plug your modem into it too.

✔ Chapter 4 has information on using a UPS and on using a power strip.

✔ Using a UPS doesn't affect the performance of your PC. The computer couldn't care less whether it's plugged into the wall or a UPS.

✔ Refer to Chapter 24 for information on configuring the PC's power management scheme to work with a UPS.

Headset

A *headset* is a pair of headphones but with the addition of a microphone. This may seem useless, until you consider how many ways such a gizmo can be used on a PC. First of all, headsets are great for playing online games. You can not only hear the sounds better, but for playing online, also speak with the rest of your team, coordinating tactics or just insulting them.

A headset works well for online communications tools like Skype or Google Hangouts. And if you desire to try Windows dictation, the headset is the preferred choice for vocal input.

Scanner

A *scanner* is essentially a digital camera designed to take pictures of flat objects. These include documents, photos, and even transparencies. I scan items all the time because my office lacks a fax. So I can receive a document, print it, sign it, scan it, and send it back. (That's for those publishers of mine who haven't figured out how to digitally sign a PDF, not that I'm picking on Wiley or anything.)

The good news is that an all-in-one printer features a scanner. The better models provide sheet feeders, so you can scan a raft of documents without having to feed in each one.

Software that comes with the scanner helps you crop incoming images, save as a certain type of graphics file, create a PDF, or transform the scanned text into an editable document.

Thumb Drives and Media Cards

The floppy diskette died long ago. The plot right next to its grave is ready for the optical disc, if the groundskeeper hasn't finished piling on the last shovelful of dirt. That leaves thumb drives and media cards as the PC's primary form of removable storage.

Thumb drives are ubiquitous. If you don't have some, go out and buy a few. Get them in packs of 2 to 5, which saves money. For capacity, buy what you can afford, although a huge capacity isn't necessary when the drives are used only for moving files between computers or for archiving purposes.

Media cards serve the same purposes as thumb drives, but this type of storage can also be used in a digital camera, smartphone, or tablet. Because of that flexibility, ensure that you get a media card that's compatible with your portable gizmos, such as the SD card or MicroSD card.

- ✔ Thumb drives need not be boring. I've seen thumb drives in the shape of a human thumb! Some drives have whimsical designs, which is fun but you pay more for those gizmos.

- ✔ Many folks keep thumb drives on their keychains so that storage is always handy.

- ✔ An alternative to transferring files to a thumb drive is to use cloud storage to share files. See Chapter 16.

- ✔ If your PC lacks a media card reader, you can pick up an external one. You can purchase an all-in-one reader, which accepts all media card formats, or get one specific to the type of media cards you use.

- ✔ Media cards are rather diminutive, similar in size and thickness to a wheat thin or postage stamp. Therefore, they're easy to lose, so I recommend keeping media cards in their plastic containers when they're not in use.

Chapter 27

Ten Tips from a PC Guru

I don't consider myself a computer expert or genius or guru, although many have referred to me by using those nasty terms. I'm just a guy who understands how computers work. Or, better than that, I understand how computer people think and I can translate it into English for you. Given that, here are some tips and suggestions so that you and your PC can go on your merry way.

Remember That You're in Charge

You bought the computer. You clean up after its messes. You press the Any key (which is the Enter key). You control the computer — simple as that.

Think of the computer as an infant. You must treat it the same way, with respect and careful attention. Don't feel that the computer is bossing you around any more than you feel that a baby is bossing you around during its 3 a.m. feedings. They're both helpless creatures, subject to your every whim. Be gentle, but be in charge.

Mind Who "Helps" You

Nothing beats getting computer help when you need it. Most computer nerds enjoy helping beginners. Sometimes, they help you at no cost, though you shouldn't abuse a good relationship by becoming a pest.

When you can't find help, use the support you paid for: from your manufacturer, computer dealer, software developer, and Internet service provider.

Above all, keep in mind that not everyone who tries to help you truly knows what they're doing. My advice is to avoid friends or (especially) relatives who offer to "fix" your PC when you haven't asked them to. That leads to big trouble.

- Treat your PC like your wallet. You wouldn't hand it over to anyone, right?

- You may like your smart nephew Victor, but don't let him near your computer. Don't let the grandkids or out-of-town relatives "play" on the Internet while they come to visit. You'll thank me later.

Give Yourself Time to Learn

Things take time. No one sits down at a computer and instantly knows everything, especially with new software. True, the boss may have given you only a day to learn how to work some new program. Such a task is unrealistic and unfair (and you can literally point to this sentence for support).

It takes about a week to become comfortable with any software. It takes longer to really figure out how it works, even if you get a good book on the topic. Honestly, I don't think that anyone out there knows *everything* about a major software product. Don't set the bar so high that you can't leap over it.

Create Separate Accounts

If two people are using one computer, make two computer accounts. That way, you can each keep your stuff separate. The issue is not secrecy but organization. Having one account for each person who uses the computer is better than having two or more people share — and mess up — the only account.

The same guideline applies to email: Get yourself separate email accounts — one for you and one for your partner or one for each human who uses the computer. That way, you receive only your mail, and you don't miss anything because someone else has read or deleted it.

- ✔ Configuring a second account on a Windows 10 PC involves some arduous steps, the most egregious of which is that the second account holder must have an email address — even for a kid's account. That's just obnoxious.

- ✔ Windows 10 uses the Setup app to add accounts. Click the Accounts button, and then choose Family & Other Users from the left side of the screen. Click the appropriate button on the right side of the screen, and be prepared to be frustrated.

- ✔ In Windows 7, use the Control Panel to add another account. Beneath the User Accounts and Family Safety heading, choose Add or Remove User Accounts.

Mind What You Download

Even after years of experience, I fall victim to not heeding my own advice: Sometimes you get into such a hurry to download a program from the Internet that you don't read everything. A box goes checked or unchecked, and the result is that unwanted software is installed on your computer.

The good news is that if you're quick, you can uninstall that software. If you don't notice — and it's easy to do — the software becomes embedded in your PC. Not even antispyware utilities can remove it. That's because you invited the software in.

The solution is to slow down! Pay attention when you download or install software. Read *every* screen. Look for options and offers. Install only what you need, not the bonus offers, toolbars, search engines, shopping assistants, or varieties of unwanted, loathsome programs.

Organize Your Files

Microsoft, as well as other software developers, has toiled endlessly to create a computer environment that fools you into believing that using a PC is fun and easy. It's really not. Though working on a computer today is easier than in the text-mode days of the MS-DOS operating system, some complex computer science issues remain.

Number one of all the basic computer science issues is file organization. You can live a digital life, completely unfettered by any need to organize your files. The result is like living in a house without closets, cupboards, or drawers: Everything is everywhere. Some people like that configuration, but it's far more effective to keep things organized.

- Properly name files when you first save them. Be short and descriptive.

- There's nothing wrong with naming a file *kill me* or *delete me*. That portends future thrills for doing file hunting and removing files you no longer need.

- Organize similar files into folders. Properly name the folders to describe their contents.

- Use subfolders to further organize files.

- See Chapter 15 for details on working with files and folders.

Don't Reinstall Windows

A myth floating around tech support sites says that the solution to all your ills is to reinstall Windows. Some tech support people even claim that it's common for most Windows users to reinstall at least once a year. That's rubbish.

You *never* need to reinstall Windows. All problems are fixable. It's just that the tech support people are urged by their bottom-line-watching overlords to get you off the line quickly. Therefore, they resort to a drastic solution rather than try to discover the true problem. If you press them, they *will* tell you what's wrong and how to fix it.

In all my years of using a computer, I have never reinstalled Windows or had to reformat the PC's primary storage device. It's not even a good idea just to refresh the bits on the hard drive or whatever other nonsense they dish up. There just isn't a need to reinstall Windows, ever. Period.

Shun the Hype

The computer industry is rife with hype. Magazines and websites tout this or that solution, crow about new trends, and preannounce standards that supposedly will make everything you have obsolete. Ignore all of it!

My gauge for hype is whether the thing that's hyped is shipping as a standard part of a PC. I check the ads. If they're shipping the item, I write about it. Otherwise, it's a myth and may not happen. Avoid being lured by the hype.

Keep on Learning

There's no reason to stop discovering new things about your PC. If you're into books (and you seem to be), consider getting another computer book on a topic that interests you. Bookstores, both physical and on the Internet, are brimming with titles covering just about every computer topic. Also peruse computer magazines and periodicals.

For example, perhaps you want to take up programming. I'm serious! If you enjoy solving puzzles, you'll probably enjoy programming. Or maybe you want to learn how to get the most from a graphics program. In a time when people try to glean knowledge from mediocre (but free) information on the Internet, why not take time to truly educate yourself?

Remember Not to Take This Computer Stuff Too Seriously

Hey, simmer down! Computers aren't part of life. They're nothing more than mineral deposits and petroleum products. Close your eyes and take a few deep breaths. Imagine that you're lying on a soft, sandy beach in the South Pacific. Having just dined on an exotic salad, you close your eyes as the sounds of the gentle surf lull you into a well-deserved, late-afternoon nap.

Next, you're getting your feet rubbed as you sip champagne and feel the bubbles explode atop your tongue. Soothing music plays as everyone who's ever said a bad thing about you in your life tosses you $100 bills.

Now, slowly open your eyes. It's just a dumb computer. Really. Don't take it too seriously.

Index

• Y •

• Z •

About the Author

Dan Gookin has been writing about technology for over 25 years. He combines his love of writing with his gizmo fascination to create books that are informative, entertaining, and not boring. Having written over 130 titles with 12 million copies in print translated into over 30 languages, Dan can attest that his method of crafting computer tomes seems to work.

Perhaps his most famous title is the original *DOS For Dummies,* published in 1991. It became the world's fastest-selling computer book, at one time moving more copies per week than the *New York Times* number-one bestseller (though, as a reference, it could not be listed on the *Times'* Best Sellers list). That book spawned the entire line of *For Dummies* books, which remains a publishing phenomenon to this day.

Dan's most popular titles include *PCs For Dummies, Word For Dummies, Laptops For Dummies,* and *Android Phones For Dummies.* He also maintains the vast and helpful website www.wambooli.com.

Dan holds a degree in Communications/Visual Arts from the University of California, San Diego. He lives in the Pacific Northwest, where he enjoys spending time with his sons playing video games indoors while they enjoy the gentle woods of Idaho.

Publisher's Acknowledgments

Acquisitions Editor: Katie Mohr

Senior Project Editor: Paul Levesque

Copy Editor: Rebecca Whitney

Technical Editor: Sharon Mealka

Editorial Assistant: Bridget Feeney

Sr. Editorial Assistant: Cherie Case

Production Editor: Kumar Chellappan

Cover Image: ©Getty Images/mbbirdy

Apple & Mac

iPad For Dummies,
5th Edition
978-1-118-72306-7

iPhone For Dummies,
7th Edition
978-1-118-69083-3

Macs All-in-One
For Dummies, 4th Edition
978-1-118-82210-4

OS X Mavericks
For Dummies
978-1-118-69188-5

Blogging & Social Media

Facebook For Dummies,
5th Edition
978-1-118-63312-0

Social Media Engagement
For Dummies
978-1-118-53019-1

WordPress For Dummies,
6th Edition
978-1-118-79161-5

Business

Stock Investing
For Dummies, 4th Edition
978-1-118-37678-2

Investing For Dummies,
6th Edition
978-0-470-90545-6

Personal Finance
For Dummies, 7th Edition
978-1-118-11785-9

QuickBooks 2014
For Dummies
978-1-118-72005-9

Small Business Marketing
Kit For Dummies,
3rd Edition
978-1-118-31183-7

Careers

Job Interviews
For Dummies, 4th Edition
978-1-118-11290-8

Job Searching with Social
Media For Dummies,
2nd Edition
978-1-118-67856-5

Personal Branding
For Dummies
978-1-118-11792-7

Resumes For Dummies,
6th Edition
978-0-470-87361-8

Starting an Etsy Business
For Dummies, 2nd Edition
978-1-118-59024-9

Diet & Nutrition

Belly Fat Diet For Dummies
978-1-118-34585-6

Mediterranean Diet
For Dummies
978-1-118-71525-3

Nutrition For Dummies,
5th Edition
978-0-470-93231-5

Digital Photography

Digital SLR Photography
All-in-One For Dummies,
2nd Edition
978-1-118-59082-9

Digital SLR Video &
Filmmaking For Dummies
978-1-118-36598-4

Photoshop Elements 12
For Dummies
978-1-118-72714-0

Gardening

Herb Gardening
For Dummies, 2nd Edition
978-0-470-61778-6

Gardening with Free-Range
Chickens For Dummies
978-1-118-54754-0

Health

Boosting Your Immunity
For Dummies
978-1-118-40200-9

Diabetes For Dummies,
4th Edition
978-1-118-29447-5

Living Paleo For Dummies
978-1-118-29405-5

Big Data

Big Data For Dummies
978-1-118-50422-2

Data Visualization
For Dummies
978-1-118-50289-1

Hadoop For Dummies
978-1-118-60755-8

Language &
Foreign Language

500 Spanish Verbs
For Dummies
978-1-118-02382-2

English Grammar
For Dummies, 2nd Edition
978-0-470-54664-2

French All-in-One
For Dummies
978-1-118-22815-9

German Essentials
For Dummies
978-1-118-18422-6

Italian For Dummies,
2nd Edition
978-1-118-00465-4

e Available in print and e-book formats.

Available wherever books are sold. **For more information or to order direct visit www.dummies.com**

nce

...r Dummies,
...tion
...0-470-55964-2

Anatomy and Physiology
For Dummies, 2nd Edition
978-0-470-92326-9

Astronomy For Dummies,
3rd Edition
978-1-118-37697-3

Biology For Dummies,
2nd Edition
978-0-470-59875-7

Chemistry For Dummies,
2nd Edition
978-1-118-00730-3

1001 Algebra II Practice
Problems For Dummies
978-1-118-44662-1

Microsoft Office

Excel 2013 For Dummies
978-1-118-51012-4

Office 2013 All-in-One
For Dummies
978-1-118-51636-2

PowerPoint 2013
For Dummies
978-1-118-50253-2

Word 2013 For Dummies
978-1-118-49123-2

Music

Blues Harmonica
For Dummies
978-1-118-25269-7

Guitar For Dummies,
3rd Edition
978-1-118-11554-1

iPod & iTunes
For Dummies, 10th Edition
978-1-118-50864-0

Programming

Beginning Programming
with C For Dummies
978-1-118-73763-7

Excel VBA Programming
For Dummies, 3rd Edition
978-1-118-49037-2

Java For Dummies,
6th Edition
978-1-118-40780-6

Religion & Inspiration

The Bible For Dummies
978-0-7645-5296-0

Buddhism For Dummies,
2nd Edition
978-1-118-02379-2

Catholicism For Dummies,
2nd Edition
978-1-118-07778-8

Self-Help & Relationships

Beating Sugar Addiction
For Dummies
978-1-118-54645-1

Meditation For Dummies,
3rd Edition
978-1-118-29144-3

Seniors

Laptops For Seniors
For Dummies, 3rd Edition
978-1-118-71105-7

Computers For Seniors
For Dummies, 3rd Edition
978-1-118-11553-4

iPad For Seniors
For Dummies, 6th Edition
978-1-118-72826-0

Social Security
For Dummies
978-1-118-20573-0

Smartphones & Tablets

Android Phones
For Dummies, 2nd Edition
978-1-118-72030-1

Nexus Tablets
For Dummies
978-1-118-77243-0

Samsung Galaxy S 4
For Dummies
978-1-118-64222-1

Samsung Galaxy Tabs
For Dummies
978-1-118-77294-2

Test Prep

ACT For Dummies,
5th Edition
978-1-118-01259-8

ASVAB For Dummies,
3rd Edition
978-0-470-63760-9

GRE For Dummies,
7th Edition
978-0-470-88921-3

Officer Candidate Tests
For Dummies
978-0-470-59876-4

Physician's Assistant Exam
For Dummies
978-1-118-11556-5

Series 7 Exam For Dummi
978-0-470-09932-2

Windows 8

Windows 8.1 All-in-One
For Dummies
978-1-118-82087-2

Windows 8.1 For Dummie
978-1-118-82121-3

Windows 8.1 For Dummie
Book + DVD Bundle
978-1-118-82107-7

e **Available in print and e-book formats.**

Available wherever books are sold. **For more information or to order direct visit www.dummies.com**

Take Dummies with you everywhere you go!

Whether you are excited about e-books, want more from the web, must have your mobile apps, or are swept up in social media, Dummies makes everything easier.

For Dummies is the global leader in the reference category and one of the most trusted and highly regarded brands in the world. No longer just focused on books, customers now have access to the For Dummies content they need in the format they want. Let us help you develop a solution that will fit your brand and help you connect with your customers.

Advertising & Sponsorships

Connect with an engaged audience on a powerful multimedia site, and position your message alongside expert how-to content.

Targeted ads • Video • Email marketing • Microsites • Sweepstakes sponsorship

21 Million Monthly Page Views & 13 Million Unique Visitors

Custom Publishing

Reach a global audience in any language by creating a solution that will differentiate you from competitors, amplify your message, and encourage customers to make a buying decision.

Apps • Books • eBooks • Video • Audio • Webinars

Brand Licensing & Content

Leverage the strength of the world's most popular reference brand to reach new audiences and channels of distribution.

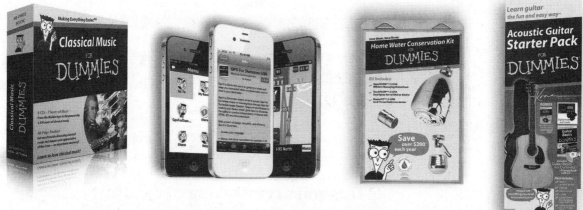

For more information, visit www.Dummies.com/biz

Dummies products make life easier!

- DIY
- Consumer Electronics
- Crafts

- Software
- Cookware
- Hobbies

- Videos
- Music
- Games
- and More!

For more information, go to **Dummies.com** and search the store by category.